Communication Works!

Communication Works!

Communication

Applications

in the

Workplace

Kathleen M. Galvin
Senior Author
Northwestern University
Evanston, Illinois

Jane Terrell
Lyndon Baines Johnson High School
Austin, Texas

National Textbook Company
a division of NTC/CONTEMPORARY PUBLISHING GROUP
Lincolnwood, Illinois USA

Cover and Interior Design: Ellen Pettengell Design

Photo acknowledgments begin on page 395, which is to be considered an extension of this copyright page.

ISBN: 0-658-00299-6

Published by National Textbook Company,
a division of NTC/Contemporary Publishing Group, Inc.
4255 W. Touhy Avenue, Lincolnwood, Illinois 60712-1975 U. S. A.
© 2001 NTC/Contemporary Publishing Group, Inc.
Manufactured in the United States of America

00 01 02 03 04 05 06 07 08 09   QB   0 9 8 7 6 5 4 3 2 1

Program Authors

Kathleen M. Galvin
Senior Author
Professor and Associate Dean
Communication Studies
  Department
Northwestern University
Evanston, Illinois

Jane Terrell
Director of Forensics
Language Arts Department
Lyndon Baines Johnson High School
Austin, Texas

Program Consultants

Jane G. Boyd
Grapevine High School
Grapevine, Texas

Ronald L. Dodson
Speech Consultant
Austin, Texas

Randy Ellis
Spring High School
Spring, Texas

Kandi King
Winston Churchill High School
San Antonio, Texas

Mary Alice Konz
Kearney High School
Kearney, Nebraska

Thomas Mahoney
Government Liaison
Ameritech

Michael Moyna
Cooper City High School
Cooper City, Florida

Ann Nicholson
Director, Communication Strategy
Information Services
Baxter International

Morris Snively
Executive Director, Communication
  Education Association
Belleville East High School
Belleville, Illinois

Joe Trevino, Jr.
Bishop High School
Bishop, Texas

Dedication

To Roy V. Wood—extraordinary friend and mentor

—KMG

To Rachel and Rebecca—daughters by birth, friends by choice

—MJT

Special thanks to Barbara Cushing, Shannon Dyer, Rebecca Wahlig, and Rachel Eichen for their research and organizational support.

Contents

Contents   **ix**

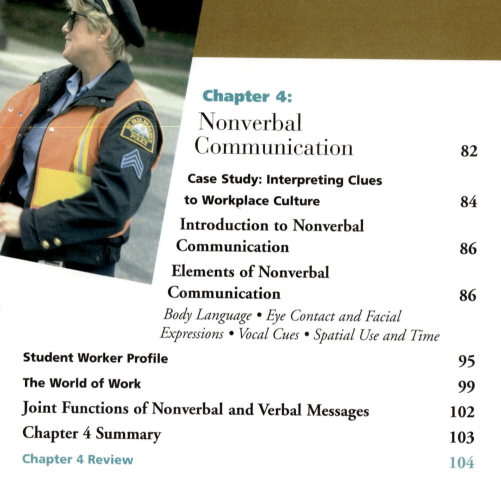

Unit 3

Interpersonal and Group Communication

Contents

Chapter 9
Conflict and Conflict Management

Unit 4 ## Presentations

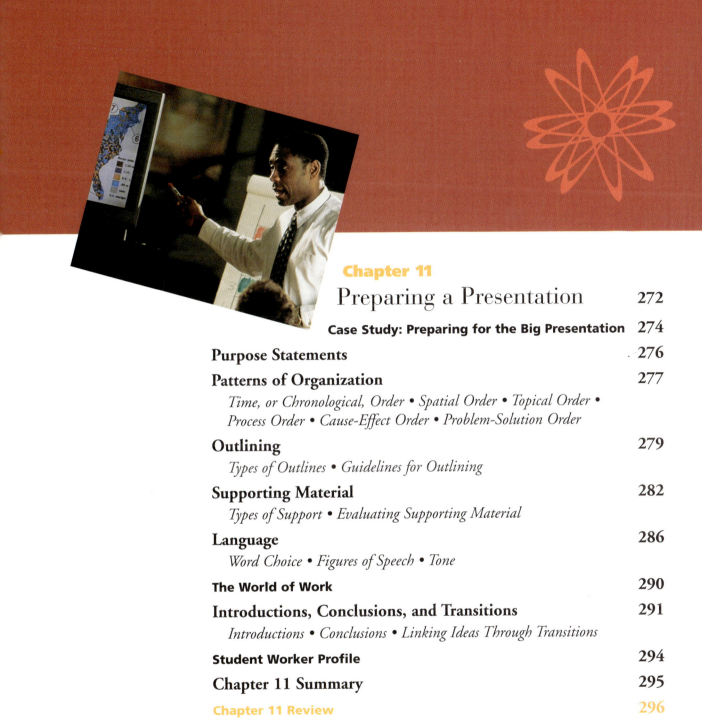

The Competent Communicator

Unit One

Communication and the Workplace

Objectives

After completing this chapter, you will be able to

- describe the importance of communication in work, service, and civic contexts
- define the communication process and explain how it works
- describe three communication situations in context
- examine your current communication skills and identify areas for growth

Key Terms

communication

context

entrepreneurs

feedback

group communication

interference

interns

interpersonal communication

public speaking

workplace

66 Communication is the lifeblood and the lifeline of relationships. **99**

—ANONYMOUS

3

Contrasting Communication Styles

The Johnson family saved for a year to visit a theme park area in a neighboring state for spring vacation. Amelia Johnson; her mother, Florence; and her two sons, Darren (7) and Derek (5) planned a four-night stay at a hotel outside the park. Florence did not have to walk far to the park entrance and could return to the hotel during the day to rest. When the Johnsons arrived, the hotel clerk informed them that, because the hotel was over-booked, he had rebooked them

at a similar hotel three miles down the road. When Mrs. Johnson complained, the clerk responded, "It's not that big a deal. There are regular shuttle buses from that hotel to the park. This happens all the time. It will be fine." Florence was upset but tried not to show it. She felt it was a big deal because she walked with a cane.

During their first day in the Water World theme park, the boys had a wonderful time in the pool, although the two women became uncomfortably hot because the children's pool area had run out of shade umbrellas. The pool next door had many extra umbrellas, but when Amelia asked a staff member about moving the umbrellas, the young man answered, "We can only give out the ones in this section. It's a problem every day. Sorry."

Later in the day Derek lost his new toy frog and started to cry very loudly. Staff members saw the situation but did not comment. Eventually, Amelia quieted her son. Although they had a park map, the Johnsons still got confused. At one point they could not figure out how to get to the synchronized-swimming arena and asked a park attendant. The attendant pointed to her left, saying, "It's

over there about ten minutes ahead. Ask someone as you get closer." After asking two more people, they finally got to the arena. Florence left early in the afternoon, waiting a half hour for the hotel shuttle, and did not come back to the park for the evening light show, since she did not want to wait in line again for the return shuttle. The Johnsons did not have the great day they had planned.

The next day the family headed off to the Movieland theme park. As they were waiting in a long line to ride on one of the roller coasters, Florence kept shifting from foot to foot and leaning against the railings. Soon a young man

in a park uniform approached and asked if she would like to sit on a bench at the front of the line until the rest of the family reached that point. Florence gratefully accepted the offer. During lunch, Darren spilled his half-finished soft drink and became upset. A cafeteria employee came over, cleaned up the mess, and arrived back with a full drink plus two cookies for the boys. She said, "We don't want you to have to be sad about anything while you are here."

Later in the day, as Amelia started to take pictures of her mother and the boys in front of movie-star cutouts, a park guide came up and suggested he take the pictures so that the whole family could be in the shots. He described landmarks to tell them how to get to the picnic grove, and then he took their map and marked a line for them to follow so that they would not get confused. Florence relaxed at the grove, and the whole family stayed to watch the evening's cartoon-character show.

The communication skills of many different persons influenced the Johnsons during their vacation. Note two instances of staff communication attempts that resulted in frustration for the Johnsons. What could those individuals have said or done differently? Note two effective communication moments. Describe what made the communication so effective in those moments.

Communication in the Workplace

At this point you may be thinking one of the following:

I can talk, so why do I need to learn to communicate?

I have a job, which I perform well, so why do I need this?

I won't have a career for years. Why should communication in the work-place affect me now?

The facts are (1) talking does not necessarily mean you are communicating, (2) your job performance can be improved if you use communication skills effectively, and (3) workplace communication issues do affect you now, and they will continue to do so in the future.

Communication Problems in the Workplace

Many business leaders are frustrated that their bright and talented new part-time and full-time employees cannot communicate effectively with each other and with the public. Frequently, customers report they are not treated well when they call a business or service organization. Others find employees in stores and restaurants to be unhelpful or unresponsive to their needs. Many employees express frustration with co-workers who are rude or, in some cases, hostile. **Entrepreneurs,** people who start up and manage their own businesses, depend heavily on employee communication skills to attract and keep customers.

Individuals who hold volunteer or community service positions face similar communication problems. Working with Habitat for Humanity, The Food Pantry, or the American Cancer Society involves everyday workplace issues. Most Americans will spend a large part of their lives in the workplace in paid or volunteer positions. Yet they may not exhibit the skills necessary for success. In a 1996 study, managers surveyed by the National Association of Colleges and Employers rated oral communication skills highest when describing what students need when entering corporate positions. Today's employers are increasingly unhappy with the skills and behaviors of high school graduates. Over 50 percent of the employers polled in a recent study said that new graduates were not respectful or polite and could not speak English properly. Employers also report that many graduates today lack writing and organizational skills.

Problems with oral communication skills are accompanied by problems with writing skills. An employee's ability to write clearly—whether in the form of a business report or electronic mail (e-mail messages)—is just one more test of that person's communication competence. Many companies are developing speaking, listening, and writing classes to help employees to improve their communication effectiveness. For example, Baxter International, a healthcare organization, offers employees classes such as How to Handle Conflict Verbally, Persuasive Speaking, and Team Building.

The Importance of Oral Communication

Why are communication skills important to you? They are important because workplace communication is or will be a major part of your life. A recent poll of adolescents by Primedia reveals that today's teenagers and young adults are independent thinkers who believe in taking responsibility for themselves. More than 80 percent of adolescents identify a well-paying job as a goal. So why do some employers believe there is a communication problem, and how can it be solved?

Of course you can communicate with some people very effectively at this point in your life, but how prepared are you to adapt to the communication demands of different people in different situations? Just because you can talk, or listen, or argue with a good friend does not mean you can communicate equally well with a boss, a newcomer to your workplace, a team member from a different culture, or a confused customer. Communication is central to

An employee's ability to write clearly is a tremendous asset in today's business world.

Steven Isoye, *Science Teacher*

Students at Highland Park High School are fortunate to have Mr. Steven Isoye as a science teacher and as the Science Department chair. His reputation as a fine teacher extends far beyond the school. He was selected as Illinois Teacher of the Year for 1998 by the Illinois State Board of Education. His own area of science is biology, though he has taught chemistry and physics during his career.

As chair of the department, Mr. Isoye spends much of his time in staff development, which means "I work with my

department in establishing goals, evaluating curriculum, and deciding where we should be going." He works with his faculty to build their knowledge and skills by encouraging them to attend conferences and workshops, and he tries to find unique opportunities to match the talents and interests of particular faculty members. In addition, he has to evaluate his faculty. Each evaluation involves a preconference, an observation of classroom teaching, and a postevaluation conference.

Mr. Isoye needs to be skilled at both written and oral communication. He suggests,

"Written communication is important because of the evaluations and reports that must be done and the number of memos that have to be sent out." Each year he has to collect data about student learning and curriculum issues, analyze the data, and present the data in written or oral form.

He needs public-speaking skills because he is called upon to give presentations to the school board, to teachers, and to parents. He also has to work one-on-one with parents, students, and teachers, which requires strong interpersonal skills.

In addition, he must help manage conflicts that arise involving students, parents, and teachers. His first move is to "make sure the student and parents talk directly to the teacher"—a strategy that frequently resolves the issue. On the occasions when that does not work, there is a need to hold a conference with the teacher, parents, the student, and a counselor. In these meet-

ings Mr. Isoye says he tries to maintain a calm voice, listen carefully, and repeat what he hears. Frequently, he relies on his strong personal listening skills and his knowledge of how to help others listen more effectively. For example, "Sometimes I will ask someone in a polite manner to say what he or she has heard so that I can check for understanding and to see that we are all on the same page and if we can come to a consensus."

Although his job is very demanding, Mr. Isoye enjoys his work because he appreciates the chance to "think out of the box" and find creative ways to solve problems and to plan for the future. He finds personal fulfillment in working with the science teachers and getting them to consider new ways to develop their own skills and to teach their specialties. Those who know and respect him would not be surprised to learn his personal belief: "I can always do better than excellent."

workplace life. A recent study by Pitney Bowes reports that workers handle over 200 messages of all types in a day. Some messages are oral; others are written. Clearly, sending and receiving messages will be part of your future workplace life. This book is concerned with your ability to become a competent communicator in the many different situations that you will encounter in the workplace.

What Is the Workplace?

You will need excellent communication skills in current and future functional contexts—this means public or semipublic situations in which your communication has consequences. Think about the term *workplace* broadly. **Workplace** refers to any situation where work is accomplished. It includes paid employment as well as unpaid work such as volunteer efforts or leadership in school and community groups. It involves working in a professional office of a national corporation or working in your local grocery store or making phone calls from home. It involves organizing your town's highway trash cleanup or volunteering on your town's ambulance crew. It also includes running your community's cable television station or working on the high school newspaper. A particular workplace communication style may be prescribed and formal, such as "Good afternoon, this is Weatherbee Products International. You have reached our Detroit office. How may I direct your call?" Or it may be very informal, such as, "Hi, Westlake Grocery."

Poor communication in the workplace can have very serious negative effects. Sales may be made or lost. Customers may return or not.

ZITS

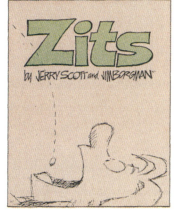

Many teens have part-time jobs at convenience stores, fast-food restaurants, movie theaters, video stores, and numerous other businesses.

Consequences are tied to a communicator's effectiveness. Sales may be made or lost; customers may return or not. Poor communication in the workplace can have very serious negative effects and, unfortunately, there is often no real way to measure the losses when a customer decides, "That salesclerk is chatting on the phone so I'm taking my business to another store" or "I won't donate to that charity because the students collecting funds could not even explain the program." In other workplace situations, misunderstandings can result in mistakes in production or incorrect orders or simply bad feelings between employees.

Teens in the Workplace

At this point in your life it is quite likely that you have major responsibilities that involve communicating with people other than your family and close friends. You may have a paying job, or you may be volunteering at a community organization. Currently one out of four high school seniors works 20 hours a week or more. It is estimated that about 25 percent of seniors work in food-service jobs and another 25 percent work in sales or as cashiers. These positions involve interacting with the public, as well as with co-workers and supervisors. In 1994–1997 more than half of all 14-year-olds worked at least part-time, mainly in jobs such as babysitting or yard work. You may be one of the countless teens who leave school each day and head to a job at a retail store, a fast-food restaurant, or a movie theater. Your summers may be spent babysitting, working at a vacation spot, doing office work, or serving as a camp counselor. You may live in a community in which most teenagers work at certain seasons of the year. This seasonal work might involve farming, holiday retail sales, or summer work at local resorts. For example, the *New York Times* reported that in 1998, 75 percent of the high school students who live on the Outer Banks of North Carolina worked year-round, while more than three-quarters worked during the May-to-September tourist season. Most mall operators report desperately trying to find student help for the holiday sales in November and December. Every year demand for teenage seasonal help grows.

Many teenagers are the backbone of community service programs, working in soup kitchens, tutoring centers, and hospitals. Some work in shelters with young children; others collect money for worthy causes. Colleges report that a high percentage of entering freshmen worked in community service during high school, and most of those students remain involved as volunteers during college. Frequently, high school and college students work as interns or do internships to gain specialized experience. Internship refers to practical supervised workplace experience. **Interns** generally are young people who are hired to gain this experience. Professionals in medicine, business, technical fields,

Many teens participate in community service programs, helping out in tutoring centers, hospitals, and daycare facilities.

and government provide paid and unpaid opportunities for young people to get firsthand experience in specialized workplaces in order to learn if that particular career area interests them.

You may have a responsible position outside the classroom. Some teens participate in conflict mediation or health education programs, function as sports team leaders, or direct children's theater companies. If you are involved in activities like these, you are part of a growing number of teens who work toward specific and valuable goals in their communities.

On the other hand, your responsibilities may be within school, religious, or political organizations. You may serve on the school board as a student member, or on a school judicial panel, or in student government. You may teach religious education classes or babysit during religious services. Or you may work for a political candidate at the local, state, or national level.

After high school you will probably head directly into a full-time job, or enroll in college, or join the armed forces. In all of these situations you will need effective communication skills.

Computer *Search*

Throughout this text you will be conducting computer searches of web sites related to careers and to communication. In order to prepare for these exercises, go to one of the following career-related sites.

www.pbs.org/insidepbs/jobs

www.cdc.gov/niosh/adoldoc.html

www.career-index.com

www.usajobs.opm.gov

After reading the material at the general site or in a more specific one that the general site leads you to, list three questions you have about your future in the work world. Write these questions down and note the web site that inspired your questions.

What Is Communication?

You have been communicating all your life, but can you define communication? Some common answers are

It's sending a message.
It's getting your point across.
It's sharing ideas and feelings.

Career Communication *Petroleum Engineer*

The career of petroleum engineer is probably not one you hear about often, but it is an important job that directly or indirectly affects most of our lives. Petroleum engineers, who usually work for oil companies, have the responsibility of looking for possible reservoirs of oil or natural gas. Once they discover such a reservoir, the engineers work to find the most efficient ways of recovering as much oil or gas as possible from it. They are continually evaluating existing equipment and developing ways to improve it in order to increase production. The majority of jobs for petroleum engineers are located in places where oil and gas are abundant, such as Texas, Oklahoma, Louisiana, and many countries overseas.

A person who would like to be a petroleum engineer should

be creative, analytical, and detail oriented. Communication skills also contribute to good performance on the job. Engineers must be able to communicate their ideas clearly both orally and in writing. They often work as part of a team of engineers to develop designs for new, more efficient equipment and to solve problems. They must interact effectively, however, with a variety of people on the job each day, including supervisors, scientists such as geologists and chemists, technicians, and drillers.

Petroleum engineers must be able to speak appropriately and make themselves understood in a wide range of situations with people of various backgrounds and educational levels. For example, they may need to discuss their latest project with another engineer, explain a scientific or technical concept or design to someone who has no science background, or listen to a report by a rig operator about what is not working on a piece of equipment. Good speaking and listening skills and clear and accurate communication can enable engineers to get things done in the most effective, efficient way possible.

Communication is the process of sending and receiving messages in order to share meanings. The communication process involves two or more people interacting verbally and nonverbally in order to understand each other's feelings, ideas, and attitudes. Sometimes they are said to be engaged in meaning making. In other words, speaker and listener are trying to understand what the other means.

What must happen for human communication to take place? The easy answer is that one person speaks and the other listens, and then they change places. This is a very simple description of a very complex process. There are six reasons why communication is complex: (1) communication is really more than speaking and listening, (2) communication is transactional, (3) commu-

Nonverbal messages rely heavily on facial expressions, body movements, appearance, and vocal tones. What nonverbal messages are being communicated in this photograph?

nication involves sharing of meanings, (4) communication depends on feedback, (5) communication is blocked by interference, and (6) communication occurs in a context. Let's look at each of these separately.

Computer *Search*

Go to an employment site on the Internet—for example, *www.Career-Index.com* or *www.quintcareers.com* and locate three job descriptions. Identify any communication-related skills listed in the description.

Communication Is More Than Speaking and Listening

Look back at the opening case study and identify moments when communication involved more than speaking and listening. You will see examples of nonverbal messages as a park attendant pointed in a direction, noticed how frustrated a child looked, or smiled at one of the boys. Human beings use words, or verbal messages, as well as nonverbal messages to connect with each other. Nonverbal messages are those expressed without words; they rely heavily on facial expressions, body movements, appearance, and vocal tones.

Check It Out

Observe two people who are deep in a conversation. They may be eating lunch together, talking in a hallway, standing in a mall, or riding on a bus. From a distance, watch the conversation for approximately five minutes, paying attention to their facial expressions; use of hand, arm, and leg movements or body shifts; and vocal tone (if you can hear them). Indicate these nonverbal messages in a notebook and make some predictions based on these messages. What do these nonverbal cues tell you about the relationship between the two people and the nature of the conversation between them? Write a paragraph in your notebook dealing with this question.

Communication Is Transactional

Communication is not just a matter of trading messages. Speakers and listeners share the responsibility for being good communicators. They don't just send messages back and forth. Transactional means that both communicators are constantly involved in and adjusting to the process. Communication works like a skilled tennis match: both tennis players are involved constantly in the game. When a good player hits the ball, he or she moves into position to prepare for the return shot. A poor player may just stand there after hitting the ball instead of anticipating the return shot. In communication, you send and receive messages simultaneously. This transactional process may be pictured in the following way:

Person One   **Person Two**
Speaking      Listening
Listening   Speaking

You can imagine how an interview, a coaching session, or a chess match works in this manner.

Communication Involves Sharing of Meanings

Look at the following messages and ask yourself how a listener might be confused by each one:

"It's a great summer job for making lots of money." (but it's *really* boring)
"The boss said there would be some heavy lifting." (He didn't say seven hours a day!)
"This team needs more motivation." (and even that may not accomplish much)
"That's really fresh." (fresh as a daisy? new and original? rude?)

Communication and the Workplace

You probably asked yourself what specifically does *lots of money* or *some heavy lifting* or *more motivation* mean. Your parents might ask what *fresh* means.

Meaning refers to the interpretation speakers and listeners place on the verbal and nonverbal messages they send out and receive. There is a wonderful expression that states, "Words don't mean, people do." What you mean by "This is a really tough job" may not be what your friend Angie means when she says it. You might be sarcastic; Angie might be overwhelmed by how long it takes. Sometimes the interpretation process is called *encoding* or *decoding* messages. Speakers encode a message by selecting the most appropriate verbal and nonverbal symbols for specific listeners. For example, clothing companies target specific audiences and create messages in their advertisements just for them. When a film student discusses a movie with her six-year-old brother, she might say, "I liked the characters of Tom and Rudy and thought the make-believe animals were awesome. The photography was good." When she discusses the same film with a friend, she might say, "I thought Tom was a well-defined character and Rudy was able to play off him as a distinct contrast. The integration of the digital creatures worked well, but they made the humans look a bit wooden. The cinematography was intriguing, since the hand-held camera segments created a defined mood." Listeners decode a message by filtering out the exact meaning of the original message. If you know the speaker is funny, you may take a remark as a joke. If you don't know the speaker, you may not think it is funny. Frequently, communication breakdowns occur when the intended message is misinterpreted by the listener. This leads to

Smiles, friendly gestures, and direct eye contact usually indicate that positive feedback is taking place. What is being communicated nonverbally in this photograph?

Chapter One

statements such as "But I thought you meant . . ." or "That's not what I said." Effective communication occurs when the listener interprets the meaning of the speaker's message the way the speaker intended it.

Communication Depends on Feedback

The term **feedback** refers to the verbal and nonverbal messages listeners send that tell speakers how they are doing. Feedback may be positive or negative. Negative feedback tells you there is a problem. You may need to change what you are doing or saying. When listeners look confused, frown, or stare into space, you probably need to adjust your message. Positive feedback tells you to continue what you are doing or saying. Smiles, nods, and direct eye contact usually indicate the listener is with you.

Assume you are trying to convince the local newspaper editor to run a free ad for the community soup kitchen's fund-raising auction. As you talk to her, you will watch her face to see if she shows signs of interest. If she looks confused, you may explain again how many lines the ad should contain. At the same time, the editor is listening to you and watching you to see how involved you are. If your voice and face convey energy and excitement about the fundraiser, she is more likely to believe you are committed to the cause. If you have a flat tone and stare at the floor, she may not believe you are really involved.

Communication Is Blocked by Interference

When a person has trouble receiving the message that is being sent, it is often because of interference, or "noise." **Interference** refers to something that blocks a listener's ability to receive a message. External distractions such as loud music, a big-screen TV, or car traffic may interfere with receiving the oral message. Internal distractions such as personal worries, daydreaming, or physical illness may also cause interference. Effective communicators work hard to reduce interference, although it's not always easy. Sometimes interference results in lost sales, accidents, or confused messages, all of which cause workplace problems.

Communication Occurs in a Context

The term **context** refers to the setting or situation in which you are communicating. You will adapt your messages to time, place, occasion, and people involved. You will consider the listener's culture and expectations. For example, you would be unlikely to talk with your best friend about a recent date in the middle of a planning meeting for the arts fair. It would not be the right time or place to do so. You will also attempt to adapt your language to your listeners. This means deciding whether to use slang or deciding how simple your words should be. Communication is a very complex process that requires careful attention in order to share meanings effectively.

Types of Communication

There are several different types of oral communication that affect the workplace. They include

- interpersonal communication
- group or team communication
- public speaking

These types of communication reflect the context for communication, especially the number of people involved and their relationships. There are other types of communication, such as intrapersonal communication or mass communication, that may also be mentioned. Intrapersonal communication refers to personal thoughts—communication with yourself that occurs within your mind. Mass communication involves one-way communication of mechanically reproduced messages to large audiences. Programs on radio and television are examples of mass communication. These types are not as relevant to human workplace communication.

Remember!

The following processes contribute to communication complexity:

▶ Creating verbal and nonverbal messages

▶ Adapting to the transactional process

▶ Creating shared meaning

▶ Reading feedback

▶ Managing interference

▶ Understanding situation or context

Kirk and Kurt Brown, *Musicians*

When Carnival Cruise Lines ships dock at the port of St. Thomas in the Virgin Islands, the passengers are in for a very pleasant surprise. They are entertained by a steel-pan orchestra made up of local musicians, including twin brothers Kirk and Kurt Brown. Kirk plays the tenna-pan, while Kurt plays the double tenna-pan. Their interest in music and some of their musical talent probably comes from their father, who also played in a steel-pan orchestra.

The twins, who have been playing since 5th grade, practice from 5 to 7 P.M. on weekdays and 9 to noon on Saturdays. According to Kirk, "It takes quite a bit of practice and perseverance in order to play really well." The twins also play for restaurants, hotels, and special occasions. Every two weeks the orchestra changes its arrangements to come up with new dances and different songs. Every show contains some cultural dances. At the end of a performance, the entire orchestra dances as the group moves offstage.

Participating in a steel-pan orchestra means more than just playing an instrument. "You must have communication skills and be well-mannered.

Being able to dance to the music is a definite plus," says Kirk. He usually introduces the band and welcomes the tourists, serving as the host or master of ceremonies. Orchestra members dress in local "tropical wear," which includes white shorts and colorful shirts. The twins frequently appear on television with the orchestra. The orchestra is a wonderful part of their lives because, according to the twins, "The atmosphere is lively and spirited. The audience gets involved and we have a great time. Tourists wear costumes, eat and drink, and really let the music take control of them."

In addition, the twins work on Graffiti Street, a PBS-sponsored teen talk show that has "regulars," performers who regularly appear on the show. Topics recently covered include teen violence, teen pregnancy, exercise, and block scheduling in schools.

According to Kurt and Kirk, their music and their media interests are likely to continue for a long time. Kurt reports that they "plan to start their own steel-pan orchestra in the future."

Student Worker Profile

19

Interpersonal Communication

When you talk with a co-worker in the office, help a customer select in-line skates, or tutor an international exchange student in English, you are taking part in **interpersonal communication,** or ongoing interaction between two people. The word *interpersonal* means "between people." Much of your day is spent talking one-on-one with other people. Although you may not be aware of it, you follow certain communication rules when you talk with another person. Your choice of words will be adapted to a specific individual. You are likely to have direct eye contact.

Group or Team Communication

Group communication is interaction among people who share an interest in the same thing or share a common purpose. In business today, employees spend many hours working in teams. Most working groups range from four to eight people, although there are many examples of larger groups. Throughout your life you will be involved in groups for a variety of reasons, including solving problems and planning events. Group discussion works best when mem-

Interpersonal communication is one-on-one interaction between two people.

Public speaking involves one speaker talking to an audience. Examples of public speaking range from formal presentations in large auditoriums to simple announcements in front of a small group.

bers follow certain rules or patterns and when leaders are prepared to help the members communicate well. A study of group communication can help you to become the best group member and leader you can be.

Public Speaking

When you present an oral report, make office announcements, or give a talk at a religious service, you are involved in public speaking. Usually **public speaking** involves one speaker or a small group of presenters talking to an audience. This may be one speaker in an auditorium addressing 60 listeners, or three committee members giving a presentation to the community college activities funding board. Speaking in public requires you to be informed and organized. You must be able to connect with your audience members. You may have to give different kinds of speeches, such as speeches to inform or to persuade. You may even have to debate with another person. A study of public speaking will help you learn how to prepare a speech, practice your public-speaking skills, and develop your listening skills.

There are many communication skills that can be associated with existing careers. However, new career areas evolve each year, and it's likely that sometime in the future you will be working as a paid employee or as a volunteer in a position that does not exist right now. There are new hot careers, which a

Communication and the Workplace

recent report predicts will grow in size and importance over the next few years. These include

- corporate intelligence officer
- extreme sports marketer
- accessibility consultant
- database integrator
- telecommuting manager
- special events planner
- multimedia training program developer
- adoption advocate
- commerce project manager

Remember!

Three types of oral communication that affect the workplace are

▶ **Interpersonal communication**

▶ **Group or team communication**

▶ **Public speaking**

Eye-to-Eye

A brief description of three hot new careers is provided below. Pick one and discuss some of the speaking and listening situations that would be part of it and the kinds of communication skills that would be needed.

Accessibility Consultant

This person interacts with others to make space more friendly for people with disabilities. It may involve consulting with small-business owners about floor layout to accommodate a wheelchair, or talking to a mall manager about accommodating blind shoppers, or helping a teacher rearrange a child's classroom to minimize distracting stimulation. Consultants need a background in design and in rehabilitation.

Corporate Intelligence Officer

This person tries to predict future trends in a particular industry and to learn what the competition is doing. He or she gathers and analyzes information from many sources—newspapers, technical journals, speeches, and futurist materials—and uses this information to project what will happen in a particular industry in the future. Companies set long-term corporate goals based on these projections. Someone working in corporate intelligence needs a background in market research and a basic understanding of a particular industry.

Telecommuting Manager

A telecommuting manager coordinates an organization's efforts to make effective use of its telecommuting employees. As more individuals work at home using e-mail, the Internet, and teleconferencing, companies need to be kept up-to-date on what computers, faxes, and modems they will need in order to equip, train, and supervise their workers. A telecommuting manager needs a background in management and information technology.

Adoption advocate is an example of a new career that will grow in size and importance in the next few years.

Self-Awareness as a Communicator

Competent workplace communicators have certain characteristics. They are sensitive to the communication needs of their jobs. They establish goals to improve their skills over time. Most important, they monitor their own communication behavior and work to develop their communication skills.

In the next chapter you will learn the steps used to become a competent communicator. The beginning of the process involves self-assessment. The following questions will help you begin the process of identifying your strengths and areas for improvement. Remember, your world will expand with each passing year, and you will have need for some skills in the future that don't seem very important right now.

Self-Inventory Form

Use this self-inventory form to analyze your current communication skills. Rate each item from 1 to 5, with 1 meaning *never* and 5 meaning *always*.

Never ▶ **Always**

1. I tend to give reasons when I disagree with another's ideas.   1   2   3   4   5

2. I pay careful attention to a person's facial expression as we discuss problems.   1   2   3   4   5

3. I monitor my speech to avoid using terms that could be offensive to another person.   1   2   3   4   5

4. I try to predict problems or confusions my listener might have and change my message to try to avoid these problems.   1   2   3   4   5

5. When giving directions, I check to see if my listener really understood what I said.   1   2   3   4   5

6. If I am surprised or concerned by what another person says, I double-check to make sure that I understood him or her correctly before responding.   1   2   3   4   5

7. If I am unclear about directions, I tend to ask questions to be sure I've got the directions right.   1   2   3   4   5

8. When I'm in a group, I try to contribute ideas and make sure that others are comfortable in contributing.   1   2   3   4   5

9. When I am dealing with customers, I try to anticipate what they might need or want.   1   2   3   4   5

10. When a newcomer enters a group, I try to make sure that person is included in the conversation.   1   2   3   4   5

11. I try to adapt my language to my listeners so that I am not too technical or confusing.   1   2   3   4   5

12. I take time to compliment others or to tell them they are doing well.   1   2   3   4   5

13. When instructing others, I try to adapt my language to their level of knowledge or background.   1   2   3   4   5

14. I pay attention to the race, gender, and age of co-workers and adapt my communication when appropriate.   1   2   3   4   5

15. I present myself well as I enter an interview situation.   1   2   3   4   5

Self-Feedback

As part of your development of communication skills, you should be involved in a self-feedback process. Self-feedback involves the messages you give yourself as you pay attention to your own behavior. Self-feedback may occur during an interaction or after an interaction is completed. For example, during a conversation you might say to yourself, "I'm using too much technical jargon for this customer" or "I'm talking too fast because I'm nervous. I should slow down." After an interview you might say to yourself, "I should have had some questions ready for the interviewer" or "I should have made my point more directly. I will next time."

Chapter 1 *Summary*

In this chapter, you learned about communication and the workplace. Effective communication is critically important to your success in the workplace—the world beyond the classroom. The workplace refers to responsible situations involving paid, volunteer, or community employment.

To understand how important communication is in the workplace, it is first necessary to recognize that the communication process is affected by a variety of complex factors, including verbal and nonverbal messages, interference, the sharing of meaning, feedback, and context.

It is also necessary to understand the basics of the communication process, be able to explain how it works, and apply it to various communication situations. Finally, the competent communicator engages in self-analysis to examine his or her own communication skills and to identify areas of growth.

Review Questions

1. What are some communication problems customers complain about?
2. What three specific skills do new graduates often lack according to business executives?
3. Define the workplace and give three examples familiar to you.
4. Name two workplace communication styles.
5. Define communication.
6. What are nonverbal messages? List four types.
7. Why does effective communication depend on feedback?
8. What two types of "noise" interfere with communication? Describe each.
9. Describe the three types of workplace communication.
10. What is self-feedback?

Critical Thinking Activities

Speaking/Doing

1. Read the help wanted pages in a local newspaper or on the Internet, or go to a specific corporate web site's job listings. Pick one position that appears to involve communication skills. Contact the company or organization and ask for a representative in Human Resources. Identify yourself and your purpose in calling. Explain that you will be brief, and ask for permission to ask just a few questions about the communication skills needed for the job advertised on the web site. Share what you learn with the class.
2. Take a poll of friends and classmates to find out how many of them hold part-time jobs after school or on weekends. Then ask those who do hold jobs to list the three most important communication skills needed to do their jobs effectively. Tally the results and share them with the class.

Writing

1. What are some consequences of poor communication in the workplace? In one or two paragraphs, describe the importance of adapting your language to the situation and explain the potential consequences of not doing so.
2. Develop a script for one of the following communication situations: a doctor talking to a patient, a librarian talking to a student, or a department-store clerk talking to a customer. Discuss with classmates how these scripts would change if you were to change the listener in each one (change the patient to another doctor, the student to another librarian, the customer to a fellow employee).

Group Activities

1. Using menus from a local restaurant, practice taking food orders. Divide the class into groups of six. One person in the group can be the "cook," one person the server, and the other four can be the diners. The server should take everyone's order on a typical order pad and then give the orders to the person in the "kitchen." That person then "fills" the orders on paper plates, writing the items

on pieces of paper and placing them on each plate. The server then takes a tray of paper plates to the diners and serves "food" properly. Have students take turns at the various roles. Discuss what mistakes where made and how they might be corrected.

2. With a partner, imagine two important communication skills needed in three of the positions listed below and give an example of each.

soccer coach   pediatrician

journalist   trial lawyer

taxi driver   police officer

Practical Application: Case Challenge

Rona, Shane, and Yuki volunteered to coordinate the Computer and Program Support Organization (CAPSO) at their high school. CAPSO is one year old and serves to provide technical support for special projects to faculty and students in the middle school and high school. Last year it served six teachers who wanted to use more web-based learning in their classroom but did not know much about the technical area. Students who were working on special science and history fair projects came to the group for help. Last year's senior coordinators all graduated. This year is just underway, and the new coordinators are finding some surprises after the first two-hour workshop in the library. Shane is complaining, "They were a terrible audience. I'm talking about the computer-graphics capabilities, and Mr. Howard kept interrupting and asking me what I meant. Then that little sixth-grade kid kept going 'I want a

web site.' The other sixth grader looked like he was totally confused."

Yuki interrupted, "Shane—you were going on about hypertext, hyperlinks, Usenet, gifs, and Java. Most of these people were here because they didn't know much about computers—I think you scared them to death. Ms. Albert said the whole thing may not be worth the effort."

When Rona gets into the conversation, she says, "We've got to figure out a way to convince these teachers and students that we can help. I just sat through most of your presentations and didn't say much. I couldn't tell what you wanted me to do or add."

"Well, what could you have done?" asked Shane.

At this point, this group needs a clearer direction and ways to communicate more effectively with their audience members. What would you advise them to consider doing in the next two weeks?

Chapter Two

Communication Competence and Workplace Culture

Objectives

After completing this chapter, you will be able to

- describe a competent communicator
- describe the five communication acts that competent communicators use
- describe the steps followed by competent communicators
- establish standards for choosing communication strategies
- begin the process of analyzing and evaluating your own communication
- begin the process of analyzing workplace culture

Key Terms

communication acts
communication strategy
competence steps
competent communicators
culture
ethics
social ritual
strategies
workplace culture

> **"** When people work to develop communication competence, they are concerned with 'putting language to work' for them. **"**
>
> —BARBARA S. WOOD, *Development of Functional Communication*

29

Learning How Workplaces Really Work

Wendy's older sister, Amanda, worked as a server at a local resort for four summers. Amanda always looked forward to her summer job because she enjoyed the guests, the other servers, and the atmosphere in the kitchen. She said the schedule—6:30 A.M. to 8:00 P.M., with an afternoon break at the pool—was tough, but she loved it. Because Amanda planned to study in Spain, she had to leave the resort almost a month early. She arranged with her boss to have Wendy fill in for her those

final four weeks. Wendy did not really know the job but figured, "How hard could it be to serve food?"

The first few days were rough. Wendy arrived at 6:35 A.M. She noticed that everyone was rushing around setting up tables and organizing their serving stations. Wendy started serving at 7:15. The early-riser guests trickled in to her six large tables. The first few older guests greeted her with "Good morning." Wendy smiled and started to pour coffee for each, as Amanda had suggested.

One woman asked, "Is that regular or decaf?" and a man said, "I don't drink coffee. Only OJ for me." Wendy got the decaf coffee and proceeded to tell the guests their three breakfast choices. When she returned with some food, the man asked, "Is the orange juice ever coming?" Wendy had forgotten he ordered it. She hurried back to the kitchen and discovered that she was surrounded by other servers shouting orders, cooks pelting her with questions, and the manager trying to inform her about two diabetic children requiring special diets at one of her tables.

By the end of the breakfast period, Wendy had heard numerous guest complaints about the slow and confused service. Several customers complained that their eggs were not prepared the way they ordered them. Their orders had to be re-filled. At 9:30 Wendy was exhausted. The lunch period didn't go well for her either. By evening, she was frustrated because she felt so much had gone wrong.

Wendy barely got through the next few days. She arrived early, raced around the dining room, slammed food on the table, and tried to avoid much direct interaction with the guests or kitchen staff. At each meal guests complained that the service was poor. On Friday Wendy told Pete, one of her co-workers, that she wanted to quit.

Pete replied, "It's clear that you're not happy, but you haven't given it a chance." This comment surprised her. Pete told her that she never asked for help, avoided the other staff, and did not relate well to the guests. He concluded, "Everybody thinks you are a snob." Wendy was shocked. Pete continued, "Look at the servers who love this job. They are friendly to everyone. They greet the guests by name, double-check the orders, give the cooks specific information, and ask questions in order to learn." He told Wendy to try to do something each day to become more competent. He suggested, for example, that she check a guest's order by repeating it back to the guest before placing it.

The next day Wendy went out of her way to greet the guests by name as they arrived in the dining room. Most seemed pleased. When she took an order, she deliberately repeated it back: "A club sandwich with extra tomato, two pickles." Sometimes she would be corrected: "Yes, but remember I said to hold the mayonnaise." Wendy worked hard to make sure she gave the cooks a full explanation of what a guest wanted. She thanked guests for their orders, and she got some smiles in return.

After another week, Wendy found herself pleased to see certain guests arrive at her table and sorry to see them go home on Saturday. She began to joke around with other staff members. The dining room manager told her she had come a long way since her first day.

Wendy's experiences probably sound familiar to you whether or not you have ever waited on tables in a restaurant. The lessons she learned can be applied to many kinds of communication situations. What observations did Pete make to be of assistance? Identify three specific changes Wendy tried to make. How would you describe the steps Wendy went through to change her behaviors?

Communication Competence

Sometimes you may think workplace behaviors involve only doing tasks correctly. So if you can pump gas, plant flowers, or fix a computer, you may think you are doing competent work. Most of the time, however, you will discover there's more to this picture! Success in most positions depends on effective communication. People who communicate effectively are called **competent communicators,** which means they are capable or skilled at speaking and listening. Competent communicators have a wide range of communication skills and know which ones to use in specific situations in order to reach their goals.

There are five **communication acts** that are the major reasons for communicating. The five acts are (1) sharing information, (2) managing persuasive messages, (3) discussing feelings, (4) following social rituals, and (5) using imagination.

Sharing Information

An important communication act is giving and getting information. Exchanging information involves giving information, giving directions, teaching a process, asking questions to get information, or checking out what someone said. Many people take this act for granted. Some speakers assume that

Exchanging information involves giving information, giving directions, teaching a process, asking questions to get information, or checking out what someone said.

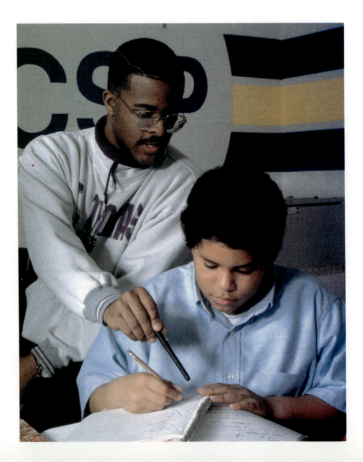

telling someone something equals teaching that person how to do something: "I told you; you should know how to do it." Others mix up steps when explaining a process or forget to include key information.

Sometimes listeners do not know they have incomplete or inaccurate information because they don't know very much about the subject. They don't know what questions to ask. Other times, they don't ask questions because they don't want to appear stupid. It is a wise listener who is able to request additional information or question a confusing point.

Eye-to-Eye

Read the following problems concerning information sharing and develop answers with your partner. What questions might a listener ask after hearing the following comments?

Situation 1

Chef to new employee on making turkey stuffing:
"After you put a bag of bread crumbs in the bowl, add chopped onion and celery. Then add two cored and peeled apples. I usually add a pinch of celery salt and black pepper. Drizzle chicken broth over it and add some small chunks of butter."

Situation 2

Coast Guard lieutenant explaining responsibilities to a new recruit:
"In this part of the country we often deal with hurricane emergencies. This means we have to get our own assets out of the area, usually sending cutters down to Yucatán. Then we start getting calls about overdue vessels. Our main job is to get all the navigational aids accounted for, to locate buoys that may have moved off course, and to get them operational. We have to clean up floating debris, and eventually we go out in the community to help them out."

Communicating to share information serves as the basis for all speaking and listening. Unless you send and receive messages accurately, you cannot get your point across, and you cannot truly understand another person's ideas.

Managing Persuasive Messages

You are often the sender and receiver of persuasive messages. Every day you try to convince other people to think or behave in a certain way, and they try to convince you. Many of your persuasive messages are directed toward your parents—for example, you try to convince them that you need a later curfew, more money, a car of your own, or new clothes. Your parents may try to per-

You send and receive persuasive messages every day. Many of them are directed toward your parents.

suade you to clean your room, study more, or earn your own spending money. Your friends regularly try to persuade you. They may encourage you to take a job where they work, join the swing chorus at school, or go to a party. As you receive persuasive messages, you will need to analyze and evaluate them against your own personal beliefs and standards.

You need to be able to manage persuasive messages effectively. For example, how would you deal with the following?

> You are a desk monitor at your community recreation center, and the evening desk supervisor has just quit. Even though you are younger than the other employees, and supervisors are usually seniors and college students, you still want the job. You want to convince the senior who is the building's night manager to hire you. What strategies will you use to persuade the supervisor to consider you? If he says, "We hire only seniors and college students in this position," what will you say?

Discussing Feelings

An important communication act is talking about your feelings and listening to others talk about theirs. Often people become uncomfortable and do not know how to respond when a conversation moves into a discussion of feelings. Yet sometimes a person who is talking about his or her feelings does not need a response but just needs someone to listen.

Chapter Two

Lena Coleman, *Choreographer*

It's not every 17-year-old who gets to tell adults, up to age 65, where to go and how to move to get there! As a member of a community dance theater, which combines acting and dancing, Lena Coleman works with all ages to create shows that teach understanding and teamwork to audiences of younger children. The goal is to model and teach acceptance and understanding for all members of the community.

Lena has been performing with the group for a long time and says, "As a performer, it's important to have good working relationships with the entire cast, so talking about respect and making sure you give it keeps the working environment pleasant."

Recently Lena has taken on a position as choreographer, which, according to her, means, "You have to command respect which is more difficult in this situation when you have such varying ages of students. You have to especially remember to speak to *everyone* on the same level." Many of her students ask questions about how to move, what the steps are, and where the motivation for certain moves comes from. She explains that "in dancing, you must take a chance, just get out there. It's all about having fun and sharing that fun with the audience." She tries to incorporate input from class members and weaves their ideas together as part of the dance.

Lena claims that listening is an important part of her work, since many people are embarrassed about being onstage and they want to talk out these feelings. Yet, on occasion, she has to persuade performers that her way is better and more effective.

Lena's work goes beyond the performing area. She has developed material for human interest stories shown on the local news. In addition she has organized promotional events such as fund-raising dinners and has developed ads for newspapers and posters.

Lena remains very excited about her work, saying, "I love performing, and, even though it sounds corny, I love it because I can touch someone with my art." She concludes, "If I do something to touch someone, I've done something worthwhile."

Student Worker Profile

Many young people who volunteer in hospitals encounter patients who want to talk about their frustrations or fears. Sometimes co-workers need to share their feelings of frustration with each other when things don't go well or their feelings of joy at a big team success. Frequently shoppers express feelings of anger if they do not believe they are being treated well or if there is something wrong with the merchandise.

How do you respond when someone else expresses a desire to talk about feelings? Do you let the person talk, or do you try to change the topic? Competent communicators are able to talk about their feelings and to listen to other people's feelings.

Following Social Rituals

Social rituals refer to a culture's rules for everyday interaction. These include communication patterns that are routinely followed in certain situations. In the United States there are rituals for greetings, for leaving, and for small talk. There are rules for talking, such as don't interrupt, look at the speaker, and don't stand very close to the other person. In Asian cultures, when you greet others you are expected to bow with little eye contact. If you are not sure what to do or say in a particular situation, you may make a poor impression or you may feel uncomfortable. Learning these rituals depends on learning from others' directions, watching and listening to others, and asking questions.

Most workplaces have rituals to follow. Some rituals are general to our society. In a store, customers ask questions about a product but not personal questions about a salesperson's life. It is unacceptable for salespeople to shout at or express anger at customers. Both customers and salespeople are expected to say "Thank you" when a sale is completed. Some social rituals are unique to a specific workplace organization; they are a part of the organization's way of life. Sometimes a senior employee will spell out expected behavior—for example, "No swearing or personal talk in front of customers." Often, however, no one tells a newcomer things like "Be sure to greet people when you show up in the morning" or "Don't disagree with the boss during a meeting. Do it later." The savvy newcomer has to learn these informal rituals by observing.

Each culture has different social rituals. Americans tend to expect listeners to maintain eye contact by looking at them directly. They also expect listeners to indicate they are paying attention by nodding and giving facial cues. In other cultures a person might look down while listening in order to be polite or might ask questions that seem very personal. In some cultures, to be on time actually means to show up 15 minutes to 2 hours after the announced time.

In the United States there are rituals for almost all social situations, including phoning for an interview, introducing a teacher to your parent, ending a conversation, and leaving a voice-mail message. Some of these rituals will be discussed later in this text.

Check It Out

Interview a volunteer who works with new immigrants or interview an immigrant (a parent, grandparent, relative, or neighbor). Ask him or her to suggest some guidelines that new immigrants might be given for how to act and speak in this country. Make a list of the suggestions.

Using Imagination

Imaginative communication occurs in storytelling, acting out a situation, or brainstorming a solution to a problem. For example, instead of lecturing a new bakery employee about how everyone is expected to pitch in when there's a deadline, a senior employee might get the point across by telling a story about the time the manager stayed late and drove the bakery van to be sure all the graduation party cakes were delivered on time. A corporate manager might coach new employees through role-plays. The manager might play the role of a difficult client to help the junior member learn effective ways to communicate with that client.

This performer is telling stories to entertain an audience, but storytelling is used informally in the workplace to teach new employees "the way we do things around here."

Remember!

Competent communicators effectively handle these communication acts:

▶ Sharing information

▶ Managing persuasive messages

▶ Discussing feelings

▶ Following social rituals

▶ Using imagination

When you and a friend are working together as a team to solve a problem, creative communication occurs. You may suggest one idea, and your friend may use your idea to create a second, which then leads to a third idea. You feed each other's imaginations. In business, this is called creative brainstorming. When you make predictions, you are using your imagination. You can make predictions about transportation in the year 2020 or about the clothes of the future. Good listeners like to hear how other people think creatively. It stimulates their thinking.

The five communication acts are important because they account for most communication situations you encounter daily. Effective speakers and listeners have many ways to use these acts. In the following section you will learn how to develop your communication competence by following four key steps.

Steps of the Competent Communicator

Competent communicators are not born with their skills. They don't know how to perform these communication acts as small children. They don't apply a secret formula. Rather, they do two things: they develop a number of strategies based on communication acts to deal with new communication situations, and they follow certain steps in order to reach their goals.

There is a piece of folk wisdom that says, "Practice makes perfect." This statement may be old, but it's not necessarily correct. Actually, practicing something over and over that is incorrect to begin with does not lead to perfection. It only makes the problem behavior permanent. People who truly wish

Wendy Chen, *Lawyer*

Wendy Chen is a lawyer who practices civil law at the small firm of Smith, Price, & Wagoner. This means that she helps people make good decisions about what to do with their property. She counsels those who are setting up wills or trusts, settles disputes about a mortgage or property title, and ensures that people's wills are carried out according to their wishes.

Chen enjoys her work. In high school she wanted to be a teacher. During her second year of college, however, she was called to sit on a jury, and the experience changed her life. "Watching the justice system at work was just fascinating to me," she remembers. "I knew immediately that I wanted to be a part of that."

Chen is convinced that good communication skills are the most important skills for a lawyer. "A lawyer's job is essentially speaking, listening, and writing," she says. Lawyers have to be able to speak clearly and form good arguments so that the judge, jury, and other lawyers will find their arguments convincing. They need to listen closely to their clients and to other lawyers in order to understand what they are really saying. Lawyers also need to be able to write well, because they often must draw up contracts, wills, or other legal documents. Chen adds, "A badly written

contract can destroy all the work of a good negotiating session, so being able to write well is an extremely important skill."

Chen says that one of the things she likes most about her job is the variety it offers. No two days are alike. She spends some days in court, presenting evidence to support a client. On other days, she meets with clients in her office to listen to their problems and counsel them on their legal rights and obligations. For example, she might advise a good course of action for a client who wants to buy property, or help a newly married couple write their first will. Other days are quieter, when she spends time in a library researching the laws behind a case or writing legal documents.

It has been six years since Chen finished law school and started working as a lawyer. When asked whether she would choose the same career if she started over again, she responds with a definite yes. "It is not always easy," she says. Some days she has to work with difficult clients and lawyers, and she often must work long hours, especially when she is in the middle of a court case. "But the satisfaction of winning a case and knowing that I have helped to make someone's life a little better makes it all worthwhile."

The World of Work

to develop good skills actively seek new ways to behave and then make an effort to practice those behaviors.

Eye-to-Eye

Discuss the two situations described below. Think of three or four ways that you could handle each situation. Then decide which one you would most likely use.

- You are selling candles three nights a week to raise money for a youth center at the local high school gymnasium. How might you convince local homeowners to contribute?
- Each Saturday you and a co-worker have total responsibility for managing a small clothing store. He comes late, leaves early, and takes long breaks. You want to tell him that this is a problem and you are angry.

Competence steps are steps that a communicator follows to select and act on a strategy for handling a particular communication situation. In order to communicate effectively in any new or complex situation, experienced communicators suggest that you use the following steps:

1. Review your communication strategies. (Think about a wide range of communication strategies you might use to handle certain situations.)
2. Select one. (Analyze the situation and choose the strategy that seems most appropriate.)
3. Act on that choice. (Actually carry out the chosen strategy.)
4. Evaluate the result. (Assess the success or failure of that strategy in terms of the responses you receive.)

Let's discuss each of these steps in more detail using a particular case. Suppose you are involved in the second situation described in the Eye-to-Eye feature above. You and Chris manage a sports store on Saturdays. Chris takes advantage of you by coming late, leaving early, and taking long breaks. You want him to recognize the problem and fix it. In what ways could you handle the situation?

Review Your Communication Strategies

Think of possible communication strategies. **Strategies** are methods or plans to reach a goal. A **communication strategy** involves using a carefully selected message to reach a goal. Some possibilities are

Customer service representatives use a variety of communication strategies to deal diplomatically with dissatisfied customers.

- leave Chris a note saying, "Please be on time next week"
- tell Chris you need to talk about the schedule because you are getting frustrated
- arrive very late to show Chris how it feels
- call the owner and ask her to talk to Chris
- other (You may have another idea.)

Reviewing possible strategies means you should always consider more than one way to deal with a situation. You need to have many options. For example, if you can only deal with an angry person by yelling, or you only respond to a helpful suggestion with "Whatever," your communication is limited. Customer service representatives rely on a variety of strategies to handle angry customers. A competent communicator might have four ways to confront anger: (1) "Let's talk about this later when we are less upset," (2) "I won't discuss this with you until you stop yelling at me," (3) "You're right—I wasn't thinking," or (4) yell back to get the other person's attention.

Select a Strategy

Selecting a strategy means choosing the best strategy from your options. Some options are better than others. You consider the situation: who is involved, the place, the occasion, and the ethics of your choice. You ask yourself questions: Is this a friend or a stranger? If this is a friend, what is she usually like? Are we in a public or private place? Are friends or strangers here? What is the reason for this occasion—a party, a study break, or a meeting?

Ethics refers to the principles you believe in regarding right or wrong conduct. These help give you ethical standards, or criteria for choosing a strategy. You need to consider your ethical standards—tell the truth, avoid hurting someone carelessly—as you select a strategy. Your final choice will depend on a variety of factors, including what you know about the other person, how public the setting is, and why you are together.

Let's look again at the example of Chris and the clothing store. You need to figure out which strategy you would choose based on the real situation. In reviewing your options, you might talk to yourself in the following way:

1. If I leave a note, Chris might ignore it and then I'd have to talk to him anyway. He might get angrier because I did not talk directly to him.
2. If I tell him I want to talk because I'm frustrated with his behavior, perhaps he will think of how to resolve things before we actually talk. Because he is a friend, I don't want to hurt him.
3. If I show up late to get my point across, I may just confuse things, and I could get in trouble with the owner.
4. If I call the owner without talking to Chris first, Chris might get very angry and it would be really unpleasant to work together.
5. Maybe if I took on one of his jobs, such as sweeping up, he'd make more of an effort to be on time.

After considering these, you may select strategy 2 in hopes of convincing Chris to treat you fairly and keeping him as a friend.

Act on the Strategy

This may seem like an unnecessary step, but guess what? Many times people do not act on the strategy they have chosen. They feel uncomfortable confronting someone, they don't want to make other people angry, or they stall, hoping that the situation will change or go away.

Suppose you select the strategy of talking with Chris instead of talking to the boss or writing notes. Now you have to really do it. Try not to let your ner-

Career Communication *Journalist*

Fine journalists need a very wide range of communication skills. Questioning is second nature to journalists, whether they are school newspaper reporters, cable TV reporters, or foreign specialists for CNN. After doing background research, they learn to ask questions that result in more than yes or no answers. They probe answers with more questions. When interviewing a source, a good reporter pays attention to nonverbal messages in addition to the verbal ones. Often journalists have to persuade people to talk to them. Some reporters

have been criticized for practicing *ambush journalism*—catching people during or following a tragic event and putting them on the spot.

Print journalists write their columns or articles with great care, using their highly devel-

oped research skills. They have a responsibility to their readers to convey as accurately and clearly as possible the stories or subjects they investigate. Broadcast journalists have the same responsibility, but they also need to pay attention to the way they deliver their stories. They must write copy that is clear and easy for listeners to understand, and they must pronounce words correctly, including difficult names such as Jakarta or Rwanda and technical words such as *Alzheimer's* or *crescendo*.

vousness get in the way. Just be ready to adapt quickly, since things often don't go exactly as you imagine they will. For example, Chris might figure out what you want to discuss and, as a result, try to avoid you.

Evaluate the Results

Evaluating the results means you decide how effective your strategy was in light of your standards. If your goals were to be honest, to get Chris to come to work on time, and to keep him as a friend, those goals will be the focus of your evaluation. After talking with Chris, you might think, "That's exactly what I should have done. He seemed to understand, and he said he'd start to wear a watch. He said he'd do better. This weekend he was on time and he seemed friendly." Or you might think, "That wasn't the way to change this situation. Chris made me feel guilty because I have a car and he rides the bus. He got really angry. He avoided me all day. I should have just let the boss handle it." In this case your evaluation would lead you to avoid the direct strategy in the future, at least with someone like Chris.

Remember!

Competent communicators follow these steps:

▶ Review strategies.

▶ Select one.

▶ Act on that choice.

▶ Evaluate the results.

When you join an organization, you have a responsibility to become familiar with its culture or personality. You will be expected to learn what it values, what its goals are, and how you should act in order to fit in.

Workplace Culture

Have you ever been a newcomer—the new person in a class or in a club, a new employee, or a new volunteer? The odds are that you did a quick study of the way things happened in your new situation and tried to figure out how you would fit in.

When you enter a new situation, such as a workplace setting, it's useful to think about it as a different culture. Try to think like an anthropologist. Anthropologists study human beings, their environment, social relations, and culture. An anthropologist is trained to enter a new culture in order to understand how the members of that culture live their lives. The anthropologist's key questions are, "How do I make sense out of everyday life in this place?" and "How do people accomplish things and communicate with each other in this culture?"

Simply put, **workplace culture** refers to the way things are done in a particular workplace. **Culture** reflects the values and beliefs of a group or organization. Sometimes culture is thought of as the personality of an organization. When you join an organization, you have the responsibility of figuring out the culture—what goals, attitudes, and tasks the organization values. Eventually you are expected to demonstrate that you've learned them. Understanding a workplace culture also involves learning the verbal and nonverbal messages to use in order to fit in. In some organizations, the employees tell newcomers how to act and, if this advice is followed, the newcomer fits in just fine. In other organizations, employees expect newcomers to figure out how to act. That raises two questions: What should I do to fit in around here? *and* Do I wish to fit in around here? You can answer both questions by watching, listening, and asking questions of your co-workers.

Read the following examples describing a newcomer's conclusions about the culture of two international travel organizations, Crossroads and Globetrek. These conclusions are based on watching, listening to, and questioning organization members. Although they are both good organizations, everyday life is somewhat different in each place. Imagine you have a summer job offer at each and have to make a choice. Which one would you choose?

Crossroads team members

- arrive on time and leave on time
- dress in slacks and shirts for men and skirts or slacks and nice tops for women
- acknowledge co-workers in a friendly way, but do not socialize
- avoid telling the boss he or she is wrong during a meeting
- knock on someone's office or cubicle before entering
- tell only their supervisor about good ideas they have
- work out a problem alone

Globetrek team members

- arrive late but stay late
- dress in jeans and T-shirts (men and women)
- socialize freely with co-workers
- disagree in a meeting if they think it's important
- walk into others' offices without knocking
- tell anyone about good ideas that they have
- ask anyone who is available to help with a problem

FOR BETTER OR FOR WORSE

© Lynn Johnston Productions Inc./Dist. by United Feature Syndicate, Inc.

Let's look at one very well-known and well-defined workplace culture: that of Disney World. When you enter one of the Disney World theme parks, you enter a very carefully defined workplace. At Disney World, employees are expected to adapt to the Disney culture. If you talk to employees of Disney World, you will quickly learn that they all describe themselves as part of a theatrical performance and see themselves as being "on stage" when they are around the visitors to the park. They are "cast in a role," not hired for a job. This dramatic metaphor—giving a performance rather than doing a job—guides how things are talked about and thought about at Disney World. The goal is to provide memorable experiences for visitors or guests.

Newcomers to the Disney culture soon learn that there are four quality standards: safety, courtesy, show, and efficiency. Safety always comes first, and cast members are given three courses in how to offer first aid to a guest who may have a health problem. They are always alert for anything that could create a safety hazard for a guest.

Courtesy is displayed by being assertively friendly—always trying to anticipate what a guest might need. For example, if a cast member sees visitors studying a map, he or she will ask them if they need directions before they have to ask for help. If a guest is having a problem, the cast member tries to fix it immediately so that the visitor will enjoy his or her time at the park.

The concept of show or "putting on a show" reflects the idea that all employees are part of a giant cast performing for guests from the time the park opens until the time it closes. Cast members wear costumes, not uniforms. Cast members learn performance tips such as eye contact, smiling at guests, squatting to be at eye level with a child, and using two fingers to point so as not to offend a visitor from another culture. The Disney appearance includes clean-shaven faces for men and limited jewelry for women, such as a simple

Employees at Disney World see themselves as being "on stage" when they are around visitors. They are "cast in a role," not hired for a job.

"Cast members" at Disney World are expected to smile at everyone, to scan crowds to see if a visitor needs anything, and to be helpful at all times.

pair of earrings. In keeping with the concept of "putting on a show," there can be no break in character—you will never hear a Disney character, such as Goofy, talk or remove a headpiece or move in ways that would be out of character. You will not see park attendants dress in anything but their uniforms or act in any way but the prescribed way.

The fourth quality, efficiency, ties things together. Cast members are expected to be on time, to move lines and attractions along efficiently, and to "work smart." Disney World employees are required to bring a high degree of professionalism to their jobs.

If you "join the show," you will learn a whole new vocabulary that will include insider terms such as "Take 5," "Pixie dust," and "Magical Moments." You will be expected to smile at everyone, scan crowds to see if a guest needs anything, pick up litter, and function as part of a large team. During off-hours, cast members are encouraged to get involved with volunteer teams that support philanthropic causes because Disney values such efforts. Disney employees tell countless stories about the valuable volunteer work other employees perform and about how co-workers inspire others by being fine role models for the Disney way.

There are many rules and regulations involved in working at Disney World. Some young people find it an exciting and rewarding place to work and have no problem with following the rules. Others may decide not to apply to work at the theme park because they do not want to work within the organization's rules.

Communication Competence and Workplace Culture

Framework for a Workplace Culture Analysis

If you become a workplace analyst, you will be able to enter a group or organization and learn how to communicate in that culture very quickly. You could sit for a few hours in Starbucks coffee shop, the principal's office, or your local soup kitchen and learn the unspoken communication rules practiced in these workplaces.

After you have completed the next three chapters on verbal communication, nonverbal communication, and listening, you will be able to do a more complete analysis of a workplace. The following workplace analysis lists some questions you would ask.

Workplace Analysis

Organization's Goals

- What is the purpose of this organization? (Is it to make money, help people, provide instruction, create art?)
- What are the organization's values or beliefs? (Animals must be protected? Education is the key to success? Business must meet the needs of the community?)

Verbal Communication Patterns

- What verbal patterns are expected of members? (Do employees greet everyone they see? Can members disagree openly?)
- How formal or informal is the language used by members? (How do people address each other? Do most members talk in technical terms? Do members joke around?)
- How do members talk with outsiders? (How are phones answered? How do members deal with the public?)

Nonverbal Communication Patterns

- What nonverbal patterns are expected of members? (How do group members dress? What tone of voice is acceptable?)
- How is time managed? (Do people have to check in and out or can they manage their own time?)
- How does office design affect communication? (Who sees each other regularly during the day? Are there places for members to socialize?)

Individual or Group Responsibility

- How much independence do members have? (Who can make decisions? Are members expected to think creatively, or are they to do only what others tell them to do?)
- How important is group communication? (Are members expected to function well in groups or on teams? Can members disagree?)

 ## *Summary*

In this chapter, you learned about communication competence and workplace culture. A competent communicator is effective in reaching his or her communication goals.

Competent communicators are skilled in the following behaviors or acts: (1) sharing information, (2) managing persuasive messages, (3) discussing feelings, (4) following social rituals, and (5) using imagination. They are able to develop communication strategies in each of these areas. In addition, competent communicators follow a four-step process to reach their goals most effectively. They review their possible communication strategies, select one based on the criteria, act on that choice, and evaluate the result.

Competent communicators ask questions and observe others to learn about the ways people in the workplace communicate with each other and manage their responsibilities.

Review Questions

1. What must a person do to become a competent communicator?
2. List the five communication acts and define each.
3. Of the five acts, which ones do you use the most often and why? (Give specific examples.)
4. Why is it important to be accurate when you share information?
5. Name three examples of persuasion in your daily life.
6 List four feelings most people like to share and four most people keep to themselves.
7. List five social rituals you notice adults use and five you notice students use. What are the differences? similarities?
8. When does "practice" not always "make perfect"?
9. Give the four steps you follow to build an effective communication act.
10. Define *workplace culture* and give examples.

Critical Thinking Activities

Speaking/Doing

1. If you could design an ideal work culture for yourself, what would it include? Describe this business management style in detail. Organize your thoughts on a few note cards and familiarize yourself with them. Then give a short impromptu talk in front of the class.
2. Interview one or both of your parents and determine what type of work culture they experience each day. Include their opinions of the work environment and what they would change if they could. Share what you learn with the class.

Writing

1. Think of a time when you were given incomplete, inadequate, or inaccurate information. In one or two paragraphs, describe that situation and the consequences. What could have been done to prevent it?
2. Choose one of the following questions and write a short essay stating your point of view. Support your point of view with reasons.

    In sending or receiving persuasive messages, who should be responsible for the outcome?

    Should advertisers be free to say or do whatever they can to convince the buyer to purchase a product or service?
3. When is it good to share feelings openly and honestly? When is it bad? Share your thoughts on this subject in a two-paragraph essay.

Group Activities

1. Work in pairs. Have one member write a set of directions to do or make something—for example, how to make a peanut butter sandwich, how to get to the water fountain, or how to tie a shoe. Choose something simple and familiar. That person will provide any "equipment" needed for his or her project. He or she will then verbally direct the other member through the process. Note problems that arise. Follow up the demonstration with discussion. What were some common problems that everyone had in completing the task? What can we do to develop more-accurate skills in communicating information?

2. In groups of three or four, visit a business and pretend you are an anthropologist. Observe and record the work culture for that business. In class, be prepared to discuss the business your group evaluated. How formal or informal was the work culture? Why is it necessary for some businesses to be more formal than others?

3. Divide into groups of five to seven. Within your group, take turns using imaginative communication to describe the world 50 years from now. What new technological and social advancements might you predict?

Practical Application: Case Challenge

Discuss the following situation with your classmates:

You are a computer lab supervisor in a library, a position that involves opening or closing the computer labs and helping students with problems such as printing, working e-mail, and so on. Near the end of each term, the labs become very busy, and the lab supervisors are pressured by students to stay later or to leave a student unattended in the room. Tonight, when you announced that the lab was closing for the night, two students begged you to let them stay longer. One student said she had about 25 minutes of work left and she had to turn in her paper early tomorrow morning. The other student said he had waited for a computer terminal for almost an hour because the lab was overcrowded. He needed a half hour to finish and argued it was the school's fault since he was at the lab but couldn't get on a machine.

How will you respond?

Unit 1 *Wrap-Up*

Work It Out!

Have a Talk Fest!

In this unit you learned that workplace communication is important. In the next three units you will study specific communication skills that can have a direct influence on your success in the workplace. Take some time now to assess what you already know about these skills and to predict how each of them can affect your job performance. Form groups of five to six students. Brainstorm answers to the following questions: What do you already know about these questions? What can you predict you will learn? Share your group's answers with the rest of the class.

Verbal, Nonverbal, and Listening Skills

- When would I need to ask questions on the job? What kind of questions work best for getting useful information?
- Are there different kinds of listening skills? Are listening skills more important in some jobs than in others? How can listening skills help me succeed in any job?
- What kind of jobs require good phone skills? good direction-giving skills? How might my phone skills and direction-giving skills affect a client? a customer? a co-worker?
- Is making introductions important? What do I know about making introductions? When would I need this skill in the workplace?
- Should I be concerned about the way I look to others? How might my appearance and body language influence my relationships with clients, customers, and co-workers?

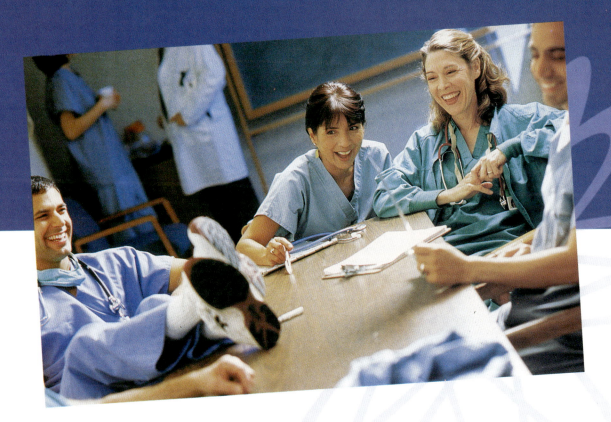

Interpersonal, Group, and Conflict-Management Skills

- What do I need to know about getting along with my co-workers? Why would it matter, as long as I do my job?
- Is interviewing for a job just a formality? (If a company wants me, they'll hire me anyway, right?) What does a company gain through a job interview? How might a job interview be valuable to me?
- What kind of jobs involve working on a team? What do I need to know about group communication to be an effective member of a work team?
- Should conflict always be avoided? (Conflict is bad, right?) What kind of work situations might involve conflict or disagreement? What strategies can I use to handle disagreements constructively?

Public-Speaking Situations

- I don't plan on accepting any job that would require me to get up in front of a large audience and deliver a formal speech, so what's the big deal? Why should I be concerned about public-speaking situations?
- On what personal/social occasions might I be called upon to "say a few words"? What information (other than where to run and hide) would be helpful to know on such occasions?
- What kind of situations at work might I encounter in which it would be valuable for me to be able to "think on my feet"? What kind of informal and formal presentations might my job require, whether I like it or not?
- What do I already know about persuasion? How can effective persuasive strategies specifically help me do my job?

Launch a Team Investigation!

Workplace cultures can differ from one another dramatically. In small groups of three to four students, investigate the workplace culture of a business or agency in your community. Choose one of following types of organizations. Try to make sure that an example of each of these types is investigated by at least one team.

- a small local business (gift shop, restaurant, etc.)
- a mid-size or large corporation (manufacturer, retail chain, etc.)
- a service organization (fire department, hospital, etc.)

Follow these guidelines for conducting your investigation:

1. Use the workplace analysis questions on pages 48–49 as a starting point. Add your own questions to help reveal as complete a picture as possible of the business you have chosen.
2. Use whatever research tools are available and appropriate, and divide responsibilities among team members. Conduct phone interviews and/or on-site interviews, and look for information on Internet web sites, in the library, in company brochures, and in newspaper and magazine advertisements.

3. When you contact a business, identify yourself, explain your purpose, and ask permission to talk with a company representative. Explain that you will not take up too much time, and remember to thank him or her for helping.
4. After gathering the information, prepare a team report and present it to the class. After all team presentations have been made, discuss the similarities and differences among the workplace cultures your class investigated.

Let Your Imagination Run Wild!

Identify your ideal job. Draw up a list of workplace behaviors that you think would be appropriate for this job. Study the Crossroads and Globetrek examples on page 45 for inspiration. Describe your ideal job and workplace culture in a two-minute talk to your classmates.

Basic
Communication
Skills

Unit Two

Chapter Three
Verbal Communication

Objectives

After completing this chapter, you will be able to

- define verbal communication
- identify and explain informal and formal language and technical language
- explain the importance of cultural language issues
- explain the importance of gender-related language issues
- develop your verbal skills—managing introductions, managing phone contacts, giving directions, asking questions, and telling stories

Key Terms

connotative meaning
denotative meaning
formal language
informal language
phone scripts
sexual harassment
slang
speech community
technical language
verbal communication

> **"** Talking and eloquence are not the same: to speak, and to speak well, are two things. A fool may talk, but a wise man speaks. **"**
>
> —BEN JONSON

Gaining Insider Status Through Language

Caitlin and Malik were hired as junior counselors for their city day camp. It was their first time working as camp counselors. Before camp opened, they attended an orientation session for new counselors, received all their information packets, and heard a discussion on topics such as employee rules, benefits, and income tax. In the afternoon all junior counselors met in groups with their specific senior counselors. Caitlin and Malik were assigned to T. J. Wells, a

fourth-year counselor, who was heading the seven- to eight-year-old group for the first time. He had four returning counselors as well as the two junior counselors.

T. J. was very excited to meet the new junior counselors and proceeded to talk to them for almost two hours. He began by telling them about counselors' responsibilities on the camp bus. "You will ride the bus from your home each day, and you must be at the bus stop 10 minutes early to talk with parents and to organize the kids. Greet every kid and parent when they arrive. Use the children's first names. When you get on the bus, be sure you spread out and make sure everyone stays in their seats. Any horseplay and the camper gets dragon points. They can sing but they can't scream or yell." He then went on about rules for arts and crafts, telling them about the supply cabinet and the rules for cleanup. He talked about the weaving space, the batik T-shirt day, and origami. Both Caitlin and Malik looked confused, but T. J. kept talking.

When T. J. stopped to chat with the camp director, Malik asked Caitlin, "Are you getting all this?"

She said, "No. I can't remember all this new stuff."

T. J. returned and began to discuss water safety. He stressed how pool supervision was critical and started to list pool rules for campers. Malik stopped him to ask, "Is this written down somewhere?"

T. J. responded, "Probably, but I'm not sure where. I'll just tell you." After five more minutes Malik and Caitlin began to interrupt.

"So the seven- and eight-year-olds can't go on the 10-foot diving board but they can use the low one?"

T. J. nodded.

"And if we see a camper dunk another, we take that camper out for the rest of the swim period."

T. J. nodded but added, "And you file a report with me, and I'll talk to the parent. This is really important because three years ago an 11-year-old dunked a 7-year-old, and she kept the kid's head underwater for over a minute. Angel, the younger one, had trouble breathing for a while. It was a counselor who saw it and stopped it."

When his cell phone rang, T. J. answered, "What's up?" After a pause he said, "Oh, Mrs. Washington, the camp day starts at 9:00. Day care starts at 7:30, I think."

As T. J. hung up, he told his junior counselors, "Always refer to parents as Mr., Mrs., or Ms., never by their first name. Also, never complain directly to a parent. If there's a problem, it's my job to talk to the parent."

By this point, what are some frustrations that Caitlin and Malik might be feeling? How did they try to clarify T. J.'s instructions? Give at least two examples of instructions that were not clear. Give at least two examples of effective communication strategies used by T. J. or the junior counselors.

Introduction to Verbal Communication

Verbal communication refers to the spoken or written words you send or receive when communicating. It involves the choice and order of words and their appropriateness for your listeners. Words are symbols that represent something but are not the thing itself. For example, you can't stand on the word *ladder* or ride on the word *motorcycle*. Most people can create an image of a motorcycle, but one listener may picture a brand new Harley-Davidson while another thinks of a 1940s vehicle used in World War II.

Words, in addition to representing objects or things, also represent ideas and beliefs. Words have great power to affect relationships between individuals, groups, or nations. The old expression "Sticks and stones may break my bones, but names will never hurt me" is wrong! Depending on the meaning of certain words to certain listeners, they can be interpreted as painful or helpful or threatening.

When you don't know what a word means, you probably look it up in a dictionary. The definition found in a dictionary is called the **denotative meaning**. Yet, sometimes words have powerful personal meanings for individuals, or they call forth an emotional response from that individual that is apart from or in addition to the dictionary meaning. A person's emotional or personal response to a word is called its **connotative meaning**.

Look at the following examples for the word *snake:*

Denotative meanings	Connotative meanings
1. scaly, limbless, long-bodied reptile	**1.** rival gang symbol
2. treacherous person	**2.** evil
	3. pet
	4. source of meat

If a speaker does not know the connotation a listener has for a certain word, serious misunderstandings may result. For example, one person may say, "You're too funny," and mean, "You have a good sense of humor." The listener may decode the message as, "You are a clown," or "You can't take things seriously."

Words can have powerful personal messages that evoke strong emotional responses in individuals.

Friends use informal language and, sometimes, slang when they hang out together in casual situations.

Eye-to-Eye

With a partner pick three of the following words. Write one or two denotative meanings for each and then brainstorm three connotative meanings for each.

liberty	skate	downsize
wheels	stepmother	diamond
brother	courtroom	smoking

Words do not have the same meanings for everyone, and even agreed-upon meanings change over time. When you create messages, you need to be precise in your selection of words. Consider how they will be understood in a given context. This increases your chances of getting your meaning across effectively to a specific listener.

Types of Verbal Communication

Let's take a look at specific types of verbal communication: formal versus informal language and technical language.

Formal Versus Informal Language

Formal language refers to the use of standard English with careful pronunciation and full sentences. Formal language is frequently used in the workplace. **Informal language** is more relaxed language usually used among friends or in casual situations. **Slang** refers to very informal language that is unique to a par-

Basic etiquette in most workplaces includes greeting your co-workers in a friendly manner.

ticular group and changes frequently. It is a type of shorthand or in-group language. When the current slang of a particular group is adopted by the general population, the group creates new slang terms. Notice the differences among the three in the following greetings:

Formal: "Good morning."
Informal: "Hi," "Mornin'," "What's new?"
Slang: "What's up?" "Yo!"

Many workplaces have guidelines that tell their employees how to speak, while others do not. In very formal settings, employees learn many rules about how to talk to clients or customers and sometimes are given scriptlike phrases to use. In many workplaces, there are strict rules that prohibit swearing or arguing with customers, clients, or co-workers. Other rules may include "Do not interrupt when someone is speaking" or "Do not talk or laugh loudly."

In very informal settings there may be few rules other than obvious ones such as not insulting or arguing with customers and clients. Employees learn acceptable greetings and leave-taking behavior by watching senior employees.

Even e-mail language may be prescribed in the workplace. In one organization an invitation to a meeting may read, "Please respond if you are coming. Feel free to call me at home." In another organization, someone might write, "pls say if ur coming-filfre to call home."

Although no one may tell you directly, businesses, especially large organizations or those that have client/customer contacts, expect their staff to use basic etiquette. This means remembering to say "Please" and "Thank you." It involves greeting co-workers and the public in a friendly manner with "Hello," "Good morning," "Good afternoon," and "Good evening," not slang terms. These rituals are part of the informal organizational culture.

Technical language is used by people who have expertise in a particular field. You encounter technical language every day in many different situations, though you are often unaware of it.

The image of any organization is conveyed through the way employees use verbal communication. It's important that your communication with co-workers and your phone, sales, or other public contact with customers and clients reflect that image.

Check It Out

Call three local businesses and analyze their phone greetings. What can you tell about each business based on the way that the representative speaks on the phone? Summarize your conclusions and share them with the class.

Technical Language

Technical language refers to specialized language used by people with expertise in a particular field. You use technical language all the time, but you may not realize it. When you discuss basketball, jazz, or new motorcycles such as a Big Dog or a Victory, you will likely use specialized terms that are unique to each of those subjects.

Almost every kind of workplace has some technical language associated with it that you will be expected to learn. If you work in a bread store, you will need to know words like *fougasse, brioche, challah, ciobatta,* and *baguette*. If you work in a coffee shop, you will need to know c*appuccino, latte, au lait,* and *espresso*.

Insiders Versus Outsiders

Sometimes you are able to function in an environment in which you do not speak or understand the technical language, but you will likely remain an outsider if you don't learn the language. Perhaps you have been asked to help the

Verbal Communication

© Lynn Johnston Productions Inc./Dist. by United Feature Syndicate, Inc.

set design team at your local community theater because you have some carpentry skill. You can help by doing exactly what the set designer tells you, but if you are going to fit in over time you will have to learn technical terms such as *Dutchman, brace, sight lines, toggles, sectional, fly space,* and *scrim* so that you will be able to give and follow directions. Knowing the technical terms will help you become a more effective member of the set design team.

If you work at a store that sells audio equipment, you had better be able to explain in simple language the value of a DVD/CD player with Dolby Digital and DB Digital audio outputs for an external decoder or why a customer would wish to consider floor speakers that are 3-way, 15-woofer – 6-5 inch inidrange 1-inch dome tweeter, 400 watts maximum, 8 ohms. As an expert on audio equipment, you will know the specific meanings of these terms, but they will sound like gibberish to most customers.

Speech Communication Ties and Language

Culture and gender influence the creation of special speech communities. A **speech community** exists when people share norms about how to talk. Shared interests, beliefs, or values affect the words people use to communicate.

Cultural Language Issues

Speech communities are influenced by race and ethnicity. Your ethnic heritage, whether European, African, Latin American, or another culture, can have an effect on how you communicate with others. When you are with people who share your cultural background, you may communicate differently from the

Ryan Tasi Francisco Alabastro, *Grocery Store Worker*

As a very busy grocery store employee, Ryan Alabastro of Pago Pago, American Samoa, has earned money and learned a great deal about business. For a number of years, Ryan has worked as a part-time stocker and bagger during the school year. In the summer he works at the store eight hours a day. He is so experienced that he has been assigned a "rookie" new employee whom Ryan is expected to train.

During the course of a day's work Ryan accomplishes many jobs. He often has to fetch boxes of groceries for customers and retrieve produce from freezers in the basement. He helps cashiers, organizing and bagging groceries for their customers. Frequently, he is expected to take care of identifying shelves that need restocking and then gathering the necessary items from the warehouse and actually stocking the shelves. Finally, at the end of a day, he may sweep the floor and dust shelves. His usual store "uniform" is a plain T-shirt, shorts, and a pair of shoes. Ryan estimates that "about 55 percent of my job is communication. I communicate with the supervisors, cus-tomers, cashiers, and friends who come through."

In the geographic region where he lives, Ryan must be able to speak a number of languages, since "My position demands that I understand the native language, which is Samoan." He does not speak Samoan regularly, since much of his work and schooling is conducted in English. On occasion Ryan encounters customers who speak his second language, Tagalog. He interacts comfortably with them in that language.

Although Ryan is a very busy store employee, he does find time for the National Honor Society, the Yearbook group, and the Marist High School Chess Club. He enjoys the chess tournaments when they play other schools. Because Marist is an all-male school, Ryan enjoys activities that are run in conjunction with their sister school, an all-female school.

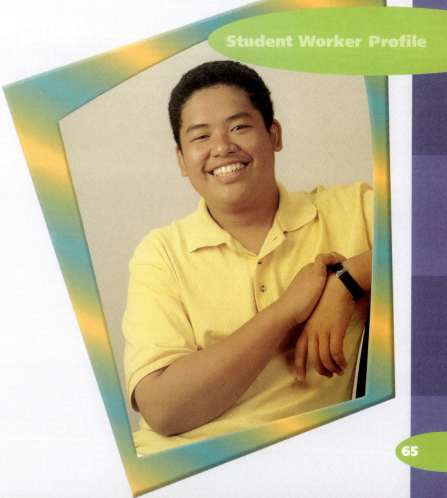

Student Worker Profile

65

way you would with people from backgrounds about which you are less familiar. With friends or co-workers from different backgrounds, you may feel the need to establish shared interests or common experiences.

Schools and workplaces in the United States are becoming more culturally diverse as the U.S. population changes and business becomes more international. For example, it is forecast that the percentage of the U.S. population that is Hispanic will continue to increase in the 21st century. Some organizations are teaching English and Spanish to their employees so that the staff can communicate effectively with one another and their customers.

Frequently standard English is not sufficient. Most of you already understand some everyday terms that have become a part of standard English from various other cultures. You may talk about beat or reggae music or order sushi or chicken almond din for lunch. You may also know of workplace situations where knowing a little bit about a second language is helpful. For example, you may work in a store in which some of your co-workers move easily between English and Spanish in their everyday conversations; you may have customers who mix English with Yiddish or Russian or Polish phrases. In these situations, it's important to learn as much as you can about the other language so that you can understand others and avoid references that might be offensive to co-workers.

By making the effort to learn something about another language and culture, you will be able to adapt quickly to situations involving cultural differences. The competent communicator is able to adapt to different speech communities, understand cross-cultural messages, and, when appropriate, integrate the use of cultural terms in everyday conversation.

Gender Language Issues

Although the lines are not rigid, males and females often create gender-based speech communities. For a long time spoken language tended to be heavily masculine. Females were assumed to be included in references that used masculine pronouns. For example, it used to be common to use the pronoun *he* to refer to either a man or a woman in statements that implied either one. ("If anyone wants to order the album, *he* can do it by phone or over the Internet.") It was common to use masculine names for particular occupations, such as policeman or fireman.

Much more attention is being given today to using nonsexist language. This includes replacing male-biased language with language that is either gender-neutral (*firefighter* instead of *fireman*) or more general (*doctor* instead of *woman doctor*). In some cases, words with strong female connotations have also been replaced with gender-neutral alternatives (*flight attendant* instead of *stewardess*). In addition, more attention is being paid today to challenging sexist stereotypes. Men and women are shown in visual images of all careers. The following chart, based on the work of Julia Wood, an expert on gender and language, indicates the way young males and females traditionally have been socialized into gender speech communities.

Socialization of Gender Speech Communities

Feminine Communication Expectations

1. Include others. Use talk to show interest in others. Respond to others' needs.
2. Use talk cooperatively. It's important to invite others into the conversation, wait your turn to speak, and respond to what others say.
3. Use talk expressively. Talk should deal with feelings, personal ideas, and problems and should build relationships with others.

Masculine Communication Expectations

1. Assert yourself. Use talk to establish your identity, expertise, knowledge, and so on.
2. Use talk competitively. Use talk to gain and hold attention, to wrest the talk stage from others. It's okay to interrupt and change topics to give your ideas attention.
3. Use talk for practical purposes. Talk should accomplish something, such as solving a problem, giving advice, or taking a stand on issues.

In everyday encounters not all males or females behave according to the expectations outlined in the chart, but these are powerful expectations historically promoted in our society and are hard to change. The person who can communicate using a combination of both sets of expectations displays more competence than a person who follows only one.

Many employers have rules that prescribe appropriate ways for men and women to talk to and about one another. Most organizations, even if they do not have specific rules, are sensitive to general workplace language and behavior that puts down a person because of his or her gender. This abuse is called **sexual harassment**, which usually occurs in a hostile environment.

In this country sexual harassment is illegal whether in schools, corporations, or community groups. Sexual harassment includes verbal and nonverbal messages such as name calling, sexual jokes, rumors, highly personal conversations and notes, and unwanted touching. The key to understanding sexual harassment is recognizing that the communication is unwelcome and unwanted. The receiver does not like it and is made to feel uncomfortable or threatened. Organizations expect employees to treat each other with respect and to create and maintain a supportive climate for differences. If one employee is sexually harassed by another, that supportive climate is replaced by a difficult or hostile working climate. Most large organizations provide training sessions for all

Verbal Communication

employees on this topic because it is so important. This topic is addressed more fully in Chapter 4.

Computer Search

Look up the sexual harassment policy on a corporation's web site. Note the problem behaviors that are outlined in the policy and the language used to describe those behaviors. You might also check the federal government's discrimination web site **www.eeoc.gov** to learn what information it provides. Report what you learn from both sites to the class.

Language and Disabilities

Speech communities are not limited to those with shared gender or cultural identity. People with disabilities share a speech community, and many of them try to encourage others to use language that is respectful. For example, they use the term *persons with disabilities,* not *disabled people,* and *persons with epilepsy,* not *epileptics.* People without disabilities aren't *normal;* they are *able-bodied.* Sometimes a speaker totalizes another person. To totalize means to refer to a person as if one label represents who he or she is—for example, "She's the cerebral palsied girl" or "Tim's the deaf kid." Responsible communicators are careful to avoid reducing others to labels. Continue to listen to people around you to identify the impact of gender, culture, or other speech communities on communication.

People with disabilities share a special speech community.

Eye-to-Eye

In groups of two or three, share your experiences of belonging to a special speech community or being on the outside of one. What are examples of verbal communication that are unique to that speech community?

Verbal Skills

Competent communicators develop sets of verbal skills for managing predictable situations.

There are five basic verbal skills that are used in all areas of everyday life, including the workplace. They are (1) managing personal introductions, (2) handling phone calls, (3) giving directions or descriptions, (4) asking questions, and (5) telling stories.

Managing Personal Introductions

There are many ways to handle introductions, ranging from informal to formal. For example, assume you are a violinist named Saylea. When you appear at your first practice for the all-district orchestra rehearsals, you might take part in an informal introduction similar to this one:

MARK: Saylea, meet Ted. Ted's also a second violin. Ted's played in this orchestra for two years. Ted, Saylea is new.

TED: Hi. Welcome.

SAYLEA: Hi, Ted.

TED: What school are you from?

If you participate in an internship program at the local hospital, you might be introduced in a more formal manner:

MARK: Dr. Mattson, I'd like you to meet Saylea Kim, a senior at Taft High School. Saylea, this is Dr. Mattson. She heads the physical therapy unit and has worked with our students before.

DR. MATTSON: *(extending her hand)* Saylea, nice to see you. It's a pleasure to have you here for the next month.

When you are the person making the introduction, you will be effective if you remember to speak clearly, pronounce the names carefully, and include any additional interesting information about each person you are introducing. This will give both people something with which to start their conversation. The general guidelines for formal introductions are as follows:

Verbal Communication

Introductions differ from group to group and from culture to culture. In the United States, people usually shake hands when they are introduced to someone.

1. Mention the name of the older person first, then the name of the younger person. Introduce the younger person to the older one.

   "Mr. Martin, I'd like you to meet Eric Martinez. He'll be serving as an interviewer for the Amigos program applicants. Eric, this is Mr. Charles Martin. He serves on the local Amigos Program Board. His daughter was a volunteer in Costa Rica for two summers."

2. Mention the name of the female first.

   "Ms. Winn, I'd like you to meet my father, Frank Diaz. Dad, this is my boss, Roberta Winn, our best salesperson."

3. Mention the name of the person who has a higher status or position of authority first.

   "Mayor Morton, this is Jake Barnes, a new American Field Service exchange student from Australia. Jake, this is Mayor Lucy Morton, who sponsored the sister city program with your city of Melbourne."

Usually you start with the most senior person in the room. In mixed groups of ages, genders, and titles, you will have to adapt. Many introductions include handshakes between the people who are being introduced. A handshake should be firm, not limp. In general, men shake hands whereas women sometimes don't. In business settings both men and women tend to shake hands. Usually, a man waits for a woman to extend her hand.

In some cultures shaking hands is not a common practice. For example, Muslim men do not shake hands with women; some Japanese will bow, while others will shake hands. We will discuss these cultural differences further in the next chapter.

Handling Phone Calls

Although you have been talking on the phone since you were very young, you may or may not have developed competent phone skills for workplace communication. Read the following phone conversation and note what Rob did well. What advice would you give him on how to improve his telephone skills?

ROB: Audio/Video Central. This is Rob. May I help you?

PAT: This is Pat Holmes. I'm still waiting for your truck. Where is it?

ROB: I'm sorry. I don't dispatch the trucks. Give me your name, phone number, and purchase order number, and I'll check on your order with the dispatcher and call you back.

PAT: I gave you my name. Pat Holmes. I don't have my purchase order here. It's a large screen TV and VCR. I'm at 555-0022.

ROB: I really need the purchase order number to track the order, and I need your area code.

PAT: *(hotly)* You people always mix up the orders.

ROB: I didn't mix up your order.

PAT: Forget it. I'll just cancel my order.

Acknowledging customer concerns is part of phone-skill training. This includes acknowledging customers' frustrations either at being kept waiting on the line or at the information they receive.

When you make a business call, you should have all the information you need at hand so that you can make a request or place an order efficiently and courteously.

Business Call Guidelines

If you have to make a business call or an informal call, you need to make a good impression. Keep the conversation short, to the point, and courteous. Follow these guidelines:

1. Identify yourself and state your business. If appropriate, you should indicate whom you work for.
2. Have all information at hand so that you may refer to notes if necessary.
3. Be brief and polite.
4. If you have a complaint, be specific with your facts and reasons. Do not be impatient or irritable. If you do not receive satisfaction, ask to speak to a supervisor and then begin again.
5. End with a "thank you" or some statement of appreciation of the person's time and help.

Phone Scripts

Phone scripts are predictable lines or scenarios that callers use for business purposes. In some cases they are sales tools; in other cases they are proven ways of getting or giving critical information. Telemarketers use detailed scripts to sell products over the phone. Skilled telemarketers, knowing that customers often are annoyed by phone solicitations, adapt their scripts to the person and the situation. Compare the following conversations:

Conversation 1

TELEMARKETER: May I speak to Mr. or Mrs. Gwinn?

DEREK: This is Derek Gwinn.

TELEMARKETER: Good evening, Mr. Gwinn. How are you tonight, sir?

DEREK: Okay.

TELEMARKETER: That's really good. Do you subscribe to any weekly magazines?

DEREK: *(curious)* What is this about?

TELEMARKETER: I'd like to know what magazines you subscribe to.

DEREK: *(angry)* If you're selling something, I'm not interested. *(hangs up)*

Conversation 2

TELEMARKETER: May I speak to Mr. or Mrs. Corral?

ELLEN: This is Ellen Corral.

TELEMARKETER: Good evening, Mrs. Corral. How are you tonight?

ELLEN: Fine, thank you.

TELEMARKETER: Glad to hear it. I'm calling from Magazine Publishers, Inc., and we are trying to determine the buying habits of homeowners in your area. Would you mind if I asked you a few questions?

ELLEN: All right. But only for a few minutes, since I am getting ready to leave.

TELEMARKETER: Thanks. I'll try to be brief.

How did the second telemarketer adapt to Ellen and the situation? Sometimes telephone scripts can have life-or-death consequences. Emergency dispatchers are trained to gain key information quickly. Read the conversation on page 74 from a 911 emergency line. Notice how effectively the dispatcher handles the situation.

Telemarketers often use very detailed phone scripts. The telemarketer in this photograph is using a script to sell symphony subscriptions.

Brian Jacobsen, *Building Engineer*

Brian Jacobsen's job at NTC/Contemporary Publishing Group is to make sure that the working environment of the three-building complex is safe, comfortable, and in good working order. His responsibilities include working on the building HVAC (heating, ventilation, and air conditioning); doing electrical, plumbing, and carpentry work; supervising the landscaping; monitoring the fire-alarm system; and maintaining the sprinkler systems and the lawn and snow equipment. Much of his work involves purchasing and fixing equipment. He believes in preventive maintenance—maintaining equipment properly to avoid the need for costly repairs.

Communication skills play an important part in Mr. Jacobsen's work. He deals regularly with concerns from co-workers in the three-building complex about leaky faucets, faulty lighting, jammed file drawers, and other aggravations. From time to time, he is forced to mediate disagreements over the temperature. "One person is cold, and the person sitting right next to him is hot. I talk to them and explain what we can do. I try to make their area more comfortable for both of them." His goal is to "make everybody happy."

Because he is responsible for contacting contractors, Mr. Jacobsen uses the telephone a lot. Frequently, it takes months of extensive phone calls and negotiations to conclude a proposal or a bid, a process that requires good negotiating skills and patience. Sometimes, when an old piece of equipment breaks down, he will spend hours calling all over the country to find the right part, a task that he describes as time-consuming but fun.

When conducting business on the phone, he is aware that he is representing the company. "I try to act in a professional way, and I appreciate it when the people I'm talking with act professionally too." He says that most contractors are easy to deal with, "But you have to be careful. There are a few suppliers who will try to take advantage of you." He once was forced to deal politely but very firmly with a supplier who threatened to take legal action if he didn't pay for lighting fixtures that had been sent to the company as free samples. "I told him we would not pay for the fixtures . . . and to have a nice day."

Mr. Jacobsen likes the challenge of new and different projects and enjoys the opportunity to use his technical skills as well as his communication skills to solve problems.

The World of Work

CALLER: I need an ambulance.

DISPATCHER: What's the matter?

CALLER: I'm having a really bad asthma attack.

DISPATCHER: Where are you?

CALLER: Two one six on Rustic Valley.

DISPATCHER: Two one six on Rustic Valley. Is that Drive or Lane?

CALLER: Lane. Hurry.

DISPATCHER: Is that a house or apartment?

CALLER: Apartment. Hurry.

DISPATCHER: We're coming. We have to find you first. What floor are you on?

CALLER: Three. Apartment 3H. Please, hurry!

DISPATCHER: The ambulance is on its way. Now I need your phone number.

Phone conversations in the workplace, whether scripted or spontaneous, serve to represent an organization to the public or to other businesspeople. Regardless of whether the organization is a small business, a large corporation, or a community group, the goal is to make a positive impression and to give and get clear, accurate information.

Giving Directions or Descriptions

Giving directions is a very important and often taken-for-granted skill. Many mistakes are prevented and hours are saved if you can do things right the first time. Which of the following sets of directions is more likely to be helpful?

All 911 dispatchers are trained to ask very specific questions in a specific order to find out everything they need to know in order to dispatch an emergency vehicle as quickly as possible.

Version A

These flowers go to Sunny Hill Resort. Go down Route 32, and just outside Freehold there's a road to your left that goes up the mountain. You go past the llama place and the Bern farm. After a while you'll see the golf course on the left. When you get into the resort, turn right and go to the back of the dining room. The flowers are for the wedding reception later today.

Version B

These flowers go to Sunny Hill Resort up on the mountain. You need to go south on Route 32 until you almost enter Freehold. On your left is a road that angles sharply back and leads up the mountain. There's a little white arrow with Sunny Hill on the right but it's hard to see. You've gone a little too far if you reach the furniture store. Turn around and you will find that the road is better marked if you are going north. Drive about three miles to the top of the mountain. You'll see a golf course on your left as you approach the resort. When you enter the resort you'll see a big parking lot on your left. Stay to your right and turn right on the first road. There are tennis courts at the turn. The second building on your right is the big dining hall. Park in the back, go in through the kitchen entrance, and ask for Billy. He's the manager. The flowers are for the wedding reception he is catering today. Now, repeat that back so we're sure you've got it.

Most people would agree that Version B is better because the directions are clearer and more complete. The speaker (1) identifies numerous visual landmarks, (2) anticipates places where the drive might become confused, (3) emphasizes specific destinations along the way, (4) identifies specific people, and (5) checks to make sure the driver has understood the directions.

Steps for Giving Directions

Chapter 13 will deal in more detail with guidelines for preparing formal presentations that involve giving directions or instructions. The following guidelines offer useful suggestions for handling directions in the many informal situations you will encounter in the workplace.

1. *Set the scene.*
   ("Here's the fastest route to the bank. Listen carefully. It's hard to find.")
2. *Use transition words to show you are moving to a new step.*
   ("Next, you mix it …")
3. *Check the listeners' understanding.*
   ("Have I lost anyone on this point?")
4. *Summarize.*
   ("Let me repeat. Donations are sent to …")

FOR BETTER OR FOR WORSE

© Lynn Johnston Productions Inc./Dist. by United Feature Syndicate, Inc.

Eye-to-Eye

Write directions to some location in your school or community that a partner might not know. Be as precise with your directions as you can. Have your partner try to follow your directions during lunch or before school. Was he or she able to go straight to the site without errors?

Asking Questions

The ability to ask intelligent and effective questions is an important verbal skill. Suppose the vice president of your club, the Mentoring Youth Club, attended a planning meeting for the high school's 25th anniversay celebration. You want to know what the role of your club will be in the event. Which questions below would be most helpful in getting the information you want?

1. How was the meeting?
2. Did they talk about the club responsibilities?
3. What responsibilities will the club have in the event?

As you might have guessed, questions 1 and 2 are of little or no help. Question 3 could be answered with useful information. This example points out the importance of asking questions that are as specific as possible. The more specific your question, the greater your chance of getting the information you want. The three questions in this example are typical of the type of questions that you deal with every day: yes/no questions, opinion questions, fact/information questions, and declarative requests.

Yes/No Questions Yes/no questions ask for the limited response of yes or no. Sometimes a yes or no answer is exactly what you are looking for, but frequently it is not enough information and you need to ask follow-up questions. "Was it a good meeting?" and "Did they talk about club responsibilities?" are basically yes/no questions.

Career Communication *Nursing*

A career in nursing demands excellence in medical knowledge, medical skills, and communication skills. Although nursing training involves years of science courses as well as studies in related areas, success depends on the application of that knowledge when dealing with patients and their families. Depending on where a nurse is employed, he or she could serve on an operating room anesthesia team, manage the care of a home-bound elderly patient, deal with illnesses or accidents in a school or corporation, or work with a team of doctors in a medical practice.

Nurses learn a wide range of technical, medical, and pharmacological (drug) terms, which they translate for patients and their families. Patients rely on nurses to explain how procedures work or how to take certain drugs. Frequently, nurses are called upon to be very careful listeners, whether it's trying to understand a patient's medical problem or dealing with an emotional reaction to illness.

Nurses frequently find themselves as part of a communication network. When the patient is a child or someone too ill to communicate effectively, the nurse often communicates directly with family members. Frequently it is the nurse who explains and follows through on procedures ordered by the doctor. Today nurses have significant responsibility for the well-being of patients. They need to make thoughtful decisions and work effectively with many other medical personnel.

Opinion Questions Opinion questions ask for another person's reaction to or feelings about a subject. Again, the more specific the question, the better chance you have of getting the information you want. "How was the meeting?" asks for another's opinion, but it may not tell you what you want to know. "Long and boring" does not tell you about the club responsibilities. You really don't want the speaker's opinion in this case.

Fact/Information Questions Fact/information questions ask for specific information, such as details that can be proven to be true. "What reponsibilities will the club have in the event?" asks for specific information. A fact/information question is the appropriate kind of question to ask in the situation described in the example involving the Mentoring Youth Club.

Declarative Requests Sometimes you can use a declarative request, called a nonquestion, to follow up an answer if you don't want to keep peppering the other person with questions or you don't know exactly what to ask. Declarative requests include statements such as "Tell me more about that," "Give some details about the project costs," or "Repeat point three for me." This encourages the speaker to elaborate on a point but does not require the listener to phrase a specific question.

Verbal Communication

The 5 W's and H

You may have heard about the 5 W's and H in writing or journalism classes. The five W's stand for *who, what, when, where,* and *why.* The H stands for *how.* These are starter words that are used at the beginning of many opinion questions and most fact/information questions. Questions that begin with these words are designed to give you very specific information:

Who will be in charge of the booth exhibits?
What kinds of materials should we display?
When do we have to give the committee our plans?
Where will our booth be located?
Why did the committee decide on booths rather than posters?
How should we go about scheduling times for participants to work at our booth?

Remember the 5 W's and H. Knowing them will help you review some of the different ways you can phrase an opinion or fact/information question to get the specific information you want.

Telling Stories

Sometimes the best way to get information across is to tell a story. Suppose you started work as a salesperson and during the first week a co-worker told you the following story:

"When we have low-performing salespeople, they get to have breakfast with Al. Al's the big sales manager—old football player, real tough. When someone slacks off, Al invites him to breakfast. He makes this invitation in the middle of a sales meeting so everyone knows what is going on. Al makes this guy show up at 6 A.M. at the Pancake House, but Al doesn't let him eat. Oh no, Al eats a huge breakfast, and he orders coffee for the guy. While Al is eating, the guy must explain why he is not meeting his sales objectives and explain his plans to turn things around. At the end of breakfast, Al decides whether or not to fire him. He has fired a few. The rest try never to eat breakfast with Al again."

What would you have learned about your new workplace from the "Breakfast with Al" story? As you probably figured out, this story was told to warn new salespeople what could happen to them if they don't work to their full potential. In the workplace, stories are passed along informally for the purpose of instructing employees about what is expected of them or about "how we do things around here." They are useful at times when giving specific advice might be seen as giving orders or lecturing someone.

Remember!

Five basic verbal skills used in the workplace are

▶ Managing personal introductions

▶ Handling phone calls

▶ Giving directions

▶ Asking questions

▶ Telling stories

In many companies, employees exchange stories in casual situations to pass along important information from one employee to another.

Guidelines for Organizational Stories

1. Have a clear point to make.
2. Keep it brief.
3. Only tell stories that are general knowledge.
4. Avoid sexist language, swearing, and offensive references.
5. Keep the story truthful. Don't exaggerate.

Chapter 3 *Summary*

In this chapter you learned about verbal communication, which is the spoken or written words you send or receive when communicating.

Formal language refers to the use of standard English. Informal language is more relaxed language usually used among friends. Technical language is a specialized language used by people with expertise in a particular field.

Both gender and culture influence the creation of special speech communities. More attention is being given today to the use of language that is gender-neutral or nonsexist.

There are five basic verbal skills that are used in everyday life: managing personal introductions, handling phone calls, giving directions or descriptions, asking questions, and telling stories.

Review Questions

1. Define verbal communication.
2. Define denotation and connotation.
3. What is the difference between formal and informal language?
4. What is technical language and who uses it?
5. Give five examples of gender-biased language and supply nonsexist alternatives for each.
6. List the guidelines for introducing people.
7. What should you do if you do not receive a satisfactory response during a business call?
8. What are the four steps for giving good directions?
9. Name three types of questions. Define each.
10. Identify the 5 W's and H. How are they useful?

Critical Thinking Activities

Speaking/Doing

1. Prepare two or three specific reasons why gender-biased language should be avoided. Give a five-minute impromptu speech in front of the class, presenting your reasons.

2. Find an article that illustrates a conflict or misunderstanding caused by poor communication skills. Bring it to class and share the piece with your classmates. Discuss what could have been done to avoid the conflict or misunderstanding.

Writing

1. In two paragraphs, discuss when it is important to use formal language and when it is appropriate to use informal language.
2. In one paragraph, explain how you should handle a business call involving a dissatisfied customer.

Group Activities

1. In groups of three or four, brainstorm situations involving misunderstandings you have experienced at school or at an after-school job. Create a story that will illustrate how to avoid a similar problem. Select one member of your group to tell the story to another group of students in your class. Afterward, evaluate whether or not they got your "message."
2. Work in pairs. Act out one of the following situations in front of the class, improvising the conversation. Afterward, discuss how communication could have been improved.
   A. A customer is dissatisfied with the work that the carpet cleaner did. A secretary at the cleaning service takes the call. (One student plays the customer. The other plays the secretary.)

B. A client is late for a meeting because he or she is having trouble finding the office. The client calls to explain the situation. The receptionist must give directions. (One student plays the client. The other plays the receptionist.)

3. Suppose you are at an orientation meeting for animal-shelter volunteers. There is a film on handling animals safely. The person in front of you is wearing a hat that is blocking your view. What will you say?

In pairs, take turns improvising this situation in front of the class. One student plays the person wearing the hat. The other student plays the person whose view is blocked. Have that student deliver one of the lines of dialogue listed below. The student wearing the hat must improvise a response to the line. Repeat the activity with a new pair of students and a different line of dialog from the list below. After all of the options have been acted out, discuss the results of each. Which ones were effective? Why?

A. "Remove your hat!"

B. "Would you please lean left or take off your hat?"

C. "Excuse me. That's a lovely hat, but I can't see the film. Would you please remove it?"

D. "I can't see the screen. Your hat's blocking my view."

Practical Application: Case Challenge

Stephanie and her cousin Ari are spending a weekend together. Four years ago Ari was in a college diving accident. He has been using a wheelchair and a cane ever since his release from the hospital rehabilitation center.

Stephanie meets Ari at the airport and notices that he is moving very slowly.

"Do you want a wheelchair?" she asks.

"No way." Ari quickly replies.

A moment later an airport security person asks Stephanie, "Does your friend want a wheelchair?"

"No," she replies. Ari looks at her oddly but says nothing.

Later, Stephanie and Ari visit a local art museum. At the entrance, Ari suggests that they rent a wheelchair because he will have to walk a long distance. When they stop for lunch in the museum's restaurant, the server takes Stephanie's order and then asks her, "And what will he have?"

Impatiently, Ari interrupts, "A BLT and a coke."

The server continues, "Does he want the BLT on toast?"

At this point Stephanie is getting very uncomfortable. What might she say or do in this situation?

Chapter Four

Nonverbal Communication

Objectives

After completing this chapter, you will be able to

- define nonverbal communication
- explain the importance of nonverbal communication
- describe the types of nonverbal communication
- explain the joint functioning between verbal and nonverbal messages
- read nonverbal communication cues to determine workplace culture

Key Terms

articulation

eye contact

facial expressions

gestures

mixed message

nonverbal communication

pitch

posture

pronunciation

proxemics

proximity

rate

spatial use

vocal quality

volume

> **"** The body is a canvas for expressing feelings and emotions; those who read it know our spirits. **"**
>
> —ANONYMOUS

Interpreting Clues to Workplace Culture

Marcus has completed a month on his summer job. He serves as an office temporary in Weissbord Automotive's general offices. Every day he reports to the main office, and he is sent to the division or area that needs him because staff members are sick or on vacation. Sometimes he stays for a day, other times for up to a week. As someone who "floats" from floor to floor and division to division, Marcus sees many different types of work groups and work spaces. Everyone who

works for Weissbord is in one large building, but the subgroups are very different. Marcus is fascinated by the differences between life on the second floor and life on the third floor.

On the third floor the offices are very quiet. The executives dress in suits, and even the secretarial staff dresses rather formally. Everyone arrives at or before 8:30 A.M. Office doors are likely to be shut if people are working inside. Offices and cubicles are filled with art and special objects representing travels. A few employees display family photos. Bulletin boards are filled with sales figures and pictures of the "Weissbord Family." People talk to each other in rather low voices; they tend to sigh or slump when they are frustrated. Staff members rarely look up when others pass by. Marcus can walk through the halls without attracting much recognition. When he comes to work on the third floor, he checks in with the receptionist and heads to a cubicle where he spends most

of the day quietly working on a computer. Usually he does not hear other employees on the phone because they talk in low tones. When Marcus makes calls, he tends to make them short and keep his voice down.

The second floor is quite different. Most employees dress in "business casual," which in the summer means almost anything but jeans and T-shirts. A few of the men are in slacks and sports shirts; others are in sweatshirts. Women are in casual tops and skirts or cargo shorts. There aren't many "real" offices; almost everyone works in cubicles filled with kids' photos and artwork, silly toys, and posters. Bulletin boards are filled with cartoons and announcements. Employees greet one another loudly each morning. They yell across cubicles and high-five each other in the hallways. When Marcus walks through the area, co-workers are sitting on each other's desks chatting. If someone is annoyed, he or she will march into another's office and confront that person face-to-face, sometimes yelling.

Usually, when staff members notice Marcus, they ask how he's doing and if he'd like a cup of coffee. When he comes to work on the second floor, he greets four or five employees, gets his coffee, and hears the latest office gossip. Some people drift in as late as 10 A.M. When he works on the second floor, he spends his day in a cubicle working on a computer and chatting about sports scores with co-workers.

Sometimes he gets distracted by the phone conversations or chatter he hears around him.

What are two messages Marcus gets from each floor that tell him how to act in each setting? Which floor would you prefer to work on and why?

Introduction to Nonverbal Communication

Nonverbal communication refers to sending and receiving messages without the use of words. It involves appearance, gestures, posture, eye contact, facial expression, voice, proxemics, objects and design, and time.

Although you may not think much about it, you depend heavily on sending and receiving wordless messages in order to communicate effectively. Researchers have estimated that between 65 and 93 percent of messages are nonverbal, especially messages that convey feelings. As you will see, nonverbal messages vary in importance and style across cultures. Yet, if you do not recognize the nonverbal component of many messages, you are likely to misinterpret the verbal message.

At this point in life, you are verbally literate. You can read, write, speak, and listen to the language of words rather effectively. You also need to be nonverbally literate, or able to "read" and interpret nonverbal cues

Nonverbal communication is a very important part of workplace cultures. Newcomers who can "read" the wordless communication of people and places are much more likely to be successful than those who miss these messages. Although this chapter will focus on the nonverbal messages you *send* to another person, remember that you interpret and make judgments based on the nonverbal messages you *receive*. Therefore, the following section will also include the nonverbal messages or nonverbal cues you "read" in order to understand workplace culture. After you have developed a competency in nonverbal language, you will readily see how verbal and nonverbal messages relate to each other.

Elements of Nonverbal Communication

There is a variety of ways to break down the types of nonverbal messages. These include body language, which includes appearance, posture, walk, gestures, and touch; eye contact and facial expression; vocal cues; and spatial use and time.

Body Language

Body language covers a number of nonverbal features, including appearance, posture and walk, gestures, and touch.

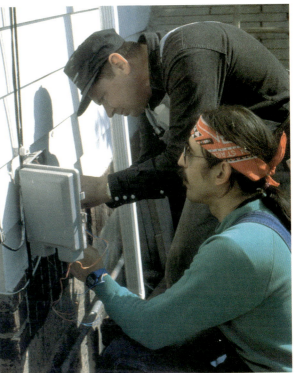

The way people are dressed can indicate what kind of work they do.

ZITS

Appearance

What message do you receive from someone who shows up on trash cleanup day dressed in slacks, shirt, and tie? Or someone who comes to a job interview in cutoffs and a T-shirt? Clothes, hairstyle, makeup, and personal decorations such as jewelry, slogan buttons, even tattoos, all send messages about how a person sees herself or himself. You make quick first judgments about others based on appearance.

Appearance may indicate mood, occupation, culture, status, or group membership. What might the following descriptions tell you about a person?

- overalls or jeans, flannel shirt, lunchbox, metal hat
- medals and stripes on a khaki uniform, standing straight
- rubber-soled athletic shoes, white slacks, loose top, stethoscope hanging around neck
- khaki shorts, white shirt with logo, green apron with pockets, an order pad and a pencil

It's likely you could make predictions of construction worker, military officer, health-care employee, and restaurant server.

When a new student joins your class, you form a first impression that is heavily based on appearance. In recent years, some schools have begun to require uniforms in order to reduce peer pressure to dress a certain way and to limit use of clothing as gang symbols.

Many companies expect employees to convey a certain image, and they provide uniforms to ensure this image. In other workplaces, employees are told, "No visible tattoos, facial piercing, jeans, or sport shoes." If you are working at a retail clothing store, you may be expected to wear certain styles or brands; if you are in a corporate office, suits or dresses may be expected. Some companies have regulations for hair, nails, makeup, and jewelry, which are expected to match the image created through clothing. Because people make snap judgments about others based on how they look, employees wish to convey a certain image to customers or clients, whether sporty, serious, or formal. They recognize that appearance matters.

Computer *Search*

Check out the following web sites to learn some tips on dressing appropriately for business-related careers. Share what you learned with your classmates.

www.townonline.com/working/careerres/js052696.html
www.collegegrad.com/book/app-a.shtml

Posture and Walk

Posture refers to your body's position as you sit or stand. Posture communicates a great deal about your mood or feelings. If you are slouching, you send a different message than if you are standing or sitting up straight. A person's posture often indicates whether or not it is a good time to start a conversation or make a request. If your supervisor is sitting slumped at the table with her head in her hand, then it's probably not the best moment to tell her that you are confused by a computer problem.

Posture can also send other messages. Models are taught to stand tall to make a good impression. Job candidates are taught to stand and sit up straight because they will appear more confident. Interviewers usually notice candidates' posture while they talk with them about their qualifications.

The way you walk also sends nonverbal messages to others. Sometimes people slouch because they are uncomfortable with their height; others think that slouching is the "in" way to walk for a certain group. When you watch people walking slowly and dragging their feet, you might decide they are tired or reluctant to get to where they are going. When you see people walking briskly, you may conclude they are anxious to get somewhere or that they are important.

Gestures and Touch

The way you use your hands, fingers, and arms adds to your nonverbal image and your effectiveness in conveying messages. These nonverbal cues include gestures and touch. **Gestures** are movements of hands and arms to help make a point. Most good speakers use gestures to visually underline something important in their message. The way gestures are used also tells others something

Nonverbal Communication

Leaning forward toward another person can show that you are interested and involved in what he or she is saying.

about a speaker's enthusiasm. Occasional gestures serve to emphasize; constant gestures tend to confuse. Some people tend to talk with their hands in motion. This habit might convey energy, but can be distracting. You may have heard someone say, "If I tied your hands behind your back, you couldn't talk."

In addition to large gestures, you use hand signals to communicate. In our culture a thumbs-up signal means "OK!" or "success." Creating a circle with thumb and index finger indicates "terrific" or "perfect." However, this is not true in other cultures, in which there may be very different meanings for such gestures.

Many work situations rely heavily on the language of gestures. The ground crew guiding airplanes to their gates uses various hand signals. Television directors cue their talent with specific hand gestures. Chefs constantly use gestures to indicate how their apprentices should prepare food.

Check It Out

Observe someone in a busy workplace for fifteen minutes—for example, a sports coach, construction worker, or teacher. Record their hand and arm movements. Note which gestures were used to convey general information and which ones were very specific to the person's job.

Touch Reaching out to touch another person sends a nonverbal message. Friends may put their arms around each other's shoulders or hug each other to indicate closeness or support. On the other hand, one person may strike another in anger. In our culture touch is related to power and status. Except in families and among friends, usually the person with the greater power or higher status initiates touch.

Touch in the workplace has become a very sensitive topic. There are times when touching another is a natural part of a job. A dance instructor may straighten the back of a pupil; an athletic trainer must wrap a sprained ankle; a nurse must touch a patient to draw blood.

When inappropriate or unwanted touching occurs, it may be considered sexual harassment. As you learned in the last chapter, unwanted or unwelcome comments or touching create a hostile environment. Therefore, many professionals ask permission to touch a student as part of instruction. A singing teacher may ask, "May I demonstrate correct breathing with you?" rather than just placing a hand on a voice student's diaphragm. If you are uncomfortable

People often use hand signals to communicate.

Nonverbal Communication

with the touch of a peer or supervisor, the first step is to say so, to say "No" or "Stop," or simply remove his or her hand firmly. Every organization has people available to handle employee complaints, and unwanted touching is a valid type of complaint.

FYI *What Is Sexual Harassment?*

Sexual harassment is unsolicited and unwanted verbal or physical conduct of a sexual nature that offends a person and interferes with that person's activities and opportunities.

What Can You Do if You Are Sexually Harassed?

- SAY NO
- Know your RIGHTS
- Keep a written, dated RECORD
- Ask for HELP
- DON'T blame yourself
- DON'T delay asking for help

Friends use touching to indicate closeness and support nonverbally.

Touch behavior is influenced by gender and culture. In our culture, women are more touch oriented than men. Women are more likely to hug and touch friends than men are. In other cultures this is different. For example, men in the Middle East or Southern Europe are more likely to hug each other than men in the United States are.

Handshakes communicate a great deal about a person. Many interviewers shake hands with prospective employees because they believe that a handshake can indicate something about the candidate that words do not. What might you tell from a handshake?

Handshakes are culture-bound. In Japan, business people usually bow to greet one another, although they may use handshakes when dealing with Americans. In Brazil, extended handshakes are common; in France, handshakes may be less firm than in the United States.

In place of the traditional handshake, friends often substitute a "high-five" when they greet one another.

Eye Contact and Facial Expressions

Facial expressions are an important part of everyday nonverbal communication. The term **facial expressions** refers to the movements of the eyes, eyebrows, and mouth that communicate our attitudes and feelings to others.

Most people expect eye contact when communicating. **Eye contact** refers to making a visual connection between people or looking someone in the eye. People's eyes meet as they speak and listen. Looking someone in the eye implies paying attention, taking the other person seriously, and being trustworthy. If you constantly avoid eye contact with another—for example, looking down at the floor or staring out a window—you risk being perceived as bored, shifty, or rude.

Making eye contact signals recognition of the other person. If you do not make eye contact, you can pretend that you did not see the other person. This "allows" you to ignore the other person.

Many messages are conveyed through eye signaling. This often involves eye contact and movement of the eyelid or eyebrow. A teacher may catch a student's eye and signal that student to be quiet without interrupting the lesson. A wink may signal flirting or a shared joke. One of the most powerful eye signals is rolling the eyes—a sign of disgust or contempt for another person or for what that person is saying (a way of saying "Duh!" soundlessly).

© Lynn Johnston Productions Inc./Dist. by United Feature Syndicate, Inc.

Eye movements are linked to eyebrow movements, another part of facial expression. You may frown and draw your eyebrows in concern or concentration. Or you can raise them in surprise.

  May indicate anger or concentration.

  May indicate curiosity or doubt.

  May indicate surprise.

Your mouth also communicates a great deal about your feelings (without saying a word). The most obvious nonverbal cue is a smile. When you encounter a new person, you usually predict if they are friendly by their smile. When you encounter a salesperson or a plumber making a service call, you are reassured if you are met by a smile. It conveys warmth, friendliness, and welcome. Smiles generally give others a feeling of being liked, while a neutral face may convey disinterest or even disapproval. Yet in other cultures people may smile even when giving bad news or saying no. This is not unusual in Japan and other parts of Asia.

Because facial expressions are the nonverbal cues that people control best, senders can hide their feelings by showing a blank face when they are really upset or by faking a smile when they are not happy. Paul Ekman, nonverbal researcher, lists the following key questions for "reading" a face. These questions can help you figure out if you are receiving the correct message.

- Does the amount of the smile or facial expression fit with what the person is saying and with the situation?
- What is the timing of the expression? Does it appear or fade too quickly to be real?
- Is the expression one that this person usually uses?

Jennifer Rosen, *Medical Aide*

When Jennifer Rosen leaves home to attend college, many local community organizations will be very sad to see her go. As an active member of her Key Club, Jennifer has become involved in a variety of long-term volunteer activities. She has made a major commitment to Horizons, an organization that serves individuals with muscular dystrophy. Last summer Jennifer worked as an attendant/companion at their camp for adults. For one week she partnered with a 42-year-old female camper who was confined to a wheel chair and needed help with eating and dressing and other daily needs. According to Jennifer, "You are basically their right hand during the week." Yet Jennifer appreciated her partner's "unbelievable sense of humor," and found the experience to be gratifying and inspiring.

Many of Horizon's clients are not able to communicate verbally, so Jennifer has learned to be sensitive to subtle nonverbal cues. She determines a camper's needs through eye contact, facial expressions, movements, and gestures. Learning to do this was a time-consuming and complex process because "to try to communicate with someone who can't speak is very challenging."

Part of the companion's role is to be an advocate and spokesperson for his or her camper, a responsibility that requires the companion to learn her partner's needs and wishes. Because of her experiences working with Horizons, Jennifer has a much deeper appreciation for the efforts made by physically challenged people to participate actively in the world around them.

Horizons is only one organization that has benefited from Jennifer's volunteer efforts. She also volunteers her services at Gilda's Club, a support center for cancer patients, and she works with friends from school to collect necessary supplies for a local battered-women's shelter. In addition, Jennifer is looking forward to training for and working at a hotline for runaway and abused teens.

Jennifer stresses how much she has grown personally through these volunteer experiences. Among other things, she says, "I've become a more effective discussion partner when talking with adults and children."

Student Worker Profile

95

Vocal Cues

How does your best friend sound when he or she is really annoyed? What vocal cues tell you someone's mood over the phone? Changes in voice can reveal a great deal about a person if the listener is sensitive to them. The four key vocal features that can convey meaning are *pitch, rate, volume,* and *quality. Articulation* is another vocal feature.

Pitch

Pitch refers to the highness or lowness of a voice. Usually males have lower-pitched voices than females. Nervous people tend to indicate their anxiety by higher-pitched voices. Sometimes employees will lower their voices to appear older over the phone. Some companies are concerned that a receptionist with a high-pitched voice will sound childish and create the wrong organizational image. Good speakers vary their pitch. When a person speaks in only one pitch, called a monotone, listeners tend to tune out or fall asleep.

Rate

Rate refers to how rapidly or slowly a person talks. Extreme differences in rate of speech may be a reflection of nervousness. A person who is tense in a particular situation will probably tend to speak more rapidly than he or she normally does. Often, very high-energy people have a rapid rate of speech. Speech rate may reflect regional speech patterns. For example, people raised in the South tend to talk more slowly and Northeasterners more rapidly than those from other parts of the country. Rapid speech is very difficult to understand for people who are not native English speakers. It also presents problems for listeners when technical language is involved.

Volume

Volume refers to the loudness or softness of a voice. Sometimes the loudness or softness may be related to a person's self-image. Soft-spoken individuals may be concerned that others do not want to listen to them. Sometimes they will raise their voice, because they think it's a way of pushing their point or that people will listen if they speak loudly.

How close you stand to other people while talking depends on how well you know them, how comfortable you are with them, and what you are talking about.

Quality

Vocal quality refers to the sound or tone of a voice. Some people have unpleasant voice qualities, such as nasal, raspy, or whining tones, that create an unfair image for them. It's easy to listen to someone with a pleasant voice, but a raspy or nasal voice creates a kind of static or interference. The message can get lost. Unpleasant voices are described as metallic, rasping, wheezing, and grating—none of which is a compliment!

Eye-to-Eye

Pair up with someone and role-play some phone calls for a charity. The speaker should try to convey one of the following attitudes: high interest, lack of interest, nervousness, or efficiency. The listener should try to identify the attitude. Create a short sales pitch for the speaker to use. The listener can improvise responses to the sales pitch.

Articulation

Vocal cues also include **articulation**, which is the clear expression of your words and sounds. This is the "Don't mumble" message. Good articulation means speaking clearly so that your listener understands your message correctly. For example, say, "Where's your mother?" not "Whrs mudder?" "Good morning" not "Morn'n," and "Did you eat?" not "Di'jeet?"

Articulation also involves good **pronunciation** or saying the words correctly. For example, say, "nuclear" *not* "nucular," "rotary" *not* "rotry," and "mother" *not* "mudder."

Nonverbal Communication

Office design and layout influence who talks to whom and the length or type of communication.

Sometimes your vocal pattern is distracting because it is filled with "like," "y'know," or "er . . . uh." This language litter clutters meanings and causes listeners to become distracted and lose interest. For example,

"We were, like, you know, going to pick up the lunches but, like, we got busy. So, you know, we tried to, like, make up time and, um, we forgot. You know what I mean."

Spatial Use and Time

Spatial Use
Spatial use refers to how space is used between persons and how the arrangement and design of space affects communication. **Proxemics** refers to the use of space and how space influences relationships and communication. It deals with **proximity**, or physical closeness or distance. What's a comfortable distance between you and a friend during a hallway conversation? How comfortable do you feel when a boss or teacher stands almost nose to nose with you?

Americans typically carry around a two-foot bubble of privacy. In other words, they generally interact with other people while standing at a distance of about two feet. The distance will vary, however, depending upon the people involved, their relationship to each other, and their purpose for being together.

The anthropologist Edward Hall identified distances at which Americans usually stand from each other. A simplified version of his work is presented here.

Toni Castro, *Distribution Manager*

Visitors may be surprised to find Toni Castro's desk right in the middle of the warehouse space, a very busy and noisy environment. But, according to this distribution manager for Illinois Tool Works (ITW), moving her desk out of an enclosed office onto the warehouse floor made a difference in her ability to manage her team. After nearly 15 years and six different positions at ITW, Toni Castro is an expert on her organization. She entered ITW as an assistant traffic coordinator, dealing with trucking companies and air-freight flights. Today she has a management position that places her at the head of a team of 18 full-time and many part-time warehouse employees. The team's goal is to provide efficient and accurate distribution of material to companies that purchase their products.

Ms. Castro says that her main responsibilities are managing and leading her team of employees, heading key projects, and participating in transportation negotiation meetings and agreements. She may find herself giving directions, explaining specific tasks to members of the warehouse team, or helping to explain a new business system for tracking the material in the warehouse. Being "out on the floor" of the warehouse is a definite plus. It places her at the center of the action and communicates to her co-workers that she is in touch and involved in the daily operations.

On a typical day, Ms. Castro arrives between 7 and 8 A.M. and stays into the evening. Much of her time is spent walking around rather than sitting at her desk. In a warehouse of 43,000 square feet, she wears out a lot of shoes! Her main concern is checking on how the team is reaching the daily goals. When a customer places a large order, it is the team's goal to ship the order in two business days with 99 percent accuracy. To ensure accuracy, warehouse staff members use hand-held scanners as they fill orders. Ms. Castro can check an audit log to see how fast things are moving and how many mistakes have been made.

ITW relies heavily on teamwork, and many employees work on cross-functional teams to solve specific problems. For example, when ITW had to find a way to get large amounts of product to a new retailer, representatives from finance,

The World of Work

sales, marketing, warehouse, and customer services came together to create a plan. In addition, all employees are encouraged to talk at open-forum meetings designed to improve the way work is done.

Toni Castro finds real pleasure in "seeing and helping people grow and develop." She is proud that her plant has been chosen as a "showcase division" in ITW, which means that people from all over the world come to see how her co-workers perform their tasks.

Intimate space is up to 1 1/2 feet. This is used for communication such as hugging, telling secrets, tickling.

Personal space is 1 1/2 to 4 feet. This is used for quiet conversations. Some touching is possible.

Social space is 4 to 12 feet. This is used for situations such as group discussions, sales meetings. Handshakes may occur.

Public space is over 12 feet. This is used when communicating across a distance, including calling, waving a greeting, or giving a speech. No touch is possible.

Although Americans are generally more comfortable interacting with others at a distance of about two feet, there are times when your "bubbles" are invaded, such as on elevators or in lines at lunch counters or in crowds. In these situations, people usually avoid making eye contact with others. By not looking at the other person, you create a psychological distance or barrier between the two of you. You do not acknowledge the other person and feel as if you have more privacy.

In other cultures, space is used differently. Businesspeople in Central and South America and the Middle East are likely to stand very close to each other while talking. When Americans encounter this closeness, they tend to back away. This makes us appear rude. In *Kiss, Bow, or Shake Hands,* a book on international business, the authors Terri Morrison, Wayne Conaway, and George Borden report that in Honduras "Conversations take place at a much closer distance than may be considered comfortable in the United States. Pulling away from your counterpart may be considered as rejection." They also describe countries such as Mexico, Spain, and Brazil, where greetings may include hugs after a few meetings.

Objects and Design The physical environment creates its own message system. People also use the physical environment to communicate nonverbally with one another. Objects that people carry, use, or display send certain messages. Pictures of children on a desk send a different message than pictures of a dog or a sailboat. Pictures tell a visitor something about the person who sits there. A display of very expensive artwork conveys the sense of power and money. Objects and art can be conversation starters. Sometimes interviewers or managers deliberately display unusual or funny objects in order to relax visitors and provide a safe topic for conversation. Office design and layout influence who talks to whom and the length or type of communication. In a large office with many desks in an open area, people are likely to talk across the open space because they see each other. In an office with high-walled cubicles or "cubbies," employees are not likely to shout over the walls. Closed or semi-closed doors send an "I'm busy" message. Open doors suggest, "You can talk with me." Office design also can influence how effectively a supervisor manages a team or group of employees. (See The World of Work, page 99.)

Nonverbal messages can reinforce what you are saying verbally. What nonverbal messages are being communicated in this photograph?

Check It Out

Walk down an office hallway in school, a public building, or a corporation. Look at the decorations (flags, pictures) and bulletin boards. Note the position of office doors or cubicle openings. Try to see how an office is decorated. Write a paragraph explaining what messages the environment sends about how to communicate in that building.

Time

The way people use time may communicate information and feelings nonverbally. What is communicated when a co-worker is always late? What is communicated when a boss always takes extra time to explain a confusing idea to you?

If you see two co-workers spending a great deal of time together, you get the message "We're good friends." If someone is always late for an appointment or forgets meetings, wasting your time, you get the message "This is not important to me." In the United States there is an emphasis on watching the clock and doing things on time. We see time as money and, therefore, as valuable.

The use of time is tied to the status or position of a person. In Western culture, a person of high status can keep someone else waiting because the other person's time is viewed as less valuable. Bosses may be late, but their staff is expected to be on time.

The way time is used differs from person to person and culture to culture. In Latin America, for example, people do not feel the same pressure to be on time. They believe that what is important will be accomplished eventually. Because time means different things to different people, you may have to know the person or the culture well to interpret the nonverbal message accurately.

Remember!

Nonverbal messages are communicated through:

▶ Body language

▶ Eye contact

▶ Facial expression

▶ Vocal cues

▶ Use of space and time

Nonverbal Communication

Career Communication *Costume Designer*

A person who works in theater costume design needs to have highly developed artistic skills, excellent interpersonal and group communication skills, and an ability to create memorable images that communicate the content and theme of a production nonverbally. Theater design is a collaborative process in which the set, lighting, and costume designers work with each other and with the director to create a unified vision for the production.

Costume designers must research the dress of the period in which the play is set. Using that research, they draft models of the costumes for the director

and others to examine. The overall color scheme of the set, lighting, and costumes helps create a mood and communicate a message to the audience. For example, a character's personality may be conveyed in part by the color and design of the costumes. Warring families may be dressed in different colors to indicate separation. Every show is a different experience, and the costume designer must be flexible, creative, and artistic.

Joint Functions of Nonverbal and Verbal Messages

It is important to understand the connection between verbal and nonverbal messages. Nonverbal messages work with or against verbal messages. The two are interconnected and function jointly in four ways.

Nonverbal messages may *support* verbal messages. For example: "We *need* (fist slammed on table, loud noise) to build a stronger defense system." Most of the time, nonverbal cues will send the same messages as the verbal cues, through the accompanying dress, facial expressions, and gestures. These similar messages may give added emphasis to the sender's intention.

Nonverbal messages may *contradict* the verbal message. For example: "Nice to see you again" (bored tone of voice, no eye contact, fishy handshake) or "I really don't want to be the group leader" (grabbing chair at head of table, smiling). In these examples, the speaker's words say one thing, but his or her nonverbal cues say something entirely different. This is called a **mixed message**—for example, "Oh go ahead without me; I don't really care" (said with a whining tone and sad look).

Nonverbal messages may *replace* verbal messages. You may find that in certain settings you use only a nonverbal message because it is impossible or inappropriate to send a verbal one. You and a friend may exchange a knowing look during a meeting when someone else claims ownership of your friend's idea.

You may discreetly nod, shrug, and roll your eyes to point out a customer who is back to try on an outfit for the fourth time.

Nonverbal messages can *regulate* verbal messages. Such nonverbal cues tell listeners when and how to speak. If someone gives you a quizzical look when you are talking, what do you do? If someone puts his hand to his ear during your presentation, what should you do? If someone looks at a watch while you are explaining a process, what might you do?

In conversations, nonverbal cues may indicate whose turn it is to speak or how long to talk. When tone lowers or a long silence occurs, you know the floor is yours. You are likely to cut your speech short if you read "hurry up" messages from your listeners. Use the following questions to help you determine whether accurate messages are being sent:

- Are the verbal and nonverbal signals sending the same message?
- Is the message specific and complete?
- Is the meaning clear?

Chapter 4 *Summary*

In this chapter, you learned about nonverbal communication, which can be broken down into four major areas: body language, including appearance, posture, walk, gestures, and touch; eye contact and facial expressions; voice; and spatial use and time.

A person's appearance is important because people make snap judgments about others based on the way they look. A person's posture, walk, gestures, and touch also communicate messages to others.

Facial expressions—the movement of the eyes, eyebrows, and mouth—communicate a person's attitudes and feelings. People use eye contact, eye signals, smiles, and frowns to connect with others as well as to communicate messages.

The four key vocal cues that convey nonverbal messages are pitch, rate, volume, and vocal quality. Articulation—the clear expression of words and sounds—is another important vocal cue. Pronunciation is closely related to articulation.

Spatial use refers to how space is used between persons. Proxemics refers to how space influences relationships and communication. People also use time to communicate information, attitudes, and feelings nonverbally.

Nonverbal and verbal messages function jointly in four ways: nonverbal messages support verbal messages, they contradict verbal messages, they regulate verbal messages, and they replace verbal messages.

Review Questions

1. What is nonverbal communication?
2. What percent of communication is nonverbal?
3. What can your posture tell an observer? Give an example.
4. How should you sit or stand to appear confident?
5. How can you avoid being accused of sexual harassment?
6. Why is eye contact important to effective communication?
7. Give examples of vocal variety.
8. What is language litter or clutter?
9. Why is it important to understand the nonverbal habits of other cultures?
10. In what four ways are nonverbal and verbal messages connected?

Critical Thinking Activities

Speaking/Doing

1. Visit a business office or a store. Note the nonverbal behavior of the employees. Make a chart that lists the types of nonverbal behavior discussed in this chapter. Fill in observations on the chart. In your chart, try to include an explanation for each example of nonverbal behavior you observe. After completing your chart, discuss your results with classmates. What similarities exist among students' charts?

2. Using the library, the Internet, or personal interviews, find out how a culture different from your own (or from a typical American culture) uses nonverbal cues to communicate. For example, in the United States, a thumbs-up signal might mean "good job" or "can I have a ride," but in a Middle Eastern country, it is an extreme insult. After you have gathered several examples, prepare a one- to three-minute speech to inform the class of your research.

3. Watch a television show, preferably one with which you are not familiar. Turn the volume off and watch the nonverbal behavior. Can you figure out what is going on? What are the relationships between the characters? After watching for 15 minutes or so, turn the volume on and check to see how accurate your observations were. Share your observations in a class discussion.

Writing

1. Go to a mall or grocery store and observe the way people walk and stand. Write down your observations. What conclusions can you draw about the people you saw just by the way they moved? Present your conclusions in a one- or two-paragraph essay.

2. Perform an experiment in proxemics. Throughout the day, have conversations with various casual friends as you normally would; however, change your normal body space with each. With some, invade their personal body space just a little; with others, draw away from them. Observe the reactions to your proxemics. Record the reactions and write one paragraph on what people's reactions are to getting too close. Write a second paragraph on their reactions when you withdraw.

Group Activities

1. In groups of eight, divide into two teams of four students. Play charades, using only gestures and facial expressions to get your team to guess the message written on a piece of paper given to you by your teacher. You will be given three minutes to get your team to figure out what message you are trying to convey. Remember, no verbal clues are allowed.

2. Work together in a small group to make a collage of pictures of people's appearances (or body postures or gestures or facial expressions). Ask your classmates what conclusions we might draw about each person in the collage. Are these conclusions fair? accurate? Use this activity as a springboard for a class discussion on stereotyping.

Practical Application: Case Challenge

Karen and Maria work as servers at an expensive restaurant. One night some business executives were so busy talking that they would not listen to the specials. Karen tried to get their attention by announcing loudly, "We have four specials," three times. Four people never even looked up. One woman smiled and shrugged apologetically. This meant Karen had to repeat the specials to each person as she asked for his or her order.

After the executives had stopped eating, Karen approached one man whose fork and knife were laid across a plate with a few vegetables left on it. She asked, "Are you finished?"

The man did not answer.

As Karen reached to remove his plate, the man grabbed her wrist and said, "I'm not done." Karen pulled her hand free and gave him a disapproving look.

Ten minutes later Maria, who had not seen Karen's situation, asked if the man was finished. Again he did not answer. When she went to remove the plate, the man grabbed her wrist, slapped her hand, and said, "I'm not finished." Maria was so startled she could hardly respond.

What messages did the diners send to Karen? to Maria? How would you feel if you were Maria? How might she respond in this situation?

Chapter Five

Listening

Objectives

After completing this chapter you will be able to

- define listening and effective listening
- explain the steps in the listening process
- explain why listening is important in the workplace
- describe types of listening
- read workplace clues through listening
- describe barriers to effective listening
- use strategies for effective listening

Key Terms

active listening

confirming message

disconfirming message

effective listening

empathic listening

external distractions

hearing

internal distractions

listening

pseudolistening

synergy

❝ But the bottom line is that almost any business situation will be handled differently, and with different results, by someone who is listening and someone who isn't. ❞

—MARK MCCORMICK,
What They Don't Teach You at Harvard Business School

107

Listening to Solve Problems

Ben, Paolo, and Alix, Senior Program Leaders, are in charge of running a training evening for parents of high school students going to Honduras and Costa Rica to perform volunteer work for six weeks of the summer. At the moment, the three are having a meeting to plan the big night.

Alix says, "OK, guys, let's stop messin' around with this stupid poster and get started. Our goal is to give parents a sense of what their children will be doing in the field during the summer and to reassure parents that their children will be safe and well. We also want to give parents a sense of what the weekly training will include and to emphasize the importance of this volunteer effort." This comment is followed by a long silence.

Finally, Ben says, "Well, just tell them that everyone always comes back safe—a little thinner, but safe."

Paolo nods. Alix stares into space.

Paolo responds, "Fine, but we have three hours to fill. How slowly can we say the goals?"

This sends Ben into a set of complaints about last year's Parent Night program. "Last year's program was too long and boring. The parents didn' t really get the picture."

"I agree," Paolo replies.

"What do you mean?" Alix asks. She is still staring into space.

"Long, boring, and unclear," repeats Ben.

Alix seems to perk up. "What was boring and unclear?"

"Well, hello! We thought you dozed off," responds Paolo.

"Last year's meeting was boring."

Alix is annoyed. "Let's not waste time putting down last year. We need to get parents involved as soon as they arrive. We could have Katie do the dental health speech that she gave to kids last summer and ask Elise to talk about working on the new school building in that little town. They could do it in Spanish and English."

Ben interrupts, "You think parents want a speech on Tommy the Tooth? Great. Duh."

"Well, at least I'm trying to find a way to create an interesting program. All you two are doing is complaining," Alix replies indignantly.

"Fine. We can have two speeches—one on teeth and one on school buildings. Then what?"

Ben continues, "The goals are for parents to relax with this idea and to help raise money for the program. Let's show them pictures of the good work our volunteers accomplish in six weeks."

"Ben, this night has nothing to do with money," Alix nearly

shouts. "We are trying to get parents on board to support their kids' participation."

Paolo is thumbing through a leader handbook.

Ben replies heatedly, "Don't get so bent out of shape. Hey Paolo, didn't they ask for money last year?"

No answer.

"Earth to Paolo . . . are you with us?"

Paolo keeps his head in the book and says, "We could do the ball exercise to get names down in Spanish and English. It's important for parents to meet each other. My mother liked that part best last year. She met Jesse's mother, and they talked to each other all summer about what each had heard from us . . ."

Alix interrupts, "And what did they say about money?"

"Huh?"

Exasperated, Ben suggests, "Hey, Alix, write a plan and we'll do whatever you say. C'mon, Paolo, let's get a burger."

Why is this group making slow progress? What advice would you give this group about listening to each other?

The Listening Process

Listening is a taken-for-granted life skill that is your most frequent communication experience. Most people equate listening and hearing, but listening and hearing are not the same. **Hearing** is a biological process created when sound waves hit your eardrum. Hearing is also part of the first step in the listening process. But listening is far more complex than just taking in sounds. **Listening** is an active process that includes receiving, interpreting, evaluating, and responding to a message. It takes effort and concentration. **Effective listening** occurs when the message sent by the speaker is the same message decoded by the listener. How often have you made a helpful suggestion that was misinterpreted, judged to be sarcastic, or responded to with a blank stare? That type of listening is frustrating to encounter. Let's take a closer look at the four steps of effective listening.

Receiving

Receiving involves taking in sense data by using your ears and eyes to gather information. Your ears take in the vocal tones and words—for example, "You signed up to work the morning shift on Saturday." As you receive a message, your eyes read the nonverbal signals, such as a frown or an annoyed glance. You watch facial expressions and gestures, and you listen to the vocal tone to get the message.

> Listening is an active process that includes receiving, interpreting, evaluating, and responding to a message. It takes effort and concentration.

Interpreting

Once you have received a message through your ears and eyes, you use your own experience to give meaning to what you just heard. This is called interpreting the message. An effective listener tries to decode the message based on what is known about the speaker. You may ask yourself questions such as

Is this my friend or a stranger?
Is this his or her normal tone, or is it different?
Is this a stressful time?
Is he or she really concerned about something else?

You will also pay attention to the words the speaker emphasizes. Consider the statement "You signed up for the morning shift on Saturday." You may interpret it as meaning *you* signed up. (No one else did it so you can't back out.) Or, "You signed up for the morning shift on *Saturday*." (What are you doing here on Friday?) There may be still other meanings, such as "I signed up for Saturday too, how great!" Nonverbal cues will provide helpful information in figuring out the intended meaning.

The special meaning of certain words also influences the interpreting process. "You look terrific," "You look splendiferous today," and "You are stylin'" all mean basically the same thing, but the listener needs to know the meaning of the words to be sure.

Finally, interpreting correctly what a speaker says depends on the speaker and listener agreeing on the meaning of certain words. If your boss tells you he'll pay you big bucks to work the morning shift on Saturday, how much will he pay you? Does *big bucks* have the same meaning for him as it does for you?

Evaluating

Evaluating involves examining a message and making a judgment. After you have interpreted a message, you need to evaluate it carefully. You have to connect the message to your own ideas or feelings about what is being said. You have to decide if you agree, disagree, or if you need more information. For example, if your boss says, "You missed work on Tuesday. What happened?" depending on how you interpreted the message, you might consider telling your boss, "Oops, I made a mistake" or "I forgot I had a debate tournament that day." On the other hand, you might be thinking, "I was hoping not to share the shift with Blake." While the other person is talking, you begin to ask yourself, "What do I think?" or "How do I feel?" or "What do I need to know?"

Eye-to-Eye

With a partner, select two of the following messages and two of the speakers. Describe how you might interpret, evaluate, and respond to these messages depending on the speaker.

Messages	Speakers
"You were supposed to be here at noon. Where were you?"	boss
	parent
"You look down. Are you OK?"	good friend
"Why didn't you tell me Isabel called?"	co-worker
"Another tattoo? Isn't one enough?"	

Speakers expect a verbal or nonverbal signal that you got the message even if you do not agree with it.

Remember!

The four steps to effective listening are

▶ Receiving

▶ Interpreting

▶ Evaluating

▶ Responding

Responding

Responding is giving verbal or nonverbal feedback to a speaker. Almost all messages require some type of response or feedback. This is illustrated in the diagram on page 15 in Chapter 1. A lack of response frustrates most speakers. The listener who gives no verbal or nonverbal feedback makes a speaker feel uncomfortable and almost nonexistent. Ignoring a speaker is called a **disconfirming message** or a message that indicates the other person is invisible. Speakers expect a verbal or nonverbal signal that you got the message even if you do not agree with it.

As a listener, you are faced with sending an appropriate or relevant response. This is called a **confirming message.** It indicates that you recognize the other person's existence. You may say, "I forgot I had a debate tournament" or "I got my dates confused. Sorry." A blank stare does not give a speaker much to work with. Whatever your verbal or nonverbal response, it tells the speaker that the message reached you. The response closes the speaking-listening loop.

The Importance of Listening

Why is effective listening important? In families and friendships, a good listener helps build relationships and a sense of connection. In the workplace, effective listening leads to success, a positive workplace climate, and money. Organizational leaders who listen well are more effective because they get the messages their co-workers are sending. In turn, their clients and customers are served well.

PEANUTS

Peanuts reprinted by permission of United Feature Syndicate.

Good listeners create a climate of support. Suppose you are concerned about money for college or how you are doing on the job. If your boss or a co-worker is a good listener, you will find it easier to come to work. Talking with someone does not solve your problem, but it will allow you to release your feelings.

If your workplace encourages honest expression of concerns or rewards good ideas, listening must be valued. A good workplace is one that allows you to raise questions and offer ideas. Successful companies listen to their employees and act on employees' suggestions.

Creativity is fostered by good listening. When employees pay attention to each other's ideas and feedback from customers and clients, exciting things happen. New ideas are created. Brainstorming or "think" sessions result in whole new ways of working. A few years ago McDonald's listened to many concerned customers and stopped using styrofoam packaging in order to help protect the environment. This decision served both the customers and McDonald's well.

Good listeners create a climate of support. A good workplace is one that allows you to raise questions and offer ideas.

Many businesspeople find that their good listening skills lead to more profits. Listening is the greatest tool in successful sales. A manager who listens to staff ideas will have a more productive workplace. In addition, good listening can lead to promotion because your work is done more efficiently. Finally, if you listen well, not only will you succeed, but your organization will find more ways to be successful.

Types of Listening

There are many types of listening. You may go into a situation knowing which type you need to use, or you may discover as you are listening that you need to use another type.

Informational Listening

An important reason to listen is to get information. Many people have problems at work or school because they do not listen carefully and miss information they need. They may miss dates, times, steps in a process, or an assignment. Often they do not ask the right questions to find out what they need to know.

Informational listening, also called deliberative listening, involves listening to learn information such as facts, directions, explanations, or news. You are listening for information when you take notes in meetings or when you pay attention to a demonstration on how to make vegetarian pizza. During television or radio news broadcasts, you listen for information about the weather, news events, and sports.

Some organizations train their employees in informational listening skills. For example, Starbucks teaches employees to listen to orders for the purpose of rearranging requests according to size, flavoring, milk, and caffeine content. This permits the staff to relay orders to each other easily and to fill orders more efficiently.

Informational listening involves listening to learn facts, directions, explanations, or news. Some jobs require very sharp informational listening skills.

Check It Out

Ask two people to describe the difference between an effective listener and a poor listener in their workplace and to give you some examples. Share these examples with the class.

FYI *Taking Good Notes*

Competent communicators listen with their eyes, ears, and sometimes with a pen or a laptop computer. Here are some guidelines for effective informational note taking:

1. *Decide what kind of notes you need to take.*
   Is your boss giving you directions on how to make something or how to get somewhere? Do you need a list, a map, or keywords?

2. *Pay attention to what is emphasized.*
   Notice if certain points are repeated or highlighted by comments such as "Remember," "Be sure to," "The key point is," or "This point is tricky." Vocal tone may also indicate importance.

3. *Make the notes your own.*
   Use symbols or codes such as stars, underlining, colors, etc., to adapt the information to yourself.

4. *Ask for more information.*
   Look for holes or gaps in the information. Try to anticipate what's missing or what could be a problem for you: "Did you say turn left at the light or turn right?" or "If I skip step 3, what will happen?"

Critical Listening

Critical listening means analyzing a message containing opinions, points of view, and attempts at persuasion and then making decisions based on your analysis. After examining a message, you need to respond actively. Perhaps you will need to ask questions to obtain further information, or you may need to think about why someone is trying to persuade you to do something. Sometimes you can link others' ideas and your ideas into a better plan.

A critical listener evaluates the other person's ideas—separating fact from opinion—before responding.

Critical listening involves separating fact from opinion and evaluating the source of a message. A fact is a statement that can be proved true or false. An opinion is a statement that is based on a belief or feeling. It is a judgment. For example, you can prove that the price of lumber went up or that the distance between Broadway and 9th Avenue is 3.5 miles. You cannot prove that lumber is too expensive or that the drive between Broadway and 9th is boring. The last two are opinions, and you can't prove or disprove opinions.

A critical listener hears the other person's ideas first; looks for facts, opinions, disagreements, and confusions; and then figures out how to respond effectively. Whether you are attending a political rally, participating in an argument, or watching a commercial on TV, your mind should be working constantly to evaluate the information you receive.

When people listen to each other creatively, they combine ideas and see new ways to do things.

What questions might a critical listener ask in response to the following statements? (Look for facts and opinions.)

- "Remi says there are only two slots for new caddies. One is already promised to Sean."
- "You should buy this car because it gets great mileage and has all the 'extras.'"
- "Matthew Wegman is a tough job interviewer. Only one out of ten candidates gets an offer."

Creative Listening

Creative listening means actively using your imagination as you interpret a message. Your imagination may create pictures, stories, or related ideas. You find yourself saying, "That's similar to the time I did . . ." or "That reminds me of . . . ." It's a process of making connections.

Often when you listen to others, your mind does amazing things. Whereas you thought there were only two ways to do something, as you listened you saw a third and better way. For example, you may hear your mother and little sister fighting over the clothes your sister wears to school. Your mother says, "You need to wear matching clothes. This does not go with that." Your sister is crying that she wants to dress herself. After listening, you may suggest that Mom lay out three outfits and let your sister choose one. Each person may find this a good idea.

Some businesses are sending their employees to comedy training to help them become more creative as presenters and listeners. Executives in these companies believe that listeners who can find humor in ideas and learn to make surprising connections between ideas will be better employees.

One specific kind of creative listening is called synergy, or cooperative interaction. **Synergy** occurs when the individual ideas of two or more persons are combined or re-formed to create something new. If you and a friend are developing a computer web site, listening to each other creatively can lead to more imaginative results.

Sometimes you can see new ways to do things in response to what other people say. Someone else's idea may inspire you to think of a related idea of your own. This is called piggybacking, and it is closely related to synergy. Suppose you are building a display for a new shipment of fall merchandise. One co-worker says, "Hang the clothes around the store from the ceiling." This idea prompts another worker to suggest hanging a display on the wall of the coffee shop next door and hanging a coffee display in your store. Someone else suggests matching clothes to blown-up photos of other stores in town, creating displays featuring clothes for certain occasions. Effective problem solvers actively use creative listening skills to see the possibilities in other people's ideas and to make the most of those ideas.

Empathic Listening

Empathic listening involves listening to another's feelings. This is a very difficult type of listening. It is not easy just to listen when others are talking about feelings. Sometimes you want to jump in to solve their problems for them. Sometimes you want to interrupt with questions or ideas. Sometimes you just want to get away from the conversation because their strong feelings make you uncomfortable.

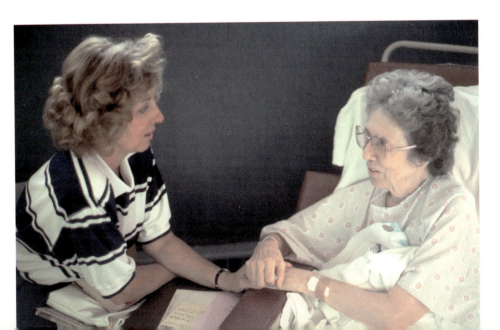

Empathic listening involves listening to another's feelings. It often requires patience and caring. Sometimes eye contact, head nodding, and touch are better responses than words.

Listening to negative feelings requires patience and caring. Talking to a friend who is angry or sad can be a challenge. Eye contact, head nodding, or touch are often better responses than words. When you do speak, it's best to paraphrase or clarify the other's ideas and feelings. This is called active listening. **Active listening** refers to the ability to really recognize another person's feelings and to reflect those feelings back to the speaker. It will take great self-control not to agree with or criticize his or her points. As a camp counselor, babysitter, or hospital volunteer, you may meet many people who want to talk about their feelings. These situations will give you the opportunity to be an empathic listener.

Eye-to-Eye

In a small group, brainstorm three careers or jobs that would require a person to demonstrate two of the four types of listening. Prepare a one-sentence explanation for each job you analyze. Use the example below as a model for your explanations.

An advertising writer needs to use creative listening and informational listening. This position requires a person to gather accurate information from others about products and consumers and to evaluate and respond to that information in creative ways.

Listening for Workplace Clues

Listening is a very important tool for reading workplace clues about how to act appropriately in a particular setting or situation. The following example demonstrates this idea.

Sarah, a college student and part-time employee at a health center, is friendly and energetic. The staff has included her in lunches and birthday parties. When they are sitting around after hours, staff members will tell slightly off-color jokes and use some four-letter words. Sarah is comfortable with the group. On the job, when Sarah is trying to register patients and the computer goes down, she is known to swear, saying, "This *%*%# machine is down again." In this situation, her co-workers frown. When Sarah is sitting behind the waiting room desk with co-workers, she sometimes tells slightly off-color jokes, but the jokes don't seem to get much of a laugh.

What might be going on here? What should Sarah be told?

Your eyes and ears help you listen to the conversations around you. If you listen attentively, you can learn what kind of talk and behavior is acceptable in the workplace, as well as what is not acceptable in the workplace.

Evan Collins, *Pharmacist*

Communication is at the heart of everyday work life for pharmacist Evan Collins. Collins is a pharmacist at Clearwater Hospital in New Jersey. His duties include filling prescriptions for in-patients and out-patients at the hospital; working with nurses, doctors, and dieticians to determine the right medication for patients; and sometimes administering medicine himself.

Collins received his Doctor of Pharmacy degree three years ago, after six years of study, and was lucky enough to find a position in a hospital right away. "A hospital is a very stimulating environment for a pharmacist to work in," he says. Pharmacists working in a hospital often become more involved in decision making regarding what drugs to prescribe for a patient than pharmacists working in other settings. Hospital pharmacists also have more direct contact with patients and other health-care professionals. This direct contact with the people they are helping can give them a better-defined sense of purpose than other pharmacists. Collins agrees, saying, "Evaluating a patient's condition, giving the right medication, and watching him or her improve is very satisfying."

Because they work with such powerful drugs, pharmacists rely on their communication skills, especially the ability to listen well. "When a doctor or nurse asks for your advice or a patient describes his or her symptoms to you, it is vital to listen closely and make sure you hear everything the person is saying—and sometimes even what he or she is not saying," Collins stresses. "Missing one vital piece of information can sometimes literally mean the difference between life and death for a patient." Pharmacists also need to be clear, patient communicators, for they are often called on to answer questions about a drug's effects or to calm someone's fears about possible side effects or interactions.

Despite the sometimes heavy responsibility that is part of the job, Collins really enjoys his work. "It's not for everyone," he admits. Potential pharmacists should have an interest in science and health, and they should enjoy interacting with people and serving the community. They should also be dedicated, enthusiastic, honest, and patient. For a person with these qualities, working as a pharmacist can be an interesting and fulfilling career. As Collins puts it, "Every day I come in to work, I help people to feel better. What could be more rewarding than that?"

The World of Work

119

Computer *Search*

Using one of the search features on the Internet, look for listening-training sites. Study the information you find at one or more of them and share what you learn with your classmates. You might start with the following site: *http://www.smartbiz.com/sbs/arts/hph15.htm*

Backstage and Frontstage Behavior

In Chapter 2 you learned that reading the workplace means acting like an anthropologist. You need to listen like a researcher. Many years ago the sociologist Erving Goffman described how to look at the roles people play in everyday life. He argued that human beings are performers who learn to manage the impressions they present to others. They do this by engaging in everyday performances. He developed the concepts of frontstage and backstage. Frontstage is the place where the performance is given. The performers are "on" and very aware of their behavior and of the image or impression they are communicating to others. Backstage is the place where performers act as themselves. They contradict their performance. They stop performing and act without monitoring every move.

Picture a nice restaurant with linen-covered tables in front for the customers and a long, cafeteria-style table for the staff in the kitchen behind swinging doors. Which of the following statements illustrate frontstage behavior? Which illustrate backstage behavior?

Servers in a fancy restaurant display frontstage behavior to their customers.

A. "Hello, my name is Rudolfo, and I will be your server tonight. How is everyone?" (smile, moderate vocal tone)

B. "Hey, Jake, quit hoggin' the ketchup and send it over here." (loud vocal tone, annoyed look)

C. "I'm sorry. We are out of salmon tonight but the whitefish is very nice." (sad facial expression, moderate vocal tone)

D. "*^%*, I had three tables mad at me because Lee screwed up ordering enough salmon steaks this week." (loud, angry tone, angry look)

As you guessed, A and C show frontstage behavior—behavior used when performing the role of a server in a nice restaurant. B and D show backstage behavior—behavior used when servers are not performing for customers but are interacting spontaneously among themselves.

Michelle Thim, *Office Clerk*

Michelle Thim studies finance at Northeastern Illinois University in Chicago. She also works as an office clerk in the editorial department at NTC/Contemporary Publishing Group. Michelle is assigned projects by various people in the editorial department, from assistant editors to the editorial director. Many of the tasks are administrative, such as copying, filing, and finding books in the company's warehouse, but she also has had the opportunity to do some editing.

Even though publishing was not a field she had thought about working in, Michelle saw an ad for the position posted on the bulletin board at her school, and she decided to apply. "The position sounded interesting," Michelle said. "I thought it would teach me some valuable job skills and give me the opportunity to work with different kinds of people." Michelle had spent a few years working for her

brother, who is an insurance agent. She liked this work and the fact that she could help her brother, but she was ready for a change.

Now Michelle has to communicate daily with a wide range of people and juggle the tasks they give her. She says that the job has helped her to improve her listening and organizational skills. She often has many projects to do at once, so she needs to be sure that the most important ones get done first but that they are all completed on time. Because she

accepts projects from different people, Michelle has had to adjust to several styles of communication and learn to listen closely to the directions of each person so that she can know how to handle the project.

Michelle says that she enjoys her work. "I don't know if I will look for a job in publishing after I graduate," she says. "I would like to find a job that utilizes my degree, such as broker or accountant. But through this job I've met some wonderful people and learned some useful skills, and those things are invaluable."

Student Worker Profile

121

Think back to the example of Sarah in the health center. Sarah moved backstage behavior into the frontstage, where she could be seen and heard by patients. That's why the other staff members frowned and didn't laugh at her jokes.

In any workplace situation, as you listen with your ears and eyes, you should ask yourself, "Is this frontstage or backstage behavior?"

Check It Out

Ask two people to describe differences in their verbal and nonverbal communication when they are in frontstage and backstage situations at their workplaces—for example, a teacher in front of class and in the teachers' lounge; a plumber on call in a house and riding in the truck with partners. Make a note of similarities and differences.

Barriers to Effective Listening

Barriers to listening often keep you from understanding a speaker's message. Five common barriers are external distractions, internal distractions, your desire to talk, personal biases, and pseudolistening. In Chapter 1 you learned about interference as part of the communication model. Each of the barriers just mentioned creates interference that prevents you from receiving a sender's message accurately.

To overcome external distractions, you have to work hard to concentrate on the message and to ignore competing sounds and signals.

Have you ever found yourself waiting impatiently for someone else to finish talking so that you could talk? Good listeners try to listen until a speaker is finished.

External Distractions

External distractions are factors outside the listener that interfere with listening. They include things like sirens outside the window, the chatter of your co-workers, or a ringing telephone, which distract your attention. To overcome the external interference, you have to work hard to concentrate on the message and to ignore the competing sounds and signals.

Internal Distractions

Internal distractions are factors inside the listener that interfere with listening. They include factors such as worries, fears, or exciting plans. If your mother is going into the hospital for surgery or you've just had a fight with your best friend, your concentration may be poor. Even good things, such as an upcoming trip or a special concert, distract your attention away from a speaker. If you don't know much about the subject of your conversation, you may find it even harder to stay focused.

Your Desire to Talk

Many people would rather talk than listen, especially if they have to listen thoughtfully to difficult ideas or feelings. You probably know someone who frequently appears to be listening but is really waiting to talk. Also, you can probably remember arguments in which you found yourself impatiently waiting for the other person to finish so that you could talk. In these situations, very little listening is going on. When people with this attitude finally get to talk, they usually just repeat their own position because they did not bother to listen to the other person's ideas. Good listeners try to listen until a speaker is finished and evaluate what the speaker has said. *Then* they respond.

Personal Biases

Personal biases tend to make a person closed-minded toward certain subjects or toward certain people. No one can be completely objective, but some people will hear only what they want to hear on certain subjects. Thus, your own perceptions may prevent you from listening seriously to certain arguments, paying attention to particular speakers, or engaging in a conversation with a new person.

Sometimes, because of a personal bias, you will "write someone off" and decide he or she has nothing worthwhile to say. This may keep you from hearing any of that person's ideas. In other situations, sensitive topics such as gender issues or religious beliefs may make you uncomfortable and you "tune out." If you always avoid discussing certain topics, you will miss the chance to become more fully informed.

Pseudolistening

Sometimes people try to cover their poor listening habits by pseudolistening. **Pseudolistening** occurs when you pretend to be listening and convey this nonverbally. A pseudolistener looks at the speaker and nods or smiles on occasion while really daydreaming or thinking about something else. Pretending to listen sometimes fools bosses and co-workers, but it can be damaging when the other person discovers that the listener has not been paying attention.

Strategies for Effective Listening

Many people think listening is a natural talent—either you have it or you don't. They watch others and think, "What a great response. I never would have thought of that." Yet listening is *not* genetically determined. You can develop a set of skills to become a more effective listener.

Use Thought Speed

Listeners have one major advantage over speakers that allows them to be active thinkers while listening. It is called thought speed. Thought speed is the amount of words a listener has the potential to understand in a set period of time. Most people speak at a rate of 120 to 150 words a minute. Yet listeners can process speech at a rate of up to 350-400 words a minute. That's a big difference! Thought speed provides the extra time listeners gain because they can process words faster than speakers can produce them. This time can be used to review the speaker's ideas, phrase a question, or form an argument.

Pay Attention to Nonverbal Cues

Use your eyes very carefully. On the basis of facial expression, how does the speaker appear—passive, determined, silly? What do his or her gestures and body movements tell you? Also note the tone of voice. Try to read the nonverbal cues.

Use Silence

You've heard the phrase "Silence is golden," but you may never have thought about what this phrase really means. When you keep your mouth shut, you often hear things you never would have heard if you kept chattering. Silence makes some individuals anxious, and they will talk to fill in the gap. Frequently, if you remain silent, the other person will fill up the gap with useful information he or she otherwise might not have thought to mention.

Use a Paraphrase Response

When speakers talk about personal problems, you may wish to paraphrase their comments. When you paraphrase what someone says, you feed back to that person in your own words what you heard. For example, "When the boss

BABY BLUES

Career Communication *Banker*

Whether helping people with their daily transactions or reviewing loan applications, banking employees make use of many communication skills in the course of their work. A bank teller must have good listening skills to understand what services a client needs. Good interpersonal skills are also important, as they are the "face" of the bank. A good or bad experience with a teller may determine whether a client continues to do business with that bank.

Bank officers meet with clients who need to perform more complicated transactions than depositing or withdrawing money—such as opening a new account or requesting a loan. The officers must be able to communicate the bank's services in a way the client can understand. They also need to listen closely to clients to make sure that the bank is offering a product that suits their needs.

You may think of banking as a good field for someone who likes figures and understands mathematical concepts such as interest rates, exchange rates, and economics. This is certainly true. A person who does not have an interest in these things will not enjoy banking. It is equally true that a person who lacks the ability to communicate well will have difficulty succeeding in the field.

treats you like that, you feel invisible" or "You're feeling pushed against a wall when Josh keeps repeating his questions, right?" These responses are a way of telling the speaker, "What I am hearing is . . ." or "You're saying that . . . ." Effective listeners paraphrase to make sure miscommunication does not occur and to help the speaker refine or clarify what he or she is saying.

Be Mindful

When listening to someone who has a problem, try to create a sense of focused attention. Empty your mind of distractions, concerns, and plans so that you can truly be attentive. This will allow you to be an empathic listener.

Chapter 5 *Summary*

In this chapter, you learned about the importance of effective listening. Listening is an active process that includes receiving, interpreting, evaluating, and responding. Effective listening occurs when the message sent by the speaker is the same message decoded by the listener.

Effective listening is important in the workplace because it creates a climate of support, encourages an honest expression of ideas and concerns, and fosters creativity.

There are four main types of listening: informational, critical, creative, and empathic.

There are five common barriers to effective communication: external distractions, internal distractions, your desire to talk, personal biases, and pseudolistening.

The following strategies can be used to become a more effective listener: using thought speed, paying attention to nonverbal cues, using silence, using a paraphrase response, and being mindful.

Review Questions

1. What is the difference between hearing and listening?
2. What will an effective listener do to interpret a message properly?
3. What three reactions are you likely to have when evaluating a message?
4. Why is effective listening important in your social life? in your business life?
5. Identify and describe the four steps of note taking.
6. What is critical listening?
7. Why is synergistic listening important in the workplace?
8. Describe a social situation in which you need an empathic listener.
9. What are some barriers to effective listening?
10. Why is paraphrasing important as a response to a speaker?

Critical Thinking Activities

Speaking/Doing

1 Prepare a one- to two-minute oral presentation on one of the following topics:
   - the importance of listening critically to advertisements
   - the importance of listening empathically in personal relationships
   - how biases and stereotyping interfere with listening

2. Make a poster of the five types of listening. Each type should be illustrated (drawings or magazine pictures), defined, and include examples. Present your poster to the class in a two- to three-minute presentation.

Writing

1. Write a two- to three-page paper on the importance of listening. Papers can focus on one of the following subtopics: listening in relationships, listening on the job, listening to foster creativity, or listening to help release feelings. Use examples from your personal world and/or from the business world to support your observations.
2. Discuss in two or three paragraphs some of the strategies that good listeners use to better understand messages.

Group Activities

1. Divide into three large groups. Role-play a business meeting within your group. Assign each group member a character with a name and a job title within a company. Have your teacher assign a specific type of listener role to each group member (informational, empathic, critical, and creative). Students should introduce themselves to each other before the meeting. Have each group discuss and solve a typical problem that faces most businesses, such as firing or laying off employees, developing a new service or product, or addressing budget issues. After a 15- to 30-minute meeting, students should return to their own "office." Each student should write a report answering these questions: Can you identify by name and job title all the corporate members? What frustrations did you face with the various types of listeners? Could you determine what type of listener each person was playing?

2. Divide into groups of five to seven students. Discuss the issue of morning announcements. Why do some students ignore them? What can be done to improve students' attention to the announcements? Prepare a report from your group that includes your recommendations. Consider offering those ideas to the sponsor in charge of announcements.

Practical Application: Case Challenge

Don Fisher runs the Community Recreation Center. He hires many local high school students to work part-time.

Miguel and Nikki coordinate the after-school program at the center, but they have gotten very frustrated with Don. Last month they proposed to operate Saturday morning basketball clinics, and Don agreed it was a good idea. Flyers were sent to the schools. When Nikki showed up on the first Saturday, Don asked what she was doing there. Nikki explained that the clinic was starting, and Don said, "What clinic?"

Nikki reminded him of the proposal and his agreement, to which Don responded, "Is that in writing?"

"No," Nikki said. "You never asked for it in writing. You just said 'Good idea. Do it.'"

"Well," Don replied, "it can't start today. I promised the gym to St. Patrick's."

When Nikki told Miguel that she had to cancel the clinic, he said, "It's hard to get through to Don. Last week he told Amy and me that we could take Wednesday afternoon off, and then he had a fit when we were both gone. The week before I had to remind him three times to unlock the ice rink early. He still arrived a half hour late and swore it was the time I told him to appear."

What strategies might Miguel and Nikki use to prevent some of these predictable problems? How might they help Don to listen more effectively?

129

Work It Out!

Help!
What Do I Do Now?

1. You work in an office. You are at a coffee hour to welcome three new employees: a young male clerk, a young female office manager, and an older female vice president. Your boss is called away suddenly. He asks you to introduce the new employees to the staff, including peers and supervisors. What will you do? (Form groups of six. Take turns doing the introductions. Three group members can be the new employees. The other members can be peers and supervisors. Allow time for each student to practice various combinations of introductions.)

2. You own a small gourmet food shop. You've just accepted an order for 100 box lunches for a business conference tomorrow. You've never had an order this big. You don't have the supplies (food and packaging) to fill it, but it is a golden opportunity to publicize your business. What will you do? (In groups of three, devise a plan of attack. What supplies will you need? Will you need additional temporary workers? Whom will you call for help? What questions will you ask? Role-play phone conversations with potential workers and suppliers. Take turns assuming the various roles.)

3. Your company makes quality furniture. You receive a call from an angry customer. The water bed he bought has sprung a leak, flooding the bedroom with water. He insists he didn't do anything to cause the leak. Your water beds never spring leaks. What will you say to the customer? (Work in pairs. Improvise a phone conversation. Take turns playing each role. As the employee, you have two goals: (1) protect the image of your company and (2) satisfy the customer.)

Attention! Attention!

You are sitting at a conference table at work. You are listening to the president of your division outline this year's work goals for your unit. Describe your posture, your eye contact, and your facial expression, and explain to your classmates why you made these choices.

Am I Overdressed?

Work in groups of three. Describe appropriate dress for the following jobs: electrician, professor, farm worker, stock person, office worker, attorney, coach, food vendor, carpenter, salesclerk, real estate agent, musician. There are no absolute "right" choices, but some choices may be more "right" than others. Might there be situations in which different clothes would be appropriate in different situations for the same job? Present your group's conclusions to the rest of the class.

Oh, No! Why Me?

You have bad news and good news for a co-worker. The bad news is that your co-worker's job has been eliminated. The good news is that you will help him or her find another job. This person is a close male peer, a close female peer, or someone you hardly know. (Choose one.) How will you conduct yourself? (Consider these factors: How close will you stand? What will your facial expression be? Will you smile? Will you look concerned? comforting? stern? Will you shake hands? Will you hug this person? put your arm around his or her shoulders? What tone of voice will you use?)

Shall I Paint It Blue?

You are an office worker, or a business executive, ranch hand, personal banker, storeowner, athletic trainer, or party consultant. (Choose one.) You have just moved into a new workspace. How will you decorate it? (Consider these factors: What will you add to help you do your job? to make the space comfortable? What restrictions will you consider? Share your choices with your classmates.)

Hold That Thought!

In a group of six, review the guidelines for note taking on page 115. Discuss how you would adapt them to suit each of the situations described. Pair up with a partner and role-play one of the situations for the group. Allow time for your partner to prepare a script. As listener, decide what kind of notes you will take. Discuss each role-play.

- You are field operations manager for a large farm. The owner is explaining how to monitor crop reports on a laptop computer.
- You have been contracted to remodel a kitchen. The customer is explaining what improvements he wants done.
- You are on a team responsible for designing software to track company inventory. The leader is explaining what the project will involve.

Am I Listening Effectively?

The four basic listening skills needed in the workplace are informational, critical, creative, and empathic skills. Which ones would be especially helpful to you in each of the following situations? Explain your choices.

- Your workplace team is responsible for planning the company picnic.

- Your office mate is having surgery, and you are taking on his work.
- Your boss is giving you your annual performance appraisal.
- A customer wants suggestions for Christmas gifts for her family.
- A co-worker with a substance-abuse problem has asked you for help.
- You and a co-worker are designing a new menu for your restaurant.
- You are at a business convention featuring speakers and workshops.

Think Before Responding

A client is unhappy with how you have handled her account. This is a complete surprise. You thought everything was fine. You have no idea why she is unhappy. While she is explaining the problem, what can/should you do? (Discuss this situation with a small group of three to four classmates. Review the strategies for effective listening on pages 124–126. Debate which of these strategies would be most helpful in this situation.)

Interpersonal and Group Communication

Unit Three

Interpersonal Communication

Objectives

After completing this chapter, you will be able to

- define interpersonal communication, functional messages, and nurturing messages, and understand their importance in the workplace
- describe the stages of relationship development
- demonstrate interpersonal skills of recognition, sharing personal information, active listening, and constructive criticism
- describe message directions and their role in the workplace
- describe the roles of humor, rumor, and gossip in the workplace
- read the interpersonal expectations in an organizational culture

Key Terms

constructive criticism

downward communication

functional messages

horizontal communication

mentor

nurturing messages

relational skills

upward communication

"Positive climates . . . result from communication patterns in which people are honest, tactful, supportive, open-minded, and oriented toward problem solving."
—CONSTANCE AND ROBERT S. STALEY II,
Communicating in Business and the Professions

Relating to Workplace Co-Workers

After graduation from the Hotel Management Program at her community college, Janelle joined the staff at the local Holiday Park Inn, a fancy 200-room hotel. She shares many of her regular front-desk shifts with Wei-Lin and Andy. After five months Janelle is questioning whether to find a position at another hotel.

The guests expect staff to be experts on all rates and specials. Last week Janelle watched as a couple arrived to check in and Wei-Lin quoted them a $90 rate. The woman said, "We were quoted a $75 rate on the phone when we made reservations."

Wei-Lin said, "They told you the wrong thing. All we have is the $90 rate this weekend."

The couple then asked about lower rates with their frequent visitor membership and an entertainment package card. Wei-Lin maintained that $90 was the only rate. They expressed frustration but paid the $90 rate. Janelle sat watching this, knowing Wei-Lin was wrong, but didn't say anything.

As the couple walked through the lobby, the man picked up a flyer advertising summer weekend special rates at $69. He walked back to the front desk. Wei-Lin was talking to another guest, so he talked with Janelle. Janelle gave him the $69 rate. The man complained loudly about how badly this whole situation was handled and said he would complain to the manager. Janelle apologized for the confusion. After the man left, Wei-Lin yelled at Janelle for making her look like a fool. Janelle wishes she did not have to work with Wei-Lin.

Janelle enjoys working with Andy, although she believes he is lazy. He arrives late and is the first one out the door at the shift's end, leaving Wei-Lin or Janelle to stay for the turnover. He disappears for long breaks to watch sports on the lounge TV. Yet he kids around and knows all the gossip—such as who is up for a promotion, who is in trouble, or which regular guests are good tippers. He treats guests well, remembering their names, greeting them as they enter each time, and going out of his way to manage any special requests. Although Janelle likes Andy, she feels taken advantage of when he leaves early. She has a two-year-old son, Dwayne, and needs to leave on time to get to the babysitter.

Each employee has a different personal style. If guests come to the desk to ask how to get to the local zoo, Wei-Lin says, "Take the #62 bus on the corner." Janelle explains where to get the #62 bus, and how often it runs. Andy goes further than Janelle, reminding them, "Don't miss the new reptile house" or "There's a great aquarium in town. It's a 15-minute walk from the zoo."

The three staffers talk to each other differently. Wei-Lin frequently orders Janelle around—for example, "Don't forget to change the schedule board," and "Didn't you do the day's receipts yet?" Andy is less bossy and more likely to ask Janelle about her son Dwayne or about her weekend plans. Although Janelle is a good listener, she seldom asks questions of the others.

Janelle's boss gave her a good three-month review and asked how Janelle liked the position. Janelle said it was fine, although it really isn't. Because she has a two-year-old son to support, she can't afford to quit this job unless she can find another one. She is wondering whether to look around for another position.

How would you characterize each shift member's style of communication? What strengths or weakness does each employee exhibit? What should Janelle do to make this situation a better working environment for her?

Interpersonal Communication

Interpersonal communication occurs when two people engage in ongoing interactions, exchanging nurturing as well as functional messages. These interactions may be voluntary or involuntary. Many workplace relationships are involuntary, meaning you would not choose to engage in regular interactions with some of the people you come into contact with at work. Yet you are expected to work well with everyone in the workplace.

In the workplace you frequently engage in functional interactions. When you call a customer to say her watch has been repaired or give directions to a doctor's office, you are involved in a practical or functional exchange. **Functional messages** deal with managing day-to-day necessities and sharing information such as travel plans, work schedules, and questions about policies. Everyday workplace communication involves many functional messages.

Most interpersonal relationships are also characterized by the exchange of nurturing, or "I care," messages. **Nurturing messages** indicate supportiveness and that the relationship is valued. Comments such as "I'm glad we're friends," "Want to hang out after work?" or "Are you feeling OK today?" are typical nurturing messages, indicating the relationship is valued. Empathic listening or nonverbal signals such as a smile or wave communicate caring.

Interpersonal relationships vary on a continuum from superficial, involving many functional messages, to very personal, involving many more nurturing messages. Most workplace messages fall between 1 and 3 along a continuum from 1 to 5 between totally functional and totally nurturing.

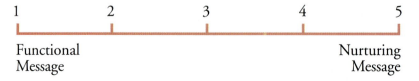

| 1 | 2 | 3 | 4 | 5 |

Functional Message   Nurturing Message

Everyday workplace communication involves many functional messages. Staffers in this *USA Today* newsroom discuss breaking stories, plan features, and monitor the day's deadlines.

Why is it important to think about everyday interpersonal relationships in the workplace? After all, you know how to relate to your friends. Eventually you may spend more waking hours in your workplace than at home or with your friends. You will want that time to be productive, pleasant, and reasonably free of conflict. Interpersonal workplace skills will also be important to you if your job involves traveling around the state or country. Finally, you may discover that your workplace provides you with potential new friends. Your interpersonal skills will help you develop those friendships.

Think about school as a workplace. Every day you exchange functional and nurturing messages with teachers, security guards, cafeteria staff, and other students. "Close the door," "Where's your pass?" and "I'd like the fries and gravy" are examples of functional messages. "Congratulations on the photo award," "Lucky day, I've seen you three times so far," and "I saved you a frozen yogurt" are examples of nurturing messages.

In the workplace you will need to use nurturing as well as functional messages. Your employer will rely on you to treat customers and clients well. Also, your employer will expect employees to treat one another well. A positive workplace climate leads to better productivity and lower employee turnover.

In the workplace, you will need to use nurturing as well as functional messages. Your boss will rely on you to treat customers and clients well.

Stages of Relationships

Research on relationship development reveals a four-stage process. As you read about these four stages, you will see how a workplace relationship is more likely to exist at the first or second level. Close friendships, or highly interpersonal relationships, exist when a relationship is at the third or fourth stage.

Interpersonal Communication

This chapter will focus more on the first two stages. The four stages are as follows: first meetings, friendly relations, involved relationships, and stable relationships. These stages should be thought of as part of a continuum.

First Meeting   Friendly   Involved   Stable

First Meetings

All relationships start at the same place—the first meeting. If you were to make a list of the social rules that guide the opening conversation between two people, you would include the following:

- Try to find some common ground for a conversation. Ask questions of the other person.
- Don't ask or answer questions about very personal topics.
- Try to present a good image (put your best foot forward). If a topic comes up that you disagree strongly about, drop it and talk about something you can discuss more easily.
- Don't tell a person you meet that you don't like him or her. Move on and meet other people.
- Talk about general things.

The term first meetings refers to the initial two or three times you meet someone. During first meetings, you usually discuss noncontroversial topics. You may spend time talking about the weather, the occasion, a current event, sports, or films. You may check to find out if you know some of the same people. You may share general information about yourself, such as where you are from and what your likes, dislikes, hobbies, and interests are. Most of your conversation stays on a superficial level. These topics are within the range of public information because they are not very personal and you are comfortable talking about them with almost anyone. No real sharing of personal information occurs.

This first stage illustrates the OAR process: Observe, Ask, and Reveal—but not too much! If you only observe, you will never develop a relationship. If you observe and ask questions, you may come across as nosy or distant. If you observe, ask questions, and reveal some information about yourself, you stand the best chance of making a connection with another person.

In this stage, your verbal and nonverbal messages will follow cultural and social rules. For example, you won't have "in" jokes to share, and you won't hug the other person. The unique you remains to be discovered in later meetings.

Ruthie Alan, *Retail Store Owner and Manager*

ing questions and listening carefully to learn their hopes or interests. She tries to learn as much as she can when she first meets a new customer, but she says, "It's never done in a first session. It requires lots of face-to-face interaction" because "some people don't know how to talk about what they like." She believes it is "fun to help people discover what represents them and not the people next door." She says 85 percent of her job in the initial meeting is listening, "even to stuff that

"I love making something beautiful out of nothing," declares Ruthie Alan, co-owner and manager of Jean Alan Interior Design Atelier. In 1994 the mother and daughter team of Jean Alan and Ruthie Alan went into business together. Their design atelier, a French term that means "a design studio workroom," is a place where, according to Ms. Alan, "People can come in and design something that they have imagined in our workroom." This is a place where old things are re-created in elegant form. Those who enter find a showroom out front where lovely finished furnishings such as lamps, custom-made pillows, and newly upholstered vintage furniture are on display. But it's in the

back where the heart of this business beats.

Behind a partition wall, clients find a large room that is the equivalent of an artist's studio. The centerpiece is a very large cutting table that displays all the fabric and trimmings that are under consideration. The walls hold shelves with bolts of fabric and crates of trims for pillows or furniture. Surrounding the table is the inventory of "before" items, such as old couch frames or table bases. It is here that a client "rediscovers the magic of older furniture."

Part of Ruthie Alan's challenge is to meet the needs of her knowledgeable customers as well as to educate the less knowledgeable customer. She helps unsure customers by ask-

doesn't have to do with decorating—because it actually does." Once she has a good sense of who a customer is, she can be much more helpful to that person.

As the business half of the team, Ms. Alan is also concerned with financial matters and is active in building a customer base. Owning one's own business is hard work, and it's on an owner's mind even when away from the store. Yet, according to Ms. Alan, the opportunity to turn "disgusting looking stuff into something beautiful" makes it all worthwhile.

By permission of Tony Cochran and Creators Syndicate.

After the first meeting, you may not wish to see the other person again. If you are working together, however, you will have to continue to deal with each other.

First meetings are important because people form first impressions based on meeting another person. First impressions can be changed but, in some cases, they are very strong and hard to overcome. Remember the saying, "You never get a second chance to make a first impression." Do your best to make your first impression a positive one.

First impressions in the workplace are hard to change. If you appear sloppy, lazy, or rude in the first days of a new job, your success and income could be negatively affected for a long time. That image, even if it is unfair, means that you have to work that much harder to be considered a competent employee.

Friendly Relations

The friendly relations stage involves ongoing interactions between people who are co-workers, casual acquaintances, or members of the same group. Most ongoing relationships remain at this stage. You enjoy seeing the other person, but there is no strong commitment to the relationship. At this stage you are more willing to talk about opinions and feelings—for example, "They can't just decide to throw Eddie out because he overslept twice" or "I feel really good when I see my younger brother becoming a success"—but not ones that are highly personal. You are probably open to discussing some personal subjects and may begin sharing some superficial evaluations of each other's behavior.

Your life is filled with relationships at the friendly-relations stage. These relationships are pleasant but not very deep. They involve a greater range of verbal and nonverbal messages than the first meetings stage. For example, you may feel comfortable using some jokes, teasing the other person, or touching

The friendly-relations stage involves ongoing interaction between co-workers or casual acquaintances. Most workplace relationships remain at this second stage.

that person to get your ideas across. At work, you may feel comfortable explaining that you really need time off because your boyfriend is in town or asking a co-worker if the boss makes him as nervous as the boss makes you. Friendly relations also involve more nurturing messages than first meetings do, but not many personal ones.

In the workplace you usually relate to supervisors, co-workers, and customers at this level, if you see them frequently. If you really like someone and want to get to know him or her better, you may begin to hold conversations that will move your relationship to the next stage.

Involved Relationships

The involved relationship stage refers to interactions between close friends or romantic partners. By the time you reach this third stage, you share much more personal information and feelings. You and your friend are able to criticize each other and disagree without one of you ending the relationship. You are able to read each other's verbal and nonverbal cues well. You will also share verbal and nonverbal cues that are unique to your relationship. These cues may be eye signals, verbal expressions, code words, and in-jokes that have a special meaning for the two of you.

Feelings are easily shared at this third stage. People around you may be able to tell that you are good friends because there is an open display of affection ranging from teasing to touching. You are committed to this relationship, and

Interpersonal Communication

you are willing to take some risks to maintain the relationship. Relationships at this stage are characterized by nurturing messages.

Although a co-worker or boss can be a good friend, it's not very common. It can be difficult to manage, especially when one supervises the other. It's hard because you may have to tell a friend what to do or give negative feedback on his or her work behaviors. Also a close friend may take advantage of you or expect greater freedom in the workplace.

Co-workers sometimes resent the tight twosome of friends who do everything together. This situation becomes even more of a problem when two employees are romantically involved. Some companies discourage employees from dating one another or working directly with a boyfriend or girlfriend because doing so can make co-workers feel uncomfortable. Also, it can be very difficult to continue to work together if a romance ends or if personal arguments between a couple spill into the workplace.

Stable Relationships

By the time a relationship has reached the stable stage, each person knows the other extremely well. The stable relationship stage refers to long-term connections between very close friends or committed romantic partners. In this stage, you share deep feelings and very private information. It's unlikely that most workplace relationships fit in this category, but some examples exist, such as close school friends working together in extracurricular activities or community service and longtime friends who apply for jobs at the same company. On occasion, adult best friends start businesses together, even though it may be a challenge to develop a successful business and maintain their relationship at the stable level.

Changes in Relationships

Remember!

Interpersonal relationships progress through four stages:

▶ First meetings

▶ Friendly relations

▶ Involved relationships

▶ Stable relationships

Just as you and another person can move forward through the relationship stages, you can also move backward through some or all of the stages. You can probably name some people who were your good friends two years ago but whom you don't know very well anymore. People may move away, change jobs, or find new interests or new friends. A relationship may be neglected for a variety of reasons. When this happens, your verbal and nonverbal messages reflect the change; they are less personal and sometimes less accurate. At some point in the future, you may move forward through the stages again and rediscover a deep friendship, or you may continue to drift apart. Communication moves the relationship through these stages, forward and backward.

Proximity influences your workplace relationships. Relationships tend to change when people no longer share the same shifts or work close to one another.

One of the key factors influencing change in workplace relationships is proximity—physical closeness or distance. In the workplace, this means sharing space and time. Workplace relationships tend to change when people no longer share the same shifts or time schedules or when they no longer work close to one another or see each other regularly.

Check It Out

Interview someone who used to work with a close friend. Ask him or her about the pros and cons of being in that situation and what happened when that close friend left the job or moved to a different shift or place.

Relational Skills

Communication serves to maintain ongoing workplace relationships and keep people connected. In addition to the basic verbal, nonverbal, and listening skills discussed in the previous chapters, there are some additional communication skills that aid building a positive workplace climate. These are called relational skills and include recognition, sharing personal information, active listening, and constructive criticism. **Relational skills** are interpersonal communication skills used to build or maintain a good relationship. They send confirming messages. Relational skills apply to workplace and non-workplace situations.

Interpersonal Communication

Recognition

Recognition includes everyday talk that confirms the existence of the other person. It is speech used for social purposes or to indicate a connection with the other person.

Greetings

Although it may seem self-evident, recognition begins with greetings. In some offices employees come in, say hello to everyone, and then get to work. In other offices employees arrive and start to work without even saying "Hi." Most co-workers appreciate being recognized unless they are on the phone or in the middle of a conversation. Greetings don't have to be verbal—a smile or a wave can serve the same purpose. Greetings are confirming behaviors. It's a very basic communication act—but a very important one. The following intern's journal entry appeared in a *New York Times* article by Richard Petrow. What effect do you think the behavior described in the entry had on the intern?

> "I have just completed my first week of work at the *New York Times*. I enter in the mornings without anyone saying hello and exit in the evenings without anyone waving good-bye. At least three people in the office pass my desk without so much as a nod or grunt in my direction. By the way, I did mention to others that the Times Square neighborhood was lively. They looked at me as if I were a two-headed dog."

Leave-taking behavior is also important. Saying "good-bye," "good night," or "see you" acknowledges the existence of your co-workers in the same way that greetings do.

Small Talk

Ongoing comments serve to keep people connected. Remarks such as "How's it going?" and "Hey, Selena, how are the college applications coming?" indicate you notice another person is there. Polite questions about plans for the weekend do the same. Discussions about sports, shopping, and kids are other ways to initiate polite and friendly conversations. This type of interaction is sometimes called water-cooler or coffee-machine conversation, so named because it often occurs when people gather at those locations. Today, this kind of conversation also occurs electronically through e-mail, connecting co-workers from building to building, state to state, and country to country.

You may discover that the best way to participate in workplace small talk is to pay attention to certain sports teams, see recent films and shows, or watch

Kara Wilkinson, *Photographer*

A recent graduate of Evanston Township High School in Evanston, Illinois, Kara Wilkinson is a college art photography major who has plans to study art in Florence before graduation. Junior-Year-Abroad programs are expensive, so she has put time and energy into helping fund this dream.

As her semester ended last spring, Kara and a friend began earning funds by developing hundreds of wedding pictures for a couple that needed sets of photos for all branches of a large family. It took six days of teamwork to finish all these high-quality prints. Kara and her friend had to agree on the quality of the shots, coordinate their times in the darkroom, and negotiate a fee with the client.

Kara makes some of her spending money taking pictures for special events. She has photographed weddings, taken publicity pictures for local rock bands, and provided parents with special photos of their small children. Good interpersonal skills are important when one is photographing individuals or small groups. When she plans a photography session with people she has not met before, Kara arrives early to try to gain a sense of who the subjects are, to observe them, and to interact with them before trying to envision the shots she hopes to get. She engages the subjects in conversation to learn about them, their interests, and their style. The more comfort-

able they feel with Kara, the more likely they will be to relax and be themselves in front of the camera. According to Kara, one of her skills is "my ability to put my subject at ease." The more a photographer learns about people, the better his or her photos will be. Last summer she worked as a photographer's assistant, a job that involved entertaining children as their pictures were being taken. Working with children is much different from working with adults, and a good photographer has to be comfortable interacting with all types of people.

As a photographer, Kara is always searching for places to display her work. Such exhibits serve two purposes— increasing her client list and building her résumé. The more people who see her photographs, the more likely it is that some will like what they see and hire her to take pictures at their special events. She has had her work displayed at her local newspaper office, the Evanston Roundtable, and at a coffeehouse near her college. Many framed pieces can be found on the walls of her friends' rooms. Kara's dream is to follow in the footsteps of

internationally renowned photographer Annie Leibowitz, whose portraits of both famous and ordinary people appear in major magazines, galleries, and museums.

As any young artist knows, finding a full-time position early in one's career is not easy. Even at this point Kara earns much of her income from working in a food service position. But Kara is optimistic. The reactions to her work so far have been good, and she hopes that the contacts she has made and will continue to make will eventually lead her to the job of her dreams.

Student Worker Profile

the stock market. In some workplaces, every Monday morning starts with comments like "How 'bout them Lakers?" or "Did you see the MTV awards last night?"

Computer Search

Computers have reduced the need for face-to-face workplace interactions. One way that computer users try to make e-mail friendlier or more personal is by using symbols for emotions or feelings. These symbols are called *emoticons*. Three common ones are shown here. Collect a set of other emoticons and share their meanings with the class.

: -) The basic smiley face turned on its side. This tells the receiver the sender has made a joke or is happy.

; -) The winky smiley. This indicates that the sender has made a sarcastic remark.

: - (The frowny smiley. This indicates that the sender did not like the last statement or is upset about something.

Sharing Personal Information

Sharing personal information means voluntarily telling someone relatively private information about yourself. It also means listening to others do the same. You *choose* to share this information; no one forces you to do so. You also take a risk, because this is private and personal—it is not information for everyone.

Many people wear masks regularly. They appear happy, tough, or even-tempered when they really feel sad, scared, or upset. When people slowly drop their masks for others, they get to know each other better. In work situations, you are likely to be selective in sharing personal information. Sometimes you will do it because you are developing a friendship with a co-worker; at other times you will do it in order to explain your behavior or a request. With a friend, this type of information is likely to be met with reciprocal or equal sharing. In workplace relationships, this may not always be the case. For example, if you request a change in your schedule, ask for time off, or explain your negative mood, you do not expect your boss or co-worker to do the same. Some guidelines for sharing personal information are

1. *Don't overtalk.* People who talk about themselves too much and too quickly sometimes have difficulty establishing successful personal and work relationships.
2. *Don't undertalk.* The person who listens to everyone else but never says anything personal can also ruin a possible relationship. If you realize that you know almost nothing about this person, you are likely to ask yourself, "Am I talking too much, or is this person unwilling to talk to me?"

3. *Choose the information you wish to share wisely.* Even friends do not have to share everything. Co-workers certainly do not. You can decide when and with whom you wish to talk about personal things.

4. *Indicate the level of privacy you prefer.* When revealing personal information in the workplace, place limits on the discussion—for example, "I need minor surgery, which will keep me out for a week. It's not serious, but I don't really want to get into it." Most supervisors and co-workers will respect your request and avoid asking further questions. You may have to restate your request for the few who probe.

Check It Out

Ask three employed people how they handle discussing personal information in the workplace. What problems have they seen when co-workers share too much? What effective strategies have they or their co-workers used to share personal information appropriately? Compare your answers with your classmates' answers. What strategies were mentioned most frequently?

Active Listening

As you learned in the last chapter, listening is hard work, especially active listening. In the workplace, it can be very hard work.

Counselors spend much of their workday listening very intently. It's a basic skill for such professionals. It is their job to help another person sort out feelings or figure out how to deal with a problem without telling that person exactly what to do. This type of listening takes patience and sensitivity. Many other careers require good personal listening skills, although those skills are not always listed in the job description. Hairstylists, bartenders, and taxi drivers

Sharing personal information with a friend or co-worker means voluntarily revealing relatively private information about yourself. In the workplace, choose what you share wisely, and place limits on what you share.

have to be good listeners because customers frequently tell them painful stories and personal worries. Some regular customers rely on restaurant servers, nurses, or salesclerks as good sources of personal support. Even airline and hotel employees need empathic listening skills to deal with frustrated customers.

Remember that active listening refers to the ability to really recognize another person's feelings and to reflect back those feelings to the speaker. It is a difficult skill to learn because it requires carefully identifying the feelings being expressed and responding sensitively to the speaker. You may have heard the expression "You have to read between the lines," which means you have to figure out what is implied but not actually stated in a written text. The same idea can be applied to spoken words. It's called "listening between the words," and it means recognizing what is implied but not actually said.

The better you know someone, the easier it is to put his or her remarks into a larger, more meaningful context. For example, imagine you heard a friend say, "I'm certainly not up for this weekend. I just wish my sister's graduation were over." You might interpret this remark in a number of ways: (1) she's jealous of all the attention her sister's getting, (2) she feels guilty because her sister is a better student, or (3) she's dreading the graduation party because she won't know what to do or say. If you know the speaker well, you will be able to interpret the feeling accurately.

Hairstylists, bartenders, taxi drivers, and other workers who deal with the public on a daily basis are experts at using active listening skills.

Career Communication *Hairstylist*

Hairstylists are often thought of as amateur psychologists. In addition to having the technical skills to create a wide range of hairstyles and provide related services such as coloring, permanents, and conditioning, a successful hairstylist must also demonstrate excellent interpersonal skills. Hairstylists are experts at relaxing a customer, finding out exactly what the customer wants, explaining the procedures, keeping the customer comfortable during the appointment, and developing a personal connection. Questions such as "How much layering do you want?" "Do you want it

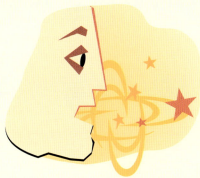

about the same length as last time?" and "Should we try for a slightly different look this time?" are common ways to engage a customer's attention and promote trust.

Hairstylists need to be sensitive listeners. Regular customers look forward to a hair-

cut as an opportunity to talk about their lives. The successful hairstylist remembers each customer and makes a point of asking about the topics that are personally important to the customer, such as school, romance, wedding plans, work, travel, the children, and health. He or she will listen empathically and support a customer's concerns. Hairstylists may also share a little bit about their own lives as they become more involved with a customer.

Constructive Criticism

Friends and co-workers need to give and receive constructive criticism. **Constructive criticism** involves stating what is not working or what is bothering you and making thoughtful suggestions for change. The purpose of constructive criticism is to identify and fix a problem and make a working relationship stronger. It is not used to put down other people. Giving constructive criticism requires self-control. It is easier to blow up or lash out at another person. Yet such behavior often leads to continued angry exchanges. The time and thought it takes to phrase criticism in a constructive way is worth the effort. The following guidelines can help you give constructive criticism:

1. *Talk to others in terms of "I."* Tell others how their behavior affects you. Think how you feel when someone says, "You were rude to me." Do you feel differently if the person says, "I felt ignored when you kept interrupting me"?
2. *Describe the behavior; don't label the person.* Rather than saying someone is lazy, stupid, or dumb, describe the behavior that upsets you. Detailed comments can tell the other person exactly what is upsetting you. Instead of saying, "You're unfair," you might say, "You always refer to our joint projects as 'my work.'"

Interpersonal Communication

3. *Stick to the present.* Don't criticize by dragging in past history. If you are upset about how someone is treating you, don't remind the person of what made you angry last month or last year. Storing things up and then telling someone everything at once is not fair. No one likes to find out that another person has been hanging on to old complaints just waiting for an opportunity to bring them up again.

Developing Relational Skills

The relational skills just discussed do not develop overnight. You need to recognize which ones you need in which situations and then work to build them. The following steps will help you:

1. *Recognize the need for improving a particular skill.* Be honest! Analyze your present communication behavior and decide what could be improved.
2. *Plan the change.* Once you have selected something to work on, decide what outcome you want. In what way will you act differently?
3. *Try it out.* Take the risk and practice the new behavior! Set a goal for how often you will practice it and in what situations you will use it.
4. *Get feedback and modify your behavior.* Find out from others how you are doing. Use this feedback to adjust your behavior.
5. *Make it your own.* Personalize the new behavior. Practice it in daily life until it becomes a common part of your communication patterns.

Workplace Interpersonal Communication Issues

There are particular interpersonal issues that all employees face in the workplace. These include recognizing message direction; managing humor, rumors, and gossip; and reading interpersonal workplace culture.

Recognizing Message Direction

Organizational messages may move in downward, upward, or horizontal directions, depending on how speakers and listeners interact. This downward, upward, or horizontal movement reflects the structure of the workplace.

Downward Communication

Downward communication occurs when superiors send messages to subordinates. These messages may be orders, policies, instructions, reprimands, or praise. They reflect a difference in power because a boss is talking to someone in the ranks below. The boss has more power over discussion, decisions, and what occurs in the workplace.

Upward Communication

Upward communication refers to messages moving from subordinates to superiors. You may initiate a conversation with a boss to make a request higher up ("I need a week of vacation time") or to offer a suggestion ("Why don't we cross-train everyone on the new computers?") or to indicate progress ("I've located 10 extra golf carts for the tournament"). It can be a risky type of communication if you are relaying a problem. Personal responsibility issues such as "We are a week behind schedule" or "I broke the deep fryer again" need to be addressed directly. Some bosses get angry at the messenger who delivers the bad news.

In the workplace, a mentor is a person who serves as a teacher or a role model to a younger or new co-worker.

Horizontal Communication

Horizontal communication occurs between peers. You may trade schedules, ask for assistance with a crowd, or compliment someone on solving a problem. This is the most frequent type of interaction in most large organizations. It is the easiest to manage because there is no power difference.

A tricky part of managing message direction is knowing when you are in a superior/subordinate situation and when you are not. For example, at a Saturday company picnic your boss might kid around and tease you in the same way a personal friend would, but on Monday morning he might reprimand you for some task you forgot to do. You may manage six employees, and although they are your classmates from school, at the recreation center they must take orders from you. Many teenagers work for bosses who are about the same age. This situation can be difficult for both parties. Frequently, it is difficult to evaluate or correct a peer. Also it can be uncomfortable to accept the authority of a peer.

An older individual in an organization may become your informal or formal mentor. A **mentor** is a person who serves as a role model or career counselor to a younger member of an organization. Mentors help younger employees learn to be successful in an organization. They discuss concerns the younger employee might have and make suggestions about handling sensitive

Peanuts reprinted by permission of United Feature Syndicate.

issues. Mentors teach junior employees to understand the organizational culture and to act appropriately within it. You may interact with your mentor on a horizontal level when you are alone but probably in a more formal manner or upward direction when in a business group.

Managing Humor, Rumors, and Gossip

Humor

Appropriate humor plays an important role in the workplace. Kidding around or joking serves to create a sense of ease and belonging. A day goes faster if you can add some humor to it. Laughter helps break up boredom and repetition. Over a period of time, funny stories can help create a sense of being an insider. Most co-workers, clients, and customers relate well to someone who can tell a good joke or share a funny personal story.

In some jobs, humor is part of a rite of passage or a sign of successful movement through an organization. For example, in the navy, fliers put on blue noses when someone flies over the North Pole for the first time, and someone dresses like King Neptune when a group of sailors cross the equator for the first time. Participation in humorous rituals like these gives everyone a sense of belonging.

The key issue with humor is "Is it appropriate?" If the humor is at another person's expense or makes fun of a group, then it is not appropriate. Sometimes a thoughtless or cruel joke has a terrible impact on the person who has been made fun of or sets up a negative image that is hard to change. Jokes or behavior that put people down because of their gender or culture represent a particularly serious form of inappropriate humor.

Rumors and Gossip

Current stories that have not been verified as true are called rumors. In the workplace they tend to be about changes in an organization that might affect employees—for example, "The new boss is coming in from the outside," "Veronica is selling the coffee shop and the new owners may not keep all the staff," or "The athletic director is going to drop girls' volleyball."

Gossip consists of rumors of a very personal nature—for example, "Anna and Gene got in a fight; that's why Gene quit" and "Quan says Beth and Luke are seeing each other." Most gossip and rumors are shared in the backspace with fellow employees but not with outsiders such as customers, clients, or strangers.

Rumors and gossip can create a sense of social connection and acceptance in a group. They can be entertaining or informative, but when they are used destructively at the expense of someone else, they are inappropriate and irresponsible. As with cruel jokes, negative gossip can devastate a person emotionally and cause great pain. It can destroy a person's reputation. The truth seldom washes away the damage of a vicious rumor. Skilled communicators know how to pass along the funny or harmless messages and stop the negative or vicious ones.

Harmless humor, rumors, or gossip can foster a sense of connection and acceptance among co-workers, but when these are used destructively, they can cause great pain and even destroy a person's reputation.

Eye-to-Eye

With a partner, develop a set of guidelines for managing gossip and rumors in a responsible and competent manner. Share your guidelines with the class.

Reading the Interpersonal Culture

Each workplace has its own interpersonal style or personality, even if it is similar to other organizations. Rizzotti's Pizza Parlor is different from Amato's Pizza Parlor. Working at Woodlands Golf Course is not the same as working at Tarryhill Golf Course. When you enter a specific workplace, pay special attention to the interpersonal communication going on around you. Paying attention to the interpersonal style will tell you a great deal about what is acceptable or unacceptable behavior there. It may also help you decide if you want to work there.

Some organizations encourage an aggressive interaction style. A risk-taking, fast-talking, competitive atmosphere means there may be lots of joking and one-upmanship going on but not much personal support. Organization members look out for themselves and concentrate on their goals. This may be a great place for self-reliant employees who enjoy competition and verbal spar-

Interpersonal Communication

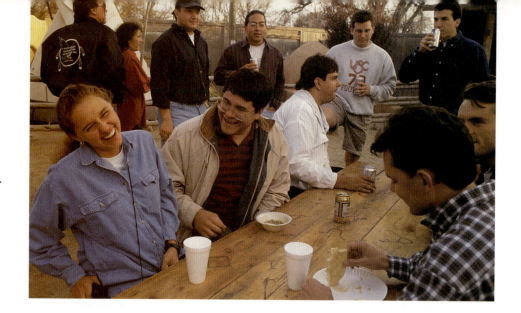

Some companies encourage a work hard/play hard environment. Employees experience a fast-paced work life and hang out together after work.

ring. Employees may not make much of an attempt to know each other well on a personal level.

Other organizations support a work-hard/play-hard culture. You push hard to make sales or deliver products, and you are expected to hang out together after work. Employees join company sports teams, support social events, and participate in company-sponsored service projects and charity events. This atmosphere may be a great place for people who want to be friendly with co-workers and who enjoy a fast-paced office life. Employees tend to know much about each other in this kind of work setting.

Still other organizations maintain a less personal culture. You come to work to complete tasks that depend on supportive working relationships and group cooperation. You may or may not socialize outside work, but in the workplace you support one another. The work flow is steady and predictable. There is time to talk during the day. Employees are discouraged from competing. Employees work at their own pace and, when needed, help each other out. This may be a good work environment for people who prefer nonpressured situations.

Finally, some organizations maintain a distant or individual culture. Each employee is a Lone Ranger—he or she functions independently. Employees are expected to do what is required, but there is little personal interaction or cooperation. Either you succeed or you leave. This is not an environment that supports nurturing communication or relational skills. It encourages functional communication, individual independence, and competition.

Evaluating Workplace Behavior

Use the following checklist to analyze your interpersonal behavior in a workplace. Rate each item from 1 to 5.

Interpersonal Behavior Checklist

	Never		▶	Always	
I greet co-workers.	1	2	3	4	5
I ask for feedback on how I am doing.	1	2	3	4	5
I double-check directions given to me.	1	2	3	4	5
I monitor how I reveal personal information.	1	2	3	4	5
I ask others questions about their weekend or other things.	1	2	3	4	5
I work at being an active listener.	1	2	3	4	5
I notice another's nonverbal cues before I begin any difficult conversation with him or her.	1	2	3	4	5
I talk with co-workers when I believe they have been rude to me.	1	2	3	4	5
I resist passing on negative gossip or vicious rumors.	1	2	3	4	5
I compliment people when they have done good work.	1	2	3	4	5

Chapter 6 *Summary*

In this chapter, you learned about interpersonal communication in the workplace. Interpersonal communication occurs when two or more people engage in ongoing interactions, exchanging nurturing as well as functional messages. Functional messages deal with managing day-to-day necessities and sharing information. Nurturing messages indicate supportiveness.

Relationships develop in four stages. They begin with first meetings, move to friendly relations, then to involved relationships, and finally to stable relationships. Most workplace relationships remain at either the first or second stage.

Relational skills are interpersonal skills used to build and maintain a good relationship with another person. Four important relational skills are recognition, sharing personal information, active listening, and constructive criticism.

Recognizing message direction; managing humor, rumors, and gossip; and reading interpersonal culture are important interpersonal issues in the workplace. Messages can travel in downward, upward, or horizontal directions. Downward communication occurs when superiors send messages to subordinates. Upward communication occurs when subordinates send messages to superiors. Horizontal communication occurs between peers. Appropriate humor in the workplace can create a sense of ease and belonging, but destructive gossip and rumors are inappropriate and irresponsible.

Every workplace has its own interpersonal style or personality. Some workplaces are aggressively competitive; others are team-oriented and highly supportive; still others are very impersonal and independence-oriented.

Interpersonal Communication

Chapter Seven

Interviewing for a Job

Objectives

After completing this chapter, you will be able to

- define *interview* and list the purpose of a job interview
- prepare a résumé
- explain the steps in preparing for an interview
- explain verbal and nonverbal messages exchanged in a job interview
- demonstrate effective interview behavior
- analyze and critique an interview

Key Terms

behavioral questions
interview
job interview
personal questions
qualifier questions
references
résumé

66 The interviewer's job is to find a reason to turn you down; your job is not to provide that reason. **99**

—JOHN L. LaFEVRE,
Interviewing: The Inside Story from a College Recruiter

Struggling Through a Job Interview

Just before high school graduation, Russell James started looking for a position that would offer full-time hours during the summer with part-time hours during the rest of the year. Russell noticed help-wanted signs in the windows of a bookstore chain that had four outlets in the city. He decided to apply, since there would be more than one location where he could work and this might give him more-flexible hours. Russell set up an appointment with the district manager,

Suzanne Marston, for the following Wednesday at 4 P.M.

On Wednesday, Russell and his girlfriend Nicole drove to the interview. They picked up soft drinks along the way. Unfortunately, they hit a pothole, and some pop spilled on Russell's good shirt, but it was too late to change clothes.

The pair arrived about five minutes late. When Russell and Nicole entered the office, the secretary told them to have a seat and gave Russell information forms to fill out. Russell asked Nicole if she had any idea what his Social Security number was or whom he should put down as a reference. Her answer was "No."

Ms. Marston came out to greet Russell. Russell said, "Hi, Ms. Martin." As they shook hands, Russell noticed that Ms. Marston was staring at his stained shirt. Although he was embarrassed, Russell said nothing about the spill. Russell explained that Nicole also hoped to work at the bookstore. He asked if she should come into the interview with him. Ms. Marston replied that

Nicole should make her own appointment.

Russell followed Ms. Marston into her office and sat in the chair closest to the door. Ms. Marston suggested he move to one next to the desk. As Ms. Marston reviewed Russell's paperwork, she asked why there were only two references rather than the requested four references. Russell said he was planning to phone in with his Social Security number and complete reference information the next day. They then discussed Russell's previous work history at the local park district. When asked about programs he enjoyed at the playground, Russell said little. In response to the question of why he was applying at the bookstore, Russell replied that the schedule looked good because he hoped for late evening hours when there would be few customers and he could study. They discussed Russell's long-range career goals, which were somewhat unclear.

Ms. Marston explained the bookstore's customer service expectations for employees;

these included recommending new books, helping customers locate books, and calling other store locations to find available copies.

Ms. Marston said, "As you may have noticed, our male employees all wear jackets. You would also have to wear a jacket. Neatness is an important part of our image." Then Ms. Marston explained, "When the store is not busy, staff members re-shelve books and move stock from the storeroom."

Near the end of the interview, Ms. Marston tried to get Russell to talk about his favorite works of fiction. Russell was vague in his responses. When Ms. Marston asked if Russell had any final questions, Russell asked two: "How much control do I have regarding vacations?" and "Do employees get discounts on the food at the store's cafe?"

As the interview ended, Russell said, " Thanks," and turned to leave. Ms. Marston followed him into the outer office, saying, "You'll hear from us when you complete your paperwork." Russell did not seem to hear her. In the hallway he reported to Nicole, "That was easy. Why don't you apply? Maybe we can get a joint schedule."

To what extent was Russell prepared for this interview? Name at least two mistakes he made. If you were to give three suggestions to Russell about how to improve his interviewing behavior, what would they be? Consider both verbal and nonverbal behavior.

The Job Interview

The word *interview* comes from the French word *entrevue*, meaning "interview" (*entre*, "between," plus *vue*, "sight"). An **interview** is a formal face-to-face meeting between two or more people to share information for a specific purpose. You will study interviewing as a research tool in Chapter 10. This chapter focuses on job interviewing.

A **job interview** is a conversation, usually between two people, to determine if one of them should join the organization the other represents. The interviewer, or person who represents the organization, shares information and asks questions to learn about the interviewee. The interviewee, or person seeking a position or membership, shares information and asks questions to decide whether to accept a position in the organization, if one is offered. When you go for an interview, your goal is to be offered a position; the interviewer's goal is to find the best candidate to take on certain responsibilities. You are trying to represent yourself to the interviewer as the person who is best qualified to meet the organization's needs. Polishing your interviewing skills is one way you can help yourself get the job that you want.

Interviews range from quite formal to informal, depending on the type of position and the situation. If you are applying for a part-time position in a law firm during your college years, you should expect a rather formal interview. If you are applying to be a photographer's assistant for the summer, you may find the interview to be more informal.

When you go to an interview, your goal is to be offered a position; the interviewer's goal is to find the best candidate for the job.

Although this chapter assumes you will be the interviewee, there are times when you will be the interviewer. You may interview applicants for staff positions at the community center summer camp, for school leadership positions, or for international exchange-student opportunities. As you read the rest of this chapter, remember to consider yourself in both roles.

Seeking a Position

Finding a position is a complicated interpersonal process that starts long before, and ends after, the actual face-to-face interview. As a result, it is vital that you prepare for an interview well in advance.

Whatever your goals are, whatever your skills are, getting a good job involves a structured and sometimes difficult process. The process begins with a job search. Where do you start looking? Vacancies may be available through traditional resources like newspaper ads or federal or state employment agencies, but more and more positions are appearing on Internet postings. Word of mouth from a friend, high school and college newspaper help-wanted ads, and signs in business windows are very useful for finding summer and part-time positions. As you begin the search, you need to read the position descriptions very carefully to determine whether or not you have the necessary qualifications.

NOW HIRING
Mega-Complex Theatre Corporation is now accepting applications for the position of night manager at our Maple Crest Theatre complex. We are looking for candidates who are customer-friendly, eager, and self-motivated. Previous management experience desired. We offer flexible hours, competitive wages, and free movies. Call 555–3280 to schedule an interview.

Read the following position descriptions and determine which one is closest to your interests and skills.

South Coast Airlines: Fleet Service Clerks
Fleet service clerks are responsible for aircraft loading and unloading; aircraft cleaning, fueling, and de-icing; and all aircraft arrival and departure activities, including pushing, towing, and related guide-person functions. Successful applicants enjoy physical labor and work well on teams.

Interviewing for a Job

Youth Advantage: Youth Mentors

Give back to the community. We need enthusiastic volunteers to hike, play sports, do arts and crafts, attend team meetings, and take field trips with our junior high youth-group members. Must be responsible, friendly, and relate well to young people. Must be willing to commit four to six hours a week.

Natural Spirit: Salesperson

New store needs salespeople for weekends and evenings. Must be willing to learn about vitamins, herbal, and natural energy supplements; manage inventory; and sell products. Friendly, health-conscious individual with customer service skills desired.

Computer *Search*

Check out two of the following web sites. At each site, select two jobs and list the skills you have that would be useful for those positions.

Job Web *(http://www.jobweb.com)*

Career Finder *(http://www.petersons/career.com)*

Help Wanted USA *(http://www.iccweb.com)*

America's Job Bank *(http://www.ajb.dni.us)*

More and more job positions are being posted in web sites on the Internet.

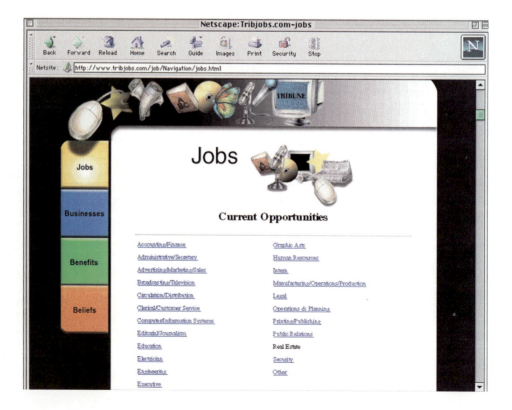

Preparing a Résumé

Once you have found an interesting job prospect, prepare a résumé of your work experience and your educational background. A **résumé** is a summary of your academic and employment background and job qualifications. It is usually one page. It contains basic information such as your name, address, phone number, e-mail address, schools attended, previous work experiences such as full-time or part-time work, major responsibilities in clubs and other volunteer organizations, and your interests and skills. It usually also includes a statement indicating that references are available upon request.

References are people who can speak about your personal and workplace qualifications. Usually, they are employers, teachers, youth group leaders, or other adults who know you well. If a potential employer requests references, you need to provide their names, addresses, and phone numbers.

Even if you are applying to a local hardware or grocery store and a formal résumé isn't necessary, you'll need certain information for your application. Look up the addresses and phone numbers of your school, former employers, and references before you apply. Call people who know you and who are not relatives, and ask their permission to be listed as a reference. Teachers make good reference choices.

Résumés should always be typed. There are many formats that are acceptable; choose one that is neat, precise, and highlights your qualities that match the organization's needs.

Sometimes you will need to develop a second version of your résumé to highlight specific qualifications for a particular job. You may have a general résumé that you will adapt to the particular position description. If you are applying to be a photographer's assistant or to work at the local cable channel, you will want to list your photo or video classes, something you might not list on another résumé. Many organizations today request that your résumé also include a brief statement indicating your goal in seeking employment with them. Goal statements are usually placed near the beginning of a résumé.

When you submit a résumé and/or a job application in person, dress for the occasion as if you were going to be interviewed. You never know when someone may decide to interview you immediately, especially for your first job experience.

Eye-to-Eye

Pair up with a partner and brainstorm the skills, responsibilities, and achievements each of you could put on a résumé in addition to your basic biographical information. Compare your lists with other classmates' lists.

Name: Marisa Martinez

Address: 360 San Bernando Drive, Apt. 8
Bernando, California

Phone: (989) 555–2365

Employment Goal:

I aim to use my talent and experience to make a contribution to the growth and betterment of children in our community as a dedicated member of your organizational team.

Skills:

Computer literate (word processing, Excel, PowerPoint); aerobics instruction; peer mediation

Education: Bernando High School, Bernando, California, 2000

Honors: National Honor Society
Who's Who Among American High School Students

Leadership: Church Youth Group, President, 1999; Vice President, 1998
Head Student Athletic Trainer, 1998-99
Amigos de Las Americas Training Staff, 1994-95

Extracurricular Activities:

Athletic Training, 9, 10, 11, 12 (5 days a week/20 hours a week)
Amigos de Las Americas Volunteer, 11, 12 (4 hours a week)

Work Experience:

1999: Volunteer for Amigos de Las Americas, Paraguay
1998: Counselor, Camp Echo
1997: Counselor, Berando Preschool Program

References: Available upon request

Preparing for the Interview

Effective job seekers do their homework. They don't just wander in to an organization spontaneously and expect to have a positive interview. They take the time first to learn what they can about an organization so that they will appear knowledgeable and make a good impression.

Researching the Organization

Researching an organization is an important pre-interview step. You may do this by calling the organization and asking if it has a brochure describing its products or services. The Internet is another good source of information. Many corporations and volunteer groups maintain web sites. The Chamber of Commerce and the Better Business Bureau also are possible research sources.

You want to know about an organization for two reasons. First, you want to know that it is reputable. Applicants are sometimes tricked by businesses that promise big earnings but actually do not pay those high wages. Remember, job hunting is a two-sided process. The company will evaluate you as a potential future employee, but you are also evaluating the company as your future employer.

The second reason for doing research is to be able to answer questions intelligently during your interview and to ask specific questions of the interviewer. You might be asked, "Why did you decide to interview with us?" or "In what ways do you think you can make a contribution to our organization?" The more you know, the better answers you can provide. In order to sell yourself to the interviewer, you must not only explain your qualifications but also outline how those qualifications directly relate to the company's specific needs. Doing research on the company is an ideal way to prepare for such answers. For example, if you were interviewing for a fund-raising job, you might say, "I understand that you need to increase donations. I was successful with our local cystic fibrosis drive last year. I have some ideas on what might improve the donations here."

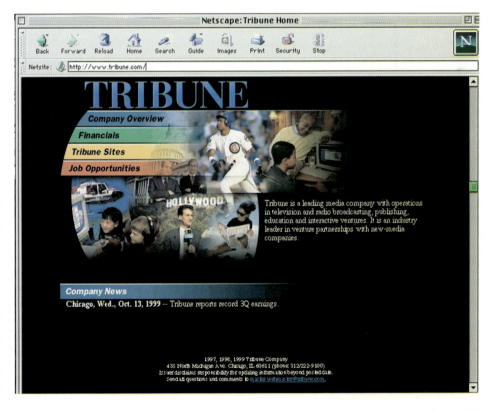

An important pre-interview step is to do research on an organization you are interested in. Many companies maintain Internet web sites that offer background information about the company.

One way to be prepared for an interview is to rehearse answers to commonly asked questions. Practicing answers will help give you more confidence when you get to the actual interview.

You should also be prepared to ask questions about the company or group. Your questions should focus on opportunities for growth and advancement, not about salary and benefits. The interviewer knows you want to earn money. But the interviewer is also looking for someone who is interested in working for that company, someone who will stay with the job. Even fast-food restaurants want to hire employees who will remain at the job at least a year. Training is expensive, and the longer an employee stays on the job, the more valuable he or she becomes to that organization. You might also ask questions about the workplace culture, employee interaction, and the environment: Is there a dress code? Do employees support one another? Is teamwork emphasized? Will I have my own desk?

Practicing Answers to Questions

Job candidates should prepare ahead of time for the interview by rehearsing answers to some commonly asked questions. As you know from giving book reports or talks, rehearsal makes a speaker seem more professional, more polished. Interviewers will be impressed by the candidate who answers questions with poise and confidence.

Qualifier Questions

The first questions are generally qualifiers. **Qualifier questions** are questions designed to determine if you meet the general qualifications for the position.

Chapter Seven

- What is your educational and/or technical background?
- What type of previous experience do you have?
- Can you work certain hours/days?
- What is your desired salary range? (This question might not be asked in a first interview.)

After it has been determined that you meet the minimum qualifications, an interviewer must then determine if you are the best candidate for the position. He or she will do this by asking a series of questions about your motivation, dependability, problem-solving skills, temperament, ability to learn, and specific job needs. These questions can be divided into two general types—personal and behavioral.

Personal Questions

Personal questions ask for the background and personal qualities of the applicant. They require a person to talk about himself or herself in a thoughtful and articulate manner. These questions help the interviewer determine if the candidate's personal qualities match with the organizational culture. Is the person a self-starter? a team player? an independent operator? Examples of personal questions include the following:

- What are your long-term career goals?
- What were your most rewarding high school experiences?
- How would your best friend describe you?

Some personal questions also serve to give more information about skills.

- What software packages can you use?
- Do you have a current driver's license?
- Are you certified in CPR?

SHERMAN'S LAGOON

Behavioral Questions

Behavioral questions are based on the concept that past behavior can predict future behavior. Employers are very interested in understanding how you handled situations in the past that may be similar to situations you might face within their organization. Behavioral questions ask for specific examples or descriptions of actions taken in the past, not what you think you might do. Answers often involve personal reports or stories.

Behavioral questions do not have a "right" answer. Sometimes they may be phrased as a declarative request and not as a question—for example, "Tell me about a time when you helped solve a problem at your last job." Note that the following examples of behavioral questions are all phrased as statements:

- Give an example of how you worked effectively with people to accomplish an important result.
- Give an example of a skill you acquired in a previous job.
- Describe a time when you achieved an important goal despite obstacles.

Eye-to-Eye

Discuss with a partner how you would answer one of the behavioral questions listed above. Give a specific example from personal experience.

FYI *Commonly Asked Questions*

If you prepare positive, thoughtful, and honest answers to questions like these before an interview, you will be one step closer to being offered a job.

General Questions

- Describe the ideal job (in terms of responsibilities, work environment, etc.).
- What would you like to avoid in a job?
- What are your long-term career goals?
- How do you see this position helping you to reach these goals?
- What is your greatest talent that helps you excel in the workplace?

Motivation/Initiative

- What work-related accomplishment are you most proud of?
- Why did you apply for this position at our company?
- Why did you choose the career for which you are preparing?
- What do you consider to be your greatest strengths and weaknesses?

Problem Solving

- If a customer complains about a faulty product, but it is clear that the product broke because of the customer's carelessness, how would you handle the situation?
- Tell me about a recent problem situation at school or work that you were useful in resolving.

Attitude/Maturity

- Tell me about a time you got angry at work and how you acted.
- Tell me about a specific area of responsibility you have enjoyed at work.
- What would you do if you knew a fellow employee was violating a policy such as stealing from the company?
- How do you deal with personality conflicts within a group?
- What characteristics are important in a manager?

Education

- Describe your most rewarding high school experience.
- What high school/college subjects did you like best/least? Why?
- What plans do you have for continued study?
- What have you learned from participation in extracurricular activities?
- What technological skills do you have?

Closing

- Do you have any questions I can answer?
- Can you think of a reason why you would be unable to perform the job?
- Why should we consider you over other candidates?

Dressing the Part

The way you dress for an interview is critical to making a good first impression. What is appropriate attire for interviewing? The answer to this varies. It depends on the job and the company's culture. Experts suggest that you try to feel great about the way you look while projecting an image that matches the job requirements and the organization.

If you're applying for a part-time position while still in school, you can probably adopt a more casual appearance than you would if you were a college graduate entering a career. The standard for young men might be slacks and button-down shirts, dress shoes, and dark socks. Shirts should be tucked in and neat, and belts should be worn. A necktie might be expected. Young women could wear dresses or skirts/slacks and blouses. Dresses and skirts should not be too short, and blouses should not be too revealing. Conservative, clean, and pressed are the general rules.

Dilbert reprinted by permission of United Feature Syndicate, Inc..

in length and neutral in color. Image is important, especially in the business world. In addition to your résumé, your dress and manners speak for you.

Check It Out

Pay attention to workplace clothing. Select three different types of organizations, such as a large business, a hobby shop, and a coffee shop or drive-in. Make a list of dress practices you observe at each organization.

The Actual Interview

When the big moment arrives, it's time for all the preparation to pay off.

Arrival

Go to the interview alone. Even if you need a parent to give you a ride, he or she should remain in the car or come back. Businesses are hiring someone mature enough to do the job by themselves, so go to the interview by yourself. Never go with friends, even if they are applying for a position as well. Businesses generally do not want to hire friends together. They are concerned that the friends would want to visit and talk rather than work at their jobs.

Arrive a few minutes early. This will make a good impression. Organizations expect workers to be prepared to begin work on time; that is what they will be paying you to do, and every minute costs them money. There may be paperwork to be filled out prior to the interview. Arriving early will allow you to get the paperwork out of the way and still start the interview on time.

Bring your résumé with you. The interviewer may not have a copy of your résumé handy. It's useful to have a résumé available even if the interviewer has asked you to fill out an application. Be ready to talk about any item on your résumé.

Conduct yourself in a professional manner. Once you open the door to an office, you have begun the interview process. Your behavior in the reception area is important. Other employees may be asked what they thought of you. Greet the office staff as if they were the people hiring you. State your name, the position for which you are applying, the time of your appointment, and the person with whom you have an interview. Smile and maintain good eye contact, and then wait and listen carefully for any instructions.

Greeting and Behavior

Your greeting is extremely important in making a good first impression. Walk confidently into the interviewer's office, and look at the interviewer as you approach. Eye contact is a key to conveying self-confidence. The handshake is also an important part of the greeting. It should be firm. A limp handshake conveys a negative image.

Greet the interviewer by name. Knowing the interviewer's name should be part of your research before the interview. If you have been unable to find out before the day of the interview, ask the secretary for the correct pronunciation. Some people are very offended when their name is mispronounced.

Listen carefully and follow directions. It is important to follow directions and to answer the exact question the interviewer asked. Most interviewers will stand to greet you and will invite you to be seated. Do not place objects on the interviewer's desk. Place purses or folders on the floor next to your chair or hold them on your lap. Also, never smoke, chew gum, or eat candy. (See Interviewers' Pet Peeves on page 180.)

Continue to maintain effective eye contact throughout the interview, but do not stare at the interviewer. Eye contact helps maintain an active listening mode, and, in our culture, looking a person in the eye conveys honesty and integrity.

Watch your body posture. Sit up straight in the chair. Leave both feet on the floor. You can cross your feet at the ankles, but you should not sit with one leg crossed over the other during a job interview. It is too casual.

Present a positive attitude. Be focused, yet friendly and personable. Remember, you need to fit in and work with a group or team. No one wants

Your greeting is an extremely important factor in making a good first impression. Walk confidently into the interviewer's office, greet the interviewer by name, and extend a firm handshake.

Interviewing for a Job

177

To create a good impression during the interview, present a positive attitude. Sit up straight and maintain eye contact. Be focused, yet friendly and personable.

to work with someone with a bad attitude or with no personality at all. Be enthusiastic. Employers want to hire individuals who are excited about their organization. Your body and your voice need to convey positive energy.

Answering Questions

If you have rehearsed the questions listed earlier in the chapter, you will probably be prepared to answer all of the questions asked. If the interviewer asks a question for which you have not prepared, take a moment to think through your answer. He or she would rather wait for a thoughtful answer than receive a quick response that might be simplistic or wrong. People who think through problems are more valuable employees.

If you have been fired in the past or have had a problem with a previous employer, be honest. It is okay to say, "I made a mistake, but I have learned from it." However, the interview is not the time or place to air your problems with a former boss. In fact, that type of response might cause the interviewer to feel that *you* are the problem and that you may be difficult to get along with.

Career Communication *Human Resources*

If you apply for a position at a medium- or large-size company, it is likely that your first contact will be with the Human Resources department. People who work in Human Resources are responsible for processing the hiring of new employees, maintaining employee records, coordinating and administering employee benefits programs, and conducting exit interviews when employees leave.

In large companies, human resources personnel conduct the initial interviews with job candidates to determine if they have the general qualifications for a particular position. They then forward a candidate's application and résumé to a manager or supervisor in the appropriate department.

Interviewing job candidates, however, is just a small part of

a Human Resources person's job. Most of his or her time is spent maintaining employee records—including performance evaluations and salary changes—and administering benefits. In very large companies, a Human Resources representative may specialize in a particular task, such as monitoring medical benefits for active and retired employees.

People who work in Human Resources need to have well-developed interpersonal skills.

They deal regularly with personal issues, advising employees, for example, on how to make use of medical benefits during times of personal crisis or how to take advantage of company out-placement services if their employment has been terminated. Effective Human Resources representatives are empathic listeners, and they take seriously their responsibility to assist employees in adjusting to a new job, managing benefits, planning for the future, and making the transition from active employment to retirement.

Answers are best when stated in a positive way. Consider the following responses to the question "Why do you want a new position?" Which answer is the more positive response?

"I want a new position so I can take on more responsibility."
"I want a new position because I get bored easily."

Answer yes/no questions with an example or explanation. Keep answers simple and to the point. Avoid long-winded responses. You will lose the interest of the interviewer, and you might get lost in your own response.

Have some questions of your own ready to ask the interviewer. You might ask "What qualities are you looking for in someone for this position?" "How much group work is expected?" "If I do well at this, are there opportunities for advancement?"

Interviewing for a Job

Group Interviews

On occasion you may be interviewed by more than one person. You may meet each interviewer individually, one after the other, or you may sit at a table with three or four interviewers at the same time. When a group of people interview you, it's important to be able to shift your focus easily to address each person directly.

On other occasions, you may find yourself part of a group of interviewees being interviewed at the same time. Some companies do this in an attempt to be efficient. More often, it is an attempt to see how well you interact with others. Some companies even schedule group games and team exercises during these interviews to analyze leadership skills. In these situations, it's especially important for you to convey self-confidence and a positive attitude.

FYI *Interviewers' Pet Peeves*

10 Ways to Bomb in a Job Interview

1. Arrive late for the interview.

2. Give a " fishy," limp handshake.

3. Chew gum.

4. Move around, wiggle constantly.

5. End every statement with "you know."

6. Appear clueless about the organization.

7. Appear interested mainly in salary or benefits.

8. Dress sloppily.

9. Talk about your social life.

10. Leave without asking any questions.

Post Interview Follow-Up

Follow-up is important. After the interview, it is important to write a thank-you letter. You want to remind the interviewer of who you are and what skills you offer. You also want to thank the interviewer for the opportunity to meet with him or her. Express again your interest in the position and state when you are available. Even if you don't get this position, another job may become available and the interviewer will remember you favorably.

In your letter, be sure to include your full name, address, phone number, and the date of the interview. A sample is shown on page 182.

Erica Lizak, *Baby Sitter, Cake Decorator, Retail Clerk*

At this point in her life, Erica Lizak has quite a list of paid positions to put on her job résumé. From ages 12 to 16, Erica earned her money by babysitting 3 to 15 hours a week, depending on her client families' needs. She changed diapers and fed babies, helped elementary-school students with homework, straightened up houses, and made dinners. According to Erica, "The most important thing to do to form good relationships with kids is to be enthusiastic, caring, and sometimes even goofy."

Her next job involved making cakes and novelties at the local Dairy Queen. At what she considers her first "real job," Erica learned punctuality, consideration for other workers and customers, and responsibility for talking to managers, when necessary. From there, Erica moved on to work at the local movie theater, acting as a ticket taker and staffing the concession stand.

Currently Erica is employed by the local T J Maxx store. The manager hired her on the spot after interviewing her. Obviously, Erica's previous work experiences and her poise and self-confidence during the interview impressed her manager.

In her 15 to 20 hours a week at work, Erika may be found handling the register, staffing the fitting room, managing the return desk, or stocking the racks. Sometimes she handles the phone calls for her section of the store and checks prices or merchandise availability. According to Erica, "It is important to keep all lines of communication open with other employees as well as with management. Talking with other employees gives you a better idea of what's going on and how you measure up to what others do."

Even while working many hours a week, Erica still finds time to be involved with the annual food drive sponsored by her school's honor society. She is also a regular server at the teachers' conference breakfasts.

Erika will graduate from high school with some hard-earned money to put toward college and a wide range of workplace skills that will help her find responsible positions in college and later.

Student Worker Profile

181

123 Your Road
Your Town, Anywhere 00000
May 5, 2001

Ms. Jean Johns
Tiger Paw Products
640 Their Road
Anywhere, 00000

Dear Ms. Johns:

Thank you for the opportunity to interview on May 4 for the warehouse position. I enjoyed speaking with you and learning more about Tiger Paw Products. The interview with you gave me a very positive impression of your company. I am confident my prior experiences and talents are a good match for this position. I would do my best to become a productive member of your team.

Again, thank you for your time and consideration. If you need any additional information, please call me at 555-4424.

Sincerely,

Albert Chang

Try to learn something from every interview experience, whether or not you get the job. Replay in your mind some of the questions and answers to see how you might improve for the next time.

Critiquing the Interview

As you review your interview experience or watch a classmate do a practice interview, use the following Interview Evaluation Form to guide your analysis and evaluation.

Interview Evaluation Form

	Yes	No	Does Not Apply
Dressed appropriately for the interview	☐	☐	☐
Greeted the interviewer by name	☐	☐	☐
Shook hands firmly	☐	☐	☐
Waited for a seating cue	☐	☐	☐
Answered the questions appropriately	☐	☐	☐
Knew something about the organization	☐	☐	☐
Knew the names of references	☐	☐	☐
Asked appropriate questions	☐	☐	☐
Maintained eye contact with the interviewer	☐	☐	☐
Thanked the interviewer when leaving	☐	☐	☐

Chapter 7   *Summary*

In this chapter, you learned about interviewing for a job. A job interview is a conversation between two people to determine if one of them should join the organization the other represents. Improving your interviewing skills can help you get the job that you want.

Once you have found an interesting job prospect, you need to prepare a résumé of your work experience and your educational background. You should also learn about the organization to find out if it is reputable and to be able to answer questions intelligently during your interview.

Before going to the interview, spend some time practicing answers to typical interview questions. Dress neatly and conservatively for the interview. Go to the interview alone, and arrive early. Greet the interviewer by name. During the interview, listen carefully and follow directions. Present a positive attitude. Maintain effective eye contact and watch your body posture.

After the interview, it is important to write a thank-you letter. Remind the interviewer of who you are and what skills you have to offer. Do a critique of the interview to see how you might improve for the next time.

Review Questions

1. Who participates in a job interview and what are their goals?
2. List at least five sources for job listings.
3. Why might you need more than one version of your résumé?
4. What are two reasons for researching a company before going to an interview?
5. List four questions you might ask at the end of the interview.
6. Give three examples of qualifier questions.
7. What do behavioral questions tell the interviewer about the applicant?
8. List four rules for interviewing for a job.
9. Why should you always go to an interview alone?
10. What should a follow-up thank-you letter include?

Critical Thinking Skills

Speaking/Doing

1. Create a poster illustrating the do's and don'ts of job interviewing attire. Present your poster to the class in a one- to two-minute presentation.
2. Interview a parent or a neighbor about his or her job. How did he or she hear about the job? What type of interview did he or she experience to get that job? What are the common interview techniques used by that company or profession? Share what you learn with the class.

Writing

Write a help-wanted ad. It should be no more that 25 words. It should describe the position, the qualifications for the job, the salary range, how to contact the company, and any other pertinent data.

Group Activities

1. Divide into groups of four or five students. Your teacher should provide you with a bowl containing job titles. One student will be the interviewee, and the remaining three or four students will be group interviewers. The interviewee should select a slip from the bowl to determine for what job he or she is interviewing. The interviewers will proceed to ask the interviewee qualifying questions, personal questions, and behavioral questions. They can use the list of commonly asked questions on

pages 172–173 to guide them. After a four- to five-minute interview, switch places. Another student will become the interviewee, and the first interviewee now becomes an interviewer. Repeat the process until each student has been both an interviewee and interviewer.

2. Divide into groups of 6 to 10 students. Plan a "fashion show" demonstrating the do's and don'ts of job interviewing attire. The "don'ts" should be reasonable, common mistakes that interviewees might make. (No one would realistically go to an interview wearing mismatched, ragged clothes.) One member of the group should be the runway announcer, describing the outfits and the do's and don'ts that they illustrate.

Practical Application: Case Challenge

When Soraya arrived home after her first year in college, most of the small businesses in town had "help wanted" signs in their windows. Her friends told her local stores and restaurants were competing for summer workers. On her way to the grocery store, Soraya decided to stop at the banquet hall. She dropped in at 4 P.M. to say she was looking for a job and ask if she could talk to someone. The hostess pointed to Sam Reston, the owner, who was setting up tables. Mr. Reston suggested that Soraya come back the next morning.

Soraya pleaded, "Can't we just talk now?"

Mr. Reston stopped, took her to his office, and asked her to summarize her past work experience. She listed her camp counseling and babysitting.

When Mr. Reston asked if Soraya had ever served the public, she looked confused and said, "I guess not." He asked for her references, but Soraya could not remember the exact names or phone numbers of the people at camp.

When Mr. Reston asked why Soraya wanted to work at the banquet hall, Soraya replied, "My friend said the tips are good."

Mr. Reston asked if her nose ring was removable.

"It hasn't been out for two years," Soraya said. "People like it."

After five minutes Mr. Reston said he had to get back to his work and he'd contact her if they had an opening. Soraya never heard from him, although her friend Natalie was hired there two weeks later.

Find examples of Soraya's lack of planning before this interview. What are three things Soyara could have handled more effectively?

Chapter Eight

Group and Team Communication

Objectives

After completing this chapter, you will be able to

- describe the types, purposes, and importance of groups and teams
- describe and demonstrate group communication skills
- describe and demonstrate group and team roles
- describe and demonstrate group problem-solving steps
- evaluate group communication
- explain group networks for communicating information
- describe duties of a leader and leadership styles
- demonstrate effective leadership skills
- evaluate leadership skills

Key Terms

agenda

brainstorming

buzz groups

cliques

committee

formal networks

forum

group

group norms

group role

informal networks

panel discussion

procedural statements

subgroups

symposium

team

> 66 The small group is clearly the tie that binds, the nucleus that holds society together. 99
>
> —LAWRENCE R. FREY, *Group Communication in Context*

Putting Teamwork into Practice

"You're sure the neighbors know we're coming at 6:30 on Sunday morning, right?" asked Matt, as they drove into the suburban neighborhood.

"I left notices in all the mailboxes on the Jeffersons' street," Mike answered.

"Did you talk to the closest neighbors like I asked you to?" Matt continued.

"Notes should do it. The Jeffersons said they would talk to the people next door. The neighbors shouldn't be surprised. The police have agreed to let us manage traffic on the block for the morning."

"Well, we'll soon find out," added Amanda, steering the grip truck with film equipment to the side of a suburban house with a basketball hoop over the garage. As Matt, Mike, and Amanda began to unload the lights, three more vehicles loaded with equipment, cast members, and food turned into the block. A few local actors were sitting on the curb waiting for the student film crew. As Amanda, the director, gathered her camera crew, Matt, the producer, headed off to talk with the Jeffersons and to give college T-shirts to the family's twins, who would be extras in the film about a basketball star's childhood. A neighbor walking a dog stopped to ask, "Who are you guys?"

"We're part of a university film group, Studio 23. We raised $12,000 to make this film. The director and other seniors are trying to add to their professional reels," one of the students replied.

"I can't believe I'm here," moaned Kevin, the audio engineer. "I was up half the night editing my directing project for Professor Danzinger."

"I was sewing the mother's dress until 2 A.M.," replied Alexandra, the costume designer. "Claudia was with me, but she missed the call this morning. I'm on my own."

"OK everyone, listen up," shouted Matt. "We will begin shooting in ten minutes. Katie, you and Zharg lock down traffic at either end of the street while we're shooting."

"Where's Jen?" The art director's head popped out of the garage where she was getting some lawn furniture for background props. Jen waved and disappeared.

"Are we ready?" asked Amanda. "Run a sound level."

"We're doing another lighting check," Scott yelled. "The clouds keep moving over just when we are set."

Just then Alexandra ran up to Matt and announced, "The basketball uniforms are missing. Claudia never packed them. They're back at the dorm."

Matt mumbled something under his breath and headed for the truck while yelling to Amanda, "I'll be back in a half hour with the uniforms."

Amanda frowned and called after him, "We shoot the team at 9:30. Drive fast." She turned and addressed the group on the lawn. "We're doing a countdown." After a quick review of the crew's responsibilities, she positioned herself behind the

camera person and yelled, "Quiet on the set."

The camera rolled as a crew member shouted, "Take 1, The Making of a Hoops Legend." He clapped the slate and shooting began.

Discuss some reasons why this group is working well. What appear to be the unwritten rules for working in this film crew? What is one group problem and how could it have been avoided?

189

Most workplace teams, like the sales team in this photograph, have specific goals and a high level of communication among members.

Groups and Their Characteristics

A **group** consists of people who communicate with each other over time and share an interest in the same things or share a common purpose. Typically, members of groups communicate regularly; participate in planning, decision making, or action; and feel connected to the other members.

Group Purpose

You have been part of many groups. You may belong to school groups, religious groups, or community groups. Their purposes vary. Some, such as the chess club or a church youth group, have a social purpose. Others, such as a community clean-up crew or student council, are task-oriented. Some of these groups work well together and accomplish a lot. Others struggle along or fall apart.

A specific type of group, frequently found in the workplace, is called a team. A **team** is a group of two or more people who coordinate their activity as they work in a task-oriented, interdependent manner toward a common goal. Teams are formed to provide an efficient way of getting work done or to solve work-related problems. Sometimes team members manage themselves. At other times, directors or managers serve as leaders. Most workplace teams have specific goals and a high level of communication among members. Examples include sales teams, rescue teams, and service teams.

Group Structure

Group structure refers to the type of organization a group needs to carry out business. Highly organized groups are characterized by a formal structure because they have set, specific rules for communication and behavior. As a member, you know which individuals will take certain responsibilities, and you can predict how the meetings will be run. Examples you are familiar with include student councils, student congresses, and extracurricular clubs governed by specific rules or procedures.

Less-organized groups tend to have an informal structure. They do not follow set, specific rules. Groups that organize quickly for specific business or social purposes, such as bike rides, good-bye parties, fund-raisers, or community cleanup projects, do not need a formal structure. You might be part of an informal lunch group, a bowling team, or a movie club.

Computer *Search*

To see how thousands of young people in all 50 states participate in volunteer groups and National Youth Service Day, check out the following web sites. Try to identify clues to the purpose and structure of the groups described at each site.

www.servenet.org

www.cns.gov/americorps

Group Norms

Group norms are the standards for behavior within a group. Norms set expectations and establish a model for how group members act. Most groups have both general norms and communication norms similar to a workplace culture. General group norms might include how to act or dress, whether it's OK to arrive late or leave early, how hard to work, whether taking a break is acceptable, and how much to help each other out. Particular communication norms within a group might include when and how to disagree, what topics are acceptable to talk about, how much to talk about personal life, how to talk to certain people (for example, a boss), and whom to talk to about certain topics.

In the opening case study, members of the film group knew what was expected of them on the set. They were prepared, knowledgeable, and cooperative. These behaviors were their group's norms. To be a productive member of any group, competent communicators select communication behavior that fits a group's norms. Communication norms are seldom spelled out explicitly to new members; usually, members learn the norms of the group by watching and asking questions.

Group and Team Communication

Group Communication Skills

To solve any group problem, each member must contribute ideas and listen carefully to the other members' ideas. Only by listening to what the others are saying will you be able to interact with them to reach a common solution. The following communication skills encourage and support good problem solving.

Giving Information

Someone has to provide information for a discussion. You may contribute factual information, quote others' ideas, clarify certain issues, or take stands to move the discussion along. It takes self-confidence to put your ideas out there and to change your ideas if others make a better point.

Questioning

Frequently, you need to question other members about the source of their information, the accuracy of a statement, the relevance of a point to the discussion, or the meaning of a statement. For example, a question such as "We were talking about ways to increase business downtown. How does your information on prisons apply?" directs the discussion to a specific person's comment and requests more information. Such questions should not be evaluative or judging but should seek explanation. In that way, discussion points can be clarified and the problem-solving process can move forward.

To solve any group problem, each member must contribute ideas and listen carefully to the ideas of others.

Supporting

You can often increase group interaction by giving positive support to other people's ideas or behaviors. When you offer additional information that further proves a point made by another person, or when you verbally or nonverbally agree with another person's opinions, you provide support. Such statements build cohesiveness among the participants by making individuals feel good about their contributions and help direct the group toward its goal.

Contradicting

What is the best way to tell someone "You're wrong"? Although you may feel comfortable when someone disagrees with you, others may feel uncomfortable. Yet disagreements do occur. A group should hear all sides before reaching consensus on a final decision. Eventually, the group will have to decide which evidence is most accurate, least biased, best supported, or most in agreement with the group's goals, but differences of opinion need to be aired. They help a group focus on issues that will determine what course of action to take.

Evaluating

During discussion, you will have to make judgments about the information presented. Such evaluations should focus on the usefulness, appropriateness, or quality of the ideas. Remarks such as "That's stupid" or "It will never work" aren't helpful. Comments such as "A toy sale would raise more money than a plant sale" or "A circus night would be a great fund-raiser, but we don't have enough members to pull it off" provide a useful explanation of your position.

Using Procedural Statements

How do you move discussion along? What are good ways for keeping a discussion on the topic? **Procedural statements** are statements that give direction to the discussion and keep the discussion on the desired path. Here are two examples: "Let's hear comments on the opposite side." "We have to wrap up discussion and make a decision. We only have 10 minutes left."

A special kind of procedural statement is the summary statement. Summarizing is a method of recapping what has been discussed and decided. A good summary should (1) be objective and brief, (2) represent the range of members' ideas, and (3) include the major points discussed.

Peanuts reprinted by permission of United Feature Syndicate.

Check It Out

Listen to a formal or informal group discussion for 15 minutes. It can be a committee meeting or friends trying to decide what to do over the weekend. Note (1) the number of times specific group communication skills are used and (2) whether members tend to use a variety of skills or use only one or two skills regularly. Write a paragraph explaining which skills are used and how often they are used.

Group Roles and Subgroups

A **group role** is a pattern of communication that characterizes one's place in a group. It reflects the group communication skills used heavily by certain members. Most members of a group behave in fairly predictable ways. Think of how you act in a group. How would you describe your behavior: funny, serious, helpful, shy, confrontational? Do you ask questions, push your ideas, or simply observe the discussion?

There are many roles people can play in a group. These roles may help or hurt movement toward the group's goal. The following list includes the most common communication roles present in any group:

1. **Experts** Experts know a great deal about a subject and actively share their knowledge with the group. They give information that provides much of the discussion content. If the experts start to take over and force ideas on other members, however, they may be looked upon as "know-it-alls." Sometimes an expert's knowledge makes others in the group feel that they have little to contribute, and, as a result, good ideas are lost.

2. **Supporters** Supporters provide positive encouragement and defend the ideas of others in the group. Sometimes they encourage a shy person to

express his or her ideas. However, if supporters never offer their own ideas, they become known as "yes-people" or "head-nodders." Often the good ideas they have go unspoken.

3. **Questioners** Questioners raise important points about the direction of the group or about specific ideas being considered. They make everyone think twice before rushing into decisions. Like the experts, they often spark discussion. However, if questioners raise issues about every topic, they can slow down a group's progress.

4. **Challengers** Challengers are willing to argue or debate ideas rather than accept them. They force the entire group to evaluate ideas and think more carefully. They may play the "devil's advocate," a person who takes an opposing position to challenge other members' analysis and ideas. If they contradict everybody just for attention, however, they can be a negative influence and slow the group's progress.

5. **Moderators** Moderators keep the group process moving by using procedural statements and by trying to make sure that everyone gets involved. They may remind the group of deadlines, provide regular summaries, or, like supporters, draw out quiet members. If they try to control the group, however, they lose their effectiveness.

6. **Collaborators** Collaborators work to find connections among ideas. They combine points and suggestions to keep the group moving forward and to bring about creative solutions. Sometimes they act as "peacemakers" by finding ways to reconcile opposing viewpoints within a group. They have to be careful not to misrepresent others' ideas or overlook their own ideas.

7. **Tension Relievers** Tension relievers keep things from getting too serious or boring. They may crack jokes, tease members, or make funny, supportive remarks. If they only act funny, however, and don't make constructive contributions, they become known as "clowns" and can be a distracting influence.

Eye-to-Eye

In groups of eight, select a discussion topic. Each person should play one of the seven group roles defined above or be the observer. The observer should not know who has been assigned each role. Discuss your topic for five to seven minutes. When you stop, ask the observer to identify each person's role; then discuss the effect of playing one major role. To what extent does it help or limit your understanding of a given topic and your effectiveness in the group?

Role Development

Although you are not locked into a group role, you may find yourself in the same role quite frequently. This situation occurs due to a number of factors. Some common factors are self-image, another's expectations, and your ability and knowledge.

Self-image

The way you view yourself influences the roles you take on. If you see yourself as helpful and supportive, but not very strong or assertive, you are likely to act as a supporter or possibly a collaborator. If you see yourself as assertive and determined, you will tend to act as a challenger or a moderator.

Others' Expectations

Others can influence the role you play by giving you feedback on how you should behave. If you receive positive feedback whenever you ask a question or challenge an idea and negative feedback when you suggest ideas, you may play the questioner or challenger role in that group. Others' expectations can limit your communication in a group. You can become stereotyped by these expectations.

Your Ability and Knowledge

You may find that your talents or knowledge influence your role. If you have marketing expertise, you may be asked questions constantly by a group trying to develop a marketing plan. When the group moves on to long-range planning, you may no longer be the expert. Roles can change within a group, and your role can change as you move from group to group. Be open to this possibility and allow yourself to be flexible!

Problems with Roles

What communication problems can arise because of group roles? If you are stereotyped into one role, people will tend to communicate with you based on that role. If you expect Jack to be a "clown," you may prevent Jack from having deeper conversations. If you are always expected to be the moderator, you may miss the opportunity to contribute ideas, questions, or challenges. The expert may not be included in some of the less serious or more social activities among group members. Encourage the "clown" or the experts of your group to make other contributions, and see what effect this has on your group's interaction.

Group roles raise gender and culture issues. A professor of workplace behavior, Leigh Thompson, says that when groups or teams form, "there is an early natural status competition based on gender, age and race." Highly skilled managers encourage all employees to contribute, and they try to help those who find it difficult to participate actively. In workplace settings, thoughtful man-

Jeff Blakely, *Structural Engineer*

For most of us, looking up at the Empire State Building or out over the Golden Gate Bridge inspires a sense of awe. When structural engineer Jeff Blakely looks at them, he thinks about what loads and forces the structures must bear and what materials were used to build them. Blakely works for a construction-and-design firm in San Francisco, California. It is his job to plan, design, and oversee the construction of the buildings and bridges that his company is hired to build. Structural engineers must understand the properties of the materials used in construction, such as steel and concrete, and must have a thorough knowledge of the concepts behind balance and geometry.

Engineers generally work as part of a group or team. As part of the team, they are expected to contribute ideas and listen to and evaluate the ideas of other team members. Structural engineers and architects work together in planning and designing projects, and during construction they must cooperate with contractors, mechanical and electrical engineers, project owners, public officials, financial specialists, and sometimes lawyers. It is essential for an engineer to get along well with a variety of people and to communicate effectively in order to perform well on the job. Blakely sees trying to satisfy all of the people working on a project as one of the most challenging aspects of his job. "Sometimes the government officials want a modern building made of the best materials, the project owner wants to keep costs to a minimum, and the architect feels changes made to the plan compromise his design," he says. "Finding a solution that is acceptable to everyone can be quite difficult."

In spite of the challenges, Blakely enjoys his career. He says that he gets great satisfaction out of seeing a building or bridge completed and knowing he played an integral role in its design. There is another aspect of his job that he likes, as well. "It's not something people usually associate with engineering," he says, "but I really feel that I am able to improve the quality of life in San Francisco through my work. Every building or bridge that I design brings new jobs into the community, or it offers someone a new home or a better way to travel. I like being able to do what I love and benefit the community at the same time."

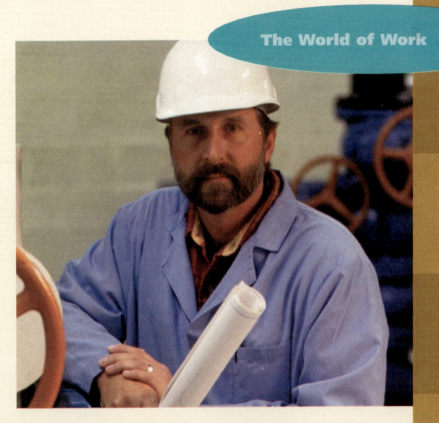

The World of Work

197

agers encourage women to contribute actively to problem-solving discussions because research shows that women sometimes do not contribute equally with men. For example, they may allow themselves to be interrupted or allow others to claim credit for their ideas. Age differences can also affect group problem solving. Sometimes younger employees are reluctant to speak up if the group has many older members. At other times, younger members might ignore or minimize the contributions of older members. Cultural differences can also influence group behavior. For example, in some Asian cultures, confronting someone directly, questioning a supervisor in public, or challenging a colleague's ideas is considered unacceptable behavior because any of these actions could result in embarrassment or loss of face.

Check It Out

Spend 20 to 30 minutes carefully watching a group interact. Identify at least three group roles and give two examples of predictable behavior. Look for any evidence of the influence of gender, age, or culture on the group's communication. Note one or two examples or note that there were no obvious examples.

Subgroups

Not all groups remain one single unit. Many groups divide into **subgroups**, or smaller units within a group. The local food pantry board may have a funding committee, a volunteer coordinating committee, and a space committee.

Workplace cliques include employees who regularly eat together, take breaks together, or hang out together after work.

Dilbert reprinted by permission of United Feature Syndicate, Inc..

The intergenerational elder-teen project may have one subgroup of music students who entertain nursing home residents, while another subgroup collects oral histories from the elderly residents. Subgroups allow people to work on specific jobs or to use special talents. Sometimes a subgroup becomes more important than the larger group from which it comes. A member may feel more attached to the subgroup and forget or de-emphasize the goals of the larger group.

One type of subgroup is called a clique. **Cliques** are subgroups whose members tend to associate with each other and avoid others. They consider themselves a closed group or an "in" group. Usually cliques make nonmembers feel like outsiders. You are already familiar with cliques at school. Workplaces have cliques too—small groups of employees often seen eating together, hanging out around a desk talking, or doing things together after work.

One unusual subunit of a group is the isolate, a person who is set apart from a group or withdraws from it. The isolate may be unwilling to participate, or the isolate may be ignored by other group members. Well-functioning groups are careful not to ignore any members, and they try to encourage reluctant or shy members to participate. Part of the responsibility for being a good communicator is to recognize the communication attempts of others and to encourage them to participate fully in discussions and decision making.

You already have experience being a member of formal and informal school groups and perhaps community or workplace groups. When you begin to work full-time, you will frequently find yourself on work teams. Your understanding of group roles and dynamics will help you and other team members work more effectively together. Your employer and co-workers will be impressed if you demonstrate the ability to stay focused on the task and contribute constructively.

Group and Team Communication

Group Meeting Procedures

It would be wonderful if group members showed up for a meeting, talked for a little while, solved a problem or made a plan, and left satisfied. Life is just not that easy! Many groups experience conflict or frustration as members struggle to reach a goal. A set of problem-solving steps and an agenda can help structure a group's meetings and keep the group moving toward a goal.

Six Steps of Problem Solving

Good problem solving involves the following steps: (1) Identify the problem. (2) Analyze the problem. (3) Set criteria for a solution. (4) Develop solutions. (5) Select a solution. (6) Evaluate the solution. Let's look briefly at each step.

Identify the Problem

Fuzzy problems result in fuzzy solutions. In other words, a group must first clearly identify what their problem is. For example, the task of finding housing for members of a high school band who are participating in the Rose Bowl Parade needs to be identified in more detail. How many rooms will be needed? How many days will the students be in Pasadena? How much money will be needed?

Analyze the Problem

Group members need to understand any background information, regulations or restrictions, and past attempts to address similar problems that worked or failed. Part of this stage is researching the issues. The student/parent housing committee needs to learn about any school rules for housing students, the available hotels in Pasadena and their rates, and so forth. They may try to learn what other school districts have done or how the school has handled sending student groups in the past. After the members have done their research, they need to establish ways to find an appropriate solution.

Effective groups analyze a problem thoroughly— researching background information, checking facts and figures, and studying past efforts at solutions.

Set Criteria for a Solution

The group then needs to decide what would make a solution workable. In other words, they have to determine the criteria or standards for a good solution. To decide how to supply housing for the band, the housing committee will have to set standards for where band members can be housed, how many students can be housed in one location, how many locations are practical, and whether or not parent chaperones will be expected to pay for their housing. The group

Justin O'Malley,
Riding Academy Attendant

Justin O'Malley spends most of his nonschool time involved in the program called Central Kentucky Riding for the Handicapped. He has ridden horses for 14 years (almost his entire life) and has never tired of it. He has worked with his instructor, John Low, for a long time and with many wonderful volunteers as well.

Justin has cerebral palsy, and he works in therapy to improve his muscle movements and his balance. He says, "When I ride horses, I feel like I'm riding with the wind. It gives me a chance to feel what it's like to walk and keep your balance. It makes me feel I'm on an even level with everybody."

Justin rides every week and continues to take lessons to improve his skill. He is able to serve as a support person at the stables, which means he helps to walk the horses and to care for them. Because Justin is so experienced at the stables, newcomers ask him questions about the horses and the program.

Although he rides quite a few horses and enjoys all of them, his special horse at the stables is "Tiny," a quarter horse that is really quite large.

He enjoys the control of being able to tell the horse what to do, but he adds that the horse and rider work together as a team and "in essence we become one."

Sometimes groups from the stables ride together, which, according to Justin, requires "a great deal of communication and teamwork to do successfully." He explains that everybody in the group needs to be able to follow instructions and know what they're supposed to do so that the group stays together. Otherwise, individuals become separated from the group and go off on their own.

When Justin is not at the stables, he can be found working as a locker room monitor at the pool, where he is expected to keep track of swimmers' belongings. He also performs general cleaning and maintenance work on the pool. In these situations, he has learned that communication is vital for dealing with the public successfully.

Student Worker Profile

may decide on the following criteria: Locate housing within a 15-mile radius of the parade site, house large groups together, and pay for parent chaperones.

Develop Solutions

Group members then try to identify solutions and evaluate them according to the criteria. The housing committee might brainstorm many ideas and narrow them to two options: rent dorm space in a local college and hold a fund-raiser to collect money for all housing expenses, or try to identify families in the Pasadena area who would be willing to house the band members for free.

Select a Solution

To decide what solution should be adopted, a group needs to determine which solutions meet the criteria and what the strengths and weaknesses of each solution are. The housing committee might decide that finding a local college to house students and parents is more practical and efficient than trying to line up many private families to serve as hosts.

Evaluate the Solution

As the group tries to implement the solution, they will be able to evaluate its success. If they find a local college within a reasonable distance, they may be very successful. If the only college is 60 miles away, they may have to try another solution. A great deal of effort goes into reaching a workable solution. Effective groups move thoughtfully through these problem-solving steps and repeat them as needed if a particular solution doesn't work.

> **Remember!**
>
> The six steps of problem solving are
>
> ▶ Identify the problem.
>
> ▶ Analyze it.
>
> ▶ Set criteria for a solution.
>
> ▶ Develop solutions
>
> ▶ Select one.
>
> ▶ Evaluate it.

An agenda gives group members a convenient structure to follow during a meeting, and it provides the leader with a framework for keeping members focused on the task.

Following an Agenda

In formal groups, particularly those that meet regularly, meetings sometimes involve announcements and reports from individual members. Usually the leader prepares an **agenda** or outline of the meeting so members know what will be discussed and in what order. Sometimes the leader includes the amount of time available to discuss a particular topic.

An agenda, available in advance of a meeting, accomplishes several purposes. It helps group members come to a meeting prepared. It allows a member who is anxious about speaking to think through his or her ideas ahead of time. It gives members a convenient structure to follow, and it provides the leader with a framework for keeping members focused on the task.

Group Evaluation

Competent communicators evaluate the effectiveness of the group process regularly, whether formally or informally. Effective groups take time to review their overall performance, and responsible members take time to review their individual contributions. Then they make changes based on what they learn to improve the effectiveness of their group interaction. The following group evaluation forms can help you do both. Use the first form to evaluate the effectiveness of a group as a whole. Use the second form to evaluate your own contributions to a group effort.

Group Evaluation Form

	Never	Sometimes	Usually	Always
Members knew what was expected of them.	☐	☐	☐	☐
Members came prepared to do their part.	☐	☐	☐	☐
Members aided each other when necessary.	☐	☐	☐	☐
Members supported and encouraged each other.	☐	☐	☐	☐
Members were willing to adjust plans as needed.	☐	☐	☐	☐

Self Evaluation in a Group

	Never	Sometimes	Usually	Always
I came prepared for what I needed to do.	☐	☐	☐	☐
I worked hard to analyze ideas.	☐	☐	☐	☐
I paid attention to others' ideas and aided others when they needed help.	☐	☐	☐	☐
I indicated when I needed help.	☐	☐	☐	☐
I played more than one role.	☐	☐	☐	☐
I supported and encouraged the efforts of others.	☐	☐	☐	☐
I rethought my ideas in order to reach the best conclusion.	☐	☐	☐	☐
I contributed actively until the task was completed.	☐	☐	☐	☐

Eye-to-Eye

In groups of three, make a plan for coordinating a visit of six international students from Thailand to your school for two days. The purpose of the visit is to understand what American students experience as their typical day in school. Your team will be totally responsible for the visiting students from 8 A.M. to 5 P.M. each day. Develop a list of the activities you would like them to experience, and list the people in school that you will need on your team to execute the plan. Make a schedule for each day.

Communication Networks

Communication networks are the means by which messages move through groups and organizations, often in predictable ways. There are two basic types of networks—formal and informal.

Formal Networks

Formal networks send information throughout an organization using downward or upward message directions. Think of a formal network as a chain of command. Formal networks are regularly used in business. They convey messages from superiors to subordinates and from subordinates to superiors. They also convey messages through announcements, procedure manuals, e-mail messages, employee handbooks, bulletin boards, and annual reports.

Informal Networks

Informal networks send information throughout an organization based on relational connections between people, not on power in an organization. Sometimes this is called the "grapevine." There are "insiders" who seem to have important information, so you turn to them for the latest news or the "right" way to do something. Rumors and gossip travel through informal networks. Very often, informal networks scoop a formal network as secrets and private information travel around before any official announcement is made. It is through informal networks that you learn that Mrs. Rajadurai won the Teacher of the Year Award or that Mitch got a promotion days before either has been officially announced. Sometimes this process is called back-channel conversation.

Check It Out

Take 15 minutes to study the message direction and network models used by an extracurricular group—the newspaper staff, a band meeting, the chess club, for example. Describe examples of specific messages moving through the group. Note who said what to whom, and identify the type of network being used.

Group Leadership

The quality of leadership strongly affects a group's ability to solve problems. Good leaders are competent communicators because they speak and listen responsibly. They recognize the strengths of group members and work to create ways for members to emphasize their strengths. Good leaders constantly think, "How can I help this group do its best work at problem solving?"

In the workplace, title, status, or expertise frequently determines who leads a team.

Becoming a Leader

There are several ways a group member might become a leader. Leaders may be appointed, they may be elected or chosen by the group, or they may gradually emerge from the group. On occasion, more than one leader will take responsibility for moving the group toward its goal.

Appointed Leaders

Sometimes a person in authority chooses group leaders. Appointed leaders are designated by someone in authority. A teacher may appoint leaders for classroom discussion groups; the president of an organization may ask another officer, such as the vice president, to head a committee. In the workplace, title, status, or expertise frequently determines who leads a group or team.

Chosen Leaders

Chosen leaders are selected by other group members. Often sports teams elect their own captain and extracurricular clubs elect their officers. Workplace team leaders may be elected or informally chosen by team members on the basis of their knowledge related to the team's task and goals. Usually, chosen leaders have strong group support, but if they are chosen on the basis of popularity, not competence, that support may disappear quickly. Effective chosen leaders frequently serve as role models or mentors to less experienced members.

Emerging Leaders

Emerging leaders move into their positions on the basis of their behavior in a group. When no one is appointed or chosen, the group may discover that one person has taken on the moderator role naturally by using procedural comments and other communication skills to guide the group through its task. In many cases this individual emerges as the leader. In other cases individual group members may resist this person's efforts and compete for the position themselves. On occasion two people might share leadership functions—one might keep the group on task while the other provides support and social connections.

Leadership Styles

Leadership styles range from high control to low control. A high-control leader, sometimes called an authoritarian, influences all group actions. He or she serves as the sole moderator and holds much of the power in decision making. A high-control leader manages all interaction and guides the group toward conclusions he or she thinks are correct.

Moderate-control leaders offer direction when the group needs it. They encourage group members to voice opinions, express disagreements, and to act in the moderator role on occasion. These leaders work to see that all members have a voice and that the discussion moves along.

Low-control leaders tend to empower group members to take control of their efforts. They attempt to locate the strengths or gifts of group members and encourage the use of these gifts. The moderator role is shared with all members. Often these leaders appear to fade into the background as the group moves along with its task.

Workplace studies reveal some gender differences in leadership style. The more masculine models of leadership are based on a competitive style and a highly rational approach. The more feminine models focus on cooperation, teamwork, and shared control. Research has shown that the most competent leaders use both styles or use more of one style based on the situation. Effective organizations support a communication climate that allows diverse leadership styles.

Leadership Responsibilities

Leadership responsibilities fall into the general areas of beginning the discussion, acting as moderator, and closing the discussion.

Beginning the Discussion

The leader begins by introducing the topic, introducing the members, or beginning the discussion. To introduce the topic, the leader may state the question or explain to the group or audience why the discussion is taking place. If team members do not know each other well, the leader may spend part of the first meeting helping members get acquainted. The leader may suggest who will speak first or what part of the topic will be discussed—for example, "First we'll discuss the problem of getting volunteers to the Special Olympics Stadium," or

"M. J. will describe our problems." If there is no designated leader, someone in the group may emerge as a leader by taking over some of these duties.

Acting as Moderator

Leaders act as moderators for all or part of the discussion. A moderator tries to keep the discussion on track and moving forward. If the group has not finished analyzing a problem, and someone interrupts with a solution, the leader might say, "That's an interesting point, Jack. Maybe you could bring that up again when we get to a discussion of solutions."

Leaders also make sure everyone contributes. This means preventing one or two members from talking all the time and encouraging quiet members to share their ideas. The leader may support valuable ideas by saying, "I'm really glad you said that. We hadn't thought of that idea."

Closing the Discussion

Leaders must watch the clock so the task can be completed before the group runs out of time. It's frustrating to spend 40 minutes discussing a problem and then to have only 10 minutes to solve it. As the group concludes its work, the leader often provides a general wrap-up or summary.

Seating Arrangements and Leadership

It is important for leaders to pay attention to how people sit in a group, because this can affect their communication within the group. Generally, when a group sits in a circle, all members are naturally included because of the directness of eye contact and equal physical distance. When the group sits at a rectangular table, the people on the ends are best able to gain eye contact with all other members. Sometimes a leader will sit in the middle of a semicircle. This is an effective arrangement for meetings that involve giving instructions or directions. Managers frequently conduct workplace meetings standing up because studies show that standing during meetings makes the meetings shorter, and the quality of decision making is just as good as when employees sit. (Employees learn to wear comfortable shoes to these meetings!) Effective group leaders choose a seating (or standing) arrangement that best suits the group's purpose.

Evaluating Leadership Skills

A good leader can always become a better leader. Competent leaders evaluate their own performances in order to improve their skills. You can use the checklist on page 209 to examine your own leadership skills.

Leadership Skills Self-Evaluation Form

	Never	Sometimes	Usually	Always
1. I try to include everyone in the discussion.	☐	☐	☐	☐
2. I guide the group through an agenda or through problem-solving steps.	☐	☐	☐	☐
3. I try to help members compromise or create new ideas.	☐	☐	☐	☐
4. I try to control excessive talkers.	☐	☐	☐	☐
5. I work to draw out quiet members.	☐	☐	☐	☐
6. I try to keep the group on the topic.	☐	☐	☐	☐
7. I encourage members to express differing opinions.	☐	☐	☐	☐
8. I encourage members to play different roles.	☐	☐	☐	☐
9. I watch the time limits.	☐	☐	☐	☐
10. I introduce the topic and close the discussion.	☐	☐	☐	☐

Public Discussion Formats

Although most groups meet in private, some groups use various public formats to discuss their ideas and reach conclusions. These formats include committees, panel discussions, and symposiums.

Committees

A **committee** is usually a subgroup formed to study or manage a specific task. If the large group has a problem for which it needs more information, it may form a committee of a few members to study the problem. That committee researches the problem and recommends an action for the group to approve.

Usually committee meetings are closed, but occasionally they are public. Although an audience may be present, audience members do not take part in the discussion.

Career Communication *Events Coordinator*

A public-relations events coordinator listens carefully, makes suggestions, negotiates, persuades, and manages teams toward one goal—satisfying the needs of a corporate client. This positon is tailor-made for those who enjoy meeting new people and who thrive on change, creativity, and stress. One month an events coordinator might be managing a convention at a hotel. Another month he or she might coordinate a national sales meeting kickoff or a corporate press conference to announce a new line of computer games.

Listening is a primary communication skill needed by an

events coordinator because he or she is responsible for creating the exact event a client desires.

Once an event is in the planning stages, the coordinator contacts specialists such as florists, rental companies, caterers, hotel managers, and theatrical and musical agents. He

or she manages a team of assistants who do most of the legwork—making deliveries, checking out convention facilities, and setting up displays. It is the coordinator's responsibility to make sure that the team is operating smoothly. During the event, the coordinator is a "trouble-shooter"—the person who handles the unexpected, last-minute problems, ranging from delayed speakers and missing flowers to broken-down buses and locked rooms. Effective coordinators solve these problems quietly, efficiently, and out of the public eye in an effort to make the client look good.

Panel Discussions

During a **panel discussion**, a subject is explored by the group members addressing an audience. A panel discussion format allows the speakers to inform or influence the audience. Most panels have four to eight members. Members of a panel make statements, ask questions, and comment on what other panel members have said. Usually a panel discussion has a leader, called a chairperson, whose job is to introduce the panel members and the subject, define important terms, call on speakers, and review points. Panel members are expected to be experts in their subject areas. At the end of a panel discussion, participants will devote time to evaluating the ideas that have been presented. Many governing bodies use panels to publicly talk about civic issues. These discussions often occur before citizen groups.

Symposiums

A **symposium** is a discussion during which members give short speeches to an audience. A symposium is more formal than a panel discussion. Each expert gives a speech representing a different point of view on the subject being discussed. Unlike a panel, speakers usually don't talk with one another unless there is a question-and-answer period following each speech. As with a panel, the leader introduces the symposium members and topics. The leader also closes the symposium by briefly summarizing the speeches.

Sometimes audience members take part in panel discussions or symposiums. When the audience becomes involved, the discussion is called a **forum**. Audience members can ask questions of the persons presenting the information. Usually the questions are asked at the end, but sometimes there is a question-and-answer period after each speaker's comments.

In some panel discussions and symposiums, time is allowed for audience members to form small groups, called buzz groups. **Buzz groups** discuss the ideas presented by the speakers and decide on possible solutions to issues raised. Buzz groups often use **brainstorming**—the process of quickly generating as many ideas as possible without evaluating them—to come up with a variety of solutions. After they have had an opportunity to discuss the issues, the audience comes back together for a final discussion.

Chapter 8 *Chapter Summary*

In this chapter you learned about group and team communication. A group consists of people who communicate with each other over time and share a common purpose. Groups can have a formal or informal structure.

Groups use the following communication skills to encourage problem solving: giving information, questioning, supporting, contradicting, evaluating, and procedural statements.

People play many roles in a group. The most common roles are experts, supporters, questioners, challengers, moderators, collaborators, and tension relievers. Some common factors that influence the role a group member plays are self-image, others' expectations, and one's ability and knowledge. Successful groups follow a six-step process for solving problems.

Formal communication networks send information upward or downward through an organization. Informal networks send information based on relational connections among people in an organization.

Group leaders may be appointed or chosen, or they may emerge gradually from the group. A leader's responsibilities include starting discussions, acting as moderator, and closing discussions. The way members are physically arranged in a meeting will influence the communication within the group.

Three common formats for public group meetings are committees, panel discussions, and symposiums. Forums are panel discussions or symposiums that include audience participation.

Review Questions

1. What is a group? What is a workplace team?
2. How are groups generally structured?
3. What are some typical norms for groups?
4. Name the types of group roles. Which role do you most often play?
5. What factors influence the roles people play in groups?
6. List the six steps of problem solving.
7. What is the difference between formal and informal networks?
8. How does a person become a leader in a group?
9. According to research, how do male and female leadership styles differ? What style should a competent leader use?
10. What are a group leader's duties?

Critical Thinking Activities

Speaking/Doing

1. Cut out pictures and photos from old newspapers and magazines that illustrate different kinds of groups—formal and informal groups, social groups, workplace teams, business groups, public forums, and so on. Present your pictures to the class, describing what you know about each group based on what each picture reveals.
2. Make a poster showing three different kinds of group seating arrangements. Identify where the leader sits in each diagram. Include information that describes the advantages and disadvantages of each arrangement.

Writing

1. Prepare an agenda for a meeting. It can be for a club to which you belong, for your church youth group, or for co-workers at your job. Plan to fill one hour with discussion and/or business.
2. In two paragraphs, describe an informal and a formal group in your school or community. What is each group's goal? How effective is each group at reaching that goal? Would changing group structure improve the effectiveness of either group?

Group Activities

1. In a group of five to seven students, plan an activity for your classmates that can be performed inside your classroom,

take no longer than 15 minutes, involve all class members, and remain within the bounds of standard class rules for noise and behavior. After the planning meeting, evaluate the effectiveness of the meeting itself. Were goals clearly set? How was leadership determined? At the end of the actual activity, evaluate the success of the group. Did the team members work well together? Did the team accomplish their goals?

2. In a group of five to seven students, discuss a current problem at your school. Use the problem-solution process to propose a solution to the problem. Write a report to your principal describing the problem and your proposed solution.

3. Form a panel of three to five students. Select a controversial topic that is important to your group. Each member of the panel should prepare a presentation discussing some aspect of the problem. Members of the panel do not need to share the same point of view on the issue. Have each panel member present his or her case in front of the class. Allow time for panel members to discuss each other's ideas. If time permits, invite questions and comments from the class.

Practical Application: Case Challenge

As part of their college work-study funding package, Carma and Renaldo agreed to set up an after-school reading program for fourth- to sixth-grade students. Two local high school students, Art and Dan, volunteered to help plan the program. Carma and Renaldo talked with faculty members at the college about how to set up such a program. One professor gave them a list of good books to consider for the age group. Another gave them advice on how to set up the program. When the four team members sat down to plan, part of the discussion sounded like this:

RENALDO: So, we have a list of recommended books, and we will order 15 of them.

ART: What are they?

RENALDO: I don't remember right now, but they are good.

DAN: Are there Goosebumps books?

CARMA: I don't think so.

DAN: My brother is that age, and he loves Harry Potter.

RENALDO: Well, I think we should use the reading list from the college. The professors know what is appropriate for kids this age.

ART: Any books on snow-boarding?

CARMA: This is supposed to be good literature. . . .

Even though this discussion has just begun, it is apparent that there are some problems with the group interaction on this team. What advice would you give the four students to help them work more efficiently as a team?

Conflict and Conflict Management

Objectives

After completing this chapter, you will be able to

- define conflict and its characteristics
- describe and give examples of different conflict styles
- describe win/win and win/lose outcomes
- describe patterns of ongoing conflict
- describe how gender, culture, and workplace culture affect conflict
- describe destructive conflict strategies
- describe and demonstrate constructive conflict strategies
- describe negotiation, mediation, and group consensus building

Key Terms

collaborating

conflict

group consensus building

gunnysacking

labeling

mediation

negotiation

win/lose outcome

win/win outcome

> 66 The best way I know how to defeat an enemy is to make him a friend. 99
>
> —ABRAHAM LINCOLN

Surviving New-Roommate Struggles

As college juniors, Cherisse and Bryan were first-year resident assistants in a student dormitory. Their jobs provided them with a way to earn free room and food, as well as the opportunity to explore a human relations career. More than 100 new RAs were selected after a long interview process, and they participated in three weeks of training before the dorms actually opened. After Cherisse and Bryan were assigned to a third-floor hall, they worked together to orient freshmen and to welcome back returning sophomores. During the opening weeks, they encountered a number of complaints, but nothing that was difficult to resolve. The residents in room 26 argued over music choices, and those in room 17 complained about noise in the hallways. Cherisse and Bryan knew from their training that the third week of the new semester marks a predictable time for differences to erupt among freshmen in the dorm. They were warned to pay careful attention to building tensions among roommates and to encourage residents to deal with their differences before they got out of hand.

By the fourth week things had heated up. Marnie asked for a transfer because her roommate, Pamela, never stayed in the room, and Marnie felt isolated. Pamela complained that Marnie was "hanging on me," and she wanted to be with her hometown friends, who were in another dorm. Adam and Nick almost came to blows because Adam, a serious pre-med student, claimed Nick regularly came back to their room loudly at 2 or 3 A.M., called his friends, and kept Adam awake. When Adam complained, Nick swore at him. Molly and Sumi argued constantly because Sumi claimed Molly was a total slob. Five rooms at the end of the hall submitted a petition to limit the constant loud music coming from a room across the courtyard.

Cherisse and Bryan held discussions—individually and together—with these residents. In one discussion, Cherisse explained to Marnie and Pamela that, according to university regulations, they had to remain together for the first eight weeks and that finding different space in the dorm for Marnie would be difficult. Cherisse encouraged Marnie and Pamela to talk about their feelings. Marnie said she had looked forward to having a roommate who would be a good friend and she felt rejected by Pamela. Pamela said she wanted to be with her high school friends but she felt pressured by Marnie to do things together. The three women discussed some ways to resolve this situation, at least for the next four weeks. The roommates talked about having dinner together in the cafeteria once a week, and Pamela asked Marnie if she wanted to go to a weekly volunteer tutoring program with Pamela and her friends. Marnie agreed and asked if Cherisse would help her connect to some other people in the dorm.

Bryan held a number of discussions with Adam and Nick, explaining that they had to find a way to work out their problems. They discussed how Nick could make phone calls in the lounge. Nick said Adam could wear earplugs, as some of the other residents did. Bryan told Nick he would have to talk with a campus counselor or Nick would be asked to leave student housing.

Bryan also talked with Molly and Sumi about their room. Sumi described how depressing it was to enter such a pigpen every day, and Molly talked about how she hated feeling guilty every time she left a shirt on the floor. They discussed options, such as totally separating the space or having a cleaning hour twice a week.

Both Cherisse and Bryan met with the residents across the courtyard and with their RAs to discuss the disturbance they were creating with their loud music. Within an hour they came up with several strategies to resolve the problem to everyone's satisfaction.

What communication skills do Cherisse and Bryan need to do their jobs well? Which strategies noted in the case study seem reasonable for the various problems described? What ideas would you suggest to any of these roommates?

Introduction to Conflict

No two people see the world exactly the same way. These differences among people frequently lead to conflict. The word *conflict* does not refer only to major fights and battles. **Conflict** occurs when two or more people believe that their beliefs or desires are incompatible. Conflicts range from minor differences of opinion, to serious disagreements, to painful, relationship-threatening battles. As you consider the relationship between conflict and communication, you need to remember three points: conflict is normal, conflict can have positive and/or negative results, and conflict can be managed.

Conflict Is Normal

Conflicts are normal because people have different needs, desires, and values. Every day you deal with small differences of opinion or times when people's desires are incompatible. It's part of life. Hiding negative feelings is unrealistic and keeps issues from being discussed or resolved.

Conflicts Have Positive and/or Negative Results

Conflict helps people grow personally and interpersonally. Your conflicts give you feedback on what is important to you and help you learn how to live and work with people who are different from you. Both interpersonal and group conflicts can help you know others better and deepen your relationships. Initial differences do not determine the future of all relationships.

When you date someone, disagreements help you know the other person better. These struggles can deepen your relationship or help you decide to end it. When your friends try to convince you to do something you don't want to do, the conversation helps you evaluate your relationship. When you disagree with someone in the workplace on how to solve a problem, the discussion may create new and valuable solutions.

On the other hand, conflict can create so much tension that people separate or avoid each other. This frequently happens when disagreements get personal and involve name calling, blaming, threats, or put-downs. Sometimes such tactics cause shame or hurt to the other person, who then retaliates with anger or force. Conflicts become negative when a disagreement between two individuals spills over to become a group battle, with friends taking sides.

When you are involved in a painful conflict in your personal life, you can deal with it by avoiding the other person. Some people do this by concentrating on their work responsibilities. They use work as a distraction from their

No two people see things exactly the same. These differences among people frequently lead to conflict.

personal conflict. When you are involved in a painful workplace conflict, however, it must be confronted. You can't avoid your co-workers.

Conflicts Can Be Managed

Some people claim, "I can't change the way I feel or how I fight. It's just the way I am." This suggests that humans cannot change. However, competent communicators know that people can improve their interactions, including the way they disagree. But changing your conflict behaviors is not easy; it requires self-analysis, self-restraint, and practice. It also requires an examination of the ethics you live by. As you will see, some ways of dealing with conflict can hurt another person; other ways may involve serious disagreement and even anger but maintain respect for the other person. Even in the heat of anger, competent communicators select constructive strategies for dealing with conflict—strategies that reflect their ethical standards.

Every year workplace managers spend millions of dollars to provide employees with educational programs on management of anger and conflict, constructive criticism, and strategies for creative conflict. These educational programs help employees find new ways to resolve differences.

Review the following statements to see how you manage conflict. Respond to each statement with *never, sometimes, usually*, or *always*.

I try to avoid conflict.
I tend to explode with anger and regret it later.
I react to criticism with defensiveness.
I take my anger out on the wrong people.
I avoid difficult people.
I hold back ideas because I don't want to have to fight for them.
I get uncomfortable when someone else yells or seems really angry.

Conflict and Conflict Management

If you responded *usually* or *always* to most of the statements in the check-list, you need to develop more constructive conflict strategies. In the following pages you will learn about different conflict styles, conflict outcomes, and conflict stages. You will also learn about ways to manage conflict. Applying some of these strategies to conflict situations of your own will help you become a more competent communicator.

Check It Out

Think about how you view conflict. What are three words that describe your reaction to being in a disagreement? You may use words from the following list or other ones. Write one sentence explaining each word choice.

excited	challenged	uncomfortable	nervous
scared	good	angry	objective

Conflict Styles

Each person develops one or more conflict styles, which are predictable ways of handling conflict. Your usual style may shift somewhat as you come into disagreement with specific people. Your style changes because of the transactional nature of communication. You adapt your style to the specific conflict and the specific person. There are five common conflict styles: competing, compromising, collaborating, giving in, and avoiding.

Competing

Competing means working to win. When you compete, you go after what you want without considering the needs or feelings of anyone else. You are concerned about yourself and about winning, whether it's a game, an argument, or getting what you want. A totally competing style implies an "I win and you lose" approach. Comments such as "You're wrong," "That's a stupid idea," or "I'm right! There is only one way" tell you that competing is going on. Competitors are not motivated to listen to other ideas because they don't acknowledge points on the other side of a conflict.

Compromising

Compromising means meeting the other person halfway or looking for the middle ground between your opposing positions. Compromising means finding a 50-50 solution. It's a half win/half lose solution that partly meets the needs of each person. Comments such as "So what do you want?" or "Let's split the difference" indicate compromise. Each person walks away partially satisfied.

Collaborating

Collaborating occurs when you are looking for a solution that will really satisfy both people. Each person is concerned about himself or herself *and* about the other person. Collaborating means trying to find a win/win or an "I win and you win" solution. It requires "out-of-the-box," or creative, thinking. Comments such as "Have you ever considered . . ." or "Let's rethink this whole thing from another angle" are signs of collaborating. When collaborators think "out of the box," it means they go beyond the obvious, limited alternatives. The goal is to find a solution that is satisfying for all individuals.

Giving In

Giving in suggests that you put the needs of the other person first. You do not look out for yourself. You are overly cooperative, denying your own needs while trying to make others happy. Comments such as "Fine. I can live with that," "Have it your way," or "I don't care" display an attempt to end a disagreement by giving in. This style may make you look good, but at times it indicates you are not taking care of yourself. It's OK to give in on occasion, but choose which battles you are going to walk away from. If you always give in, you may find that people will take advantage of you.

Avoiding

Avoiding suggests that you withdraw and do not participate in disagreements. You move away either by physically leaving or by emotionally shutting down and ignoring the other person. You become passive and do not make an effort

A totally competing style implies an "I win and you lose" approach. Competitors in the workplace don't acknowledge arguments on the other side of a conflict.

Remember!

Five common conflict styles are

▶ Competing

▶ Compromising

▶ Collaborating

▶ Giving in

▶ Avoiding

to resolve the conflict. Comments such as "You don't need me" and "Just decide and tell me later," or nonverbal cues such as physically leaving, turning away, closing a notebook and capping a pen, or staring into space indicate that the person is avoiding the disagreement. Avoiding conflict is a very destructive strategy. It can be thought of as an "I lose and you lose" situation. It leaves both you and the other person unsatisfied and frustrated.

Factors That Influence Conflict Styles

Gender and culture, as well as specific workplace cultures, influence styles of conflict. In our culture many, but not all, males and females receive different messages from their families and society about dealing with conflict. Traditionally, males are taught not to talk about problems. But they are also taught to assert their opinions and, if necessary, to use a competing style to win. Traditionally, females are taught to talk about problems as a way of resolving conflicts. They are more likely to use a compromising or giving-in style. Yet, each person is different, and you may find that these general statements do not apply to you or some of your friends.

Culture can also influence conflict style, especially if one has a very strong ethnic heritage. Just as with gender issues, cultural issues do not apply to every member of a group. Various cultures value different approaches to dealing with conflict. For example, Japanese culture stresses harmony, saving face, and avoiding direct conflict. Nonverbal cues may be used to indicate displeasure.

Workplace culture also affects how employees manage conflicts. Although in most workplaces people try to get along and find workable solutions to their conflicts, in some places employees withdraw or yell at each other regularly. In most workplaces, emotional displays such as crying or yelling are unacceptable, but in some workplaces open conflict is common. In high-stress, deadline-driven organizations such as sales, theater, advertising, and journalism, it is predictable that employees will experience times of direct conflict. Often, the personality of a boss sets the tone. If the boss yells or argues loudly, it may be seen as acceptable workplace behavior.

Eye-to-Eye

With a partner, watch a film involving an interpersonal conflict, or observe different people as they deal with disagreements. Identify one or two conflict styles that are exhibited in each disagreement. Include some sample comments or actions to justify your decisions.

Out-of-the-box thinking has a win/win goal. It reflects a collaborative approach to resolving conflict. Everybody wins. Nobody loses.

Win/Lose vs. Win/Win Outcomes

A **win/lose outcome** means that a conflict is resolved with only one person being satisfied. The other person is left unsatisfied. A **win/win outcome** means that the conflict is resolved to the mutual satisfaction of all individuals. Outcomes of conflicts are sometimes talked about using the metaphor of a box. A box suggests a closed approach. If one person wins, the other must lose. Even if a compromise is reached, it still leaves both individuals only half satisfied.

The key question is "Can the box be opened up?" In other words, can you find a new way to think about the problem so that both people go away completely satisfied and neither has to lose? This type of thinking is called *out-of-the-box* thinking.

Out-of-the-box thinking has a win/win goal. It often reflects a collaborating approach. Collaboration involves hard work and a certain amount of risk. A classic story illustrating this approach involves a quarrel over 40 crates of oranges:

Two businesspeople, A and B, each wanted the same 40 crates of oranges. This conflict was seen as a win/lose situation. After much argument, A finally asked B why he needed the oranges. B answered, "I need the rind for the spices I make." "What do you do with the pulp?" asked A. "I throw it out," B replied. A explained, "I need the oranges for my juice company. I use the pulp and throw away the rind." Suddenly inspiration struck. A and B realized each needed different parts of the same oranges. They agreed to split the costs of the oranges, and each was happy. A got all the pulp, and B got all the rind.

Conflict and Conflict Management

This simple example demonstrates the value of understanding what each person really wants in a conflict situation.

Consider the following example of a win/win outcome. Suppose you and a co-worker both want the Fourth of July off. You and Blake work the afternoon shift in a small restaurant, and your boss wants to keep the restaurant open. It's a big day in your community, and you both want to go to the parade with your friends, but your boss has indicated that at least one of you will have to work that day. You each think this is a win/lose situation. If you get the Fourth of July off, Blake has to work. If Blake gets it off, you have to work. That's a closed-box situation: one person gets everything and the other gets nothing. Each of you is thinking of reasons why you should have the day off and the other person should work. Instead of thinking this way, what else might you consider? How might you change the outcome from a win/lose one to a win/win one? Possibilities include the following:

- One of you can trade the Fourth of July for another holiday you want more, such as Thanksgiving or New Year's Eve.
- You can ask another co-worker to work for both of you that day.
- You can suggest that your boss close the restaurant for a few hours, since customers will be at the parade.
- What else could you suggest?

Review the following statements to see how often you try to create win/win outcomes. Respond to each statement with *never, sometimes, usually,* or *always.*

I discuss issues with others to find a solution we can all live with.
I exchange information with others so that we can solve a problem effectively.
I try to find ways to integrate conflicting ideas.
I try to think creatively (out of the box) to find better solutions.

Often people in conflict with each other believe there are only two options: my way or your way. As you've seen so far, if you try to take a more collaborative approach, you may find there are five or six ways to reach mutually satisfying goals, but both parties have to be willing to consider them.

Eye-to-Eye

With a partner, try some out-of-the-box brainstorming for solutions to the following conflict between Jack and Jill, 17-year-old twins who share a car. What questions would you ask them? What possible solutions to their conflict might you explore?

Chapter Nine

> **Jill:** But I have to have the car on Friday night at 7. I'm driving four people to the Ani de Franco concert. Its 40 miles away, and we have tickets.
>
> **Jack:** The problem is, I'm working. Max said he'd pay me double to work Friday night, and I can't get there without a car. I agreed to close the recreation hall at 1 A.M., and I certainly can't walk home at 2 A.M.

Stages of Repeated Conflict

Many conflicts are actually ongoing problems that reappear regularly. You argue or fight over the same old things again and again. How many times does your mother or father get angry because you haven't cleaned your room? How often do you and a close friend get into a disagreement because one of you feels left out or put down? Look at the following model of stages of ongoing or predictable conflicts:

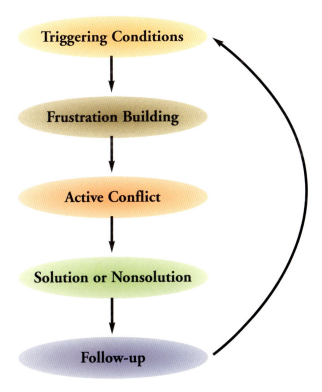

Triggering Conditions

Triggering conditions are comments or events that predictably occur before active disagreements. Triggers can be phrases such as "I don't want to hear that music in this house" or "You never listen to me." When statements like these are said in a negative tone by a particular person, you get angry. Certain events trigger tension. In the workplace, tension is created when unexpected crowds need to be served, when everyone is working toward a big deadline, or when your co-worker is late *again*. Competent communicators learn to recognize potential triggers. They may discuss solutions with others to try to reduce the tension that builds. For example, "Let's each buy only one person a gift" or "Let's use a number system so customers aren't yelling that they're next."

Frustration Building

Frustration building describes the period during which tensions rise. As you read the verbal or nonverbal signals of those around you, it becomes clear when they are getting upset. Your mother slams doors, your friend avoids you, or your boss starts to talk in an abrupt "yes" or "no" style. You may be sending out negative nonverbal or verbal cues but be unaware of your own tension. A friend says, "I can always tell when you are upset because you act all businesslike and don't smile." A co-worker says, "I can tell you're upset because you talk very fast and loud." Competent communicators recognize these signals. They try to stop the conflict from moving to the next stage. They may describe what they see by saying, "You seem upset. Want to talk about it?" or "Well, I guess we are back to doing inventory again. I hate it. How do you feel?" If attempts to discuss the tension are successful, the active conflict might be avoided because the tensions have been recognized and reduced.

Active Conflict

Active conflict occurs when all persons involved in the conflict recognize that a conflict exists. At this point, how the conflict is handled varies from one situation to another. Some co-workers stop talking to each other, some make sar-

When tensions begin to rise, you may be unaware that you are sending out negative nonverbal signals to your co-workers.

castic remarks, and some yell at one another. A friend either stops calling or tells you how angry he feels. You experience long silences or lengthy heated discussions.

Solution or Nonsolution

When you reach a solution or nonsolution, you either have found a way to settle the conflict, at least for the moment, or you have suspended the conflict because one of you is avoiding the issue or because both of you refuse to alter your positions. You have reached a solution when a co-worker says, "I'm sorry I yelled. I just got overwhelmed by pushy customers. You were right" or "Ignore me. I'm having a can't-do-anything-right day. I'll get over it." You have reached a nonsolution when one person says, "Don't bug me about this. I'm not feeling well. I'm going home," or "I refuse to deal with this now. I have to go to class," or when both of you insist, "I'm right and you're wrong. That's all there is to it!" Walking away from a conflict and refusing to look for ways to resolve the conflict in a mutually satisfying way are nonsolutions because, in both cases, nothing is resolved.

Follow-Up

At the follow-up stage, people reestablish connections. Friends might write a note or call each other. Co-workers might act more thoughtfully—for example, "I'll finish the billing" or "You want coffee?" Sometimes individuals will act formal or distant for a few days before things get back to normal. Usually, things are fine for a while, at least until another trigger condition appears, at which point these stages of conflict are acted out all over again.

Destructive Conflict Strategies

Destructive conflict strategies are attacks or attempts to hurt the other person in order to win. Such strategies include verbal attacks, gunnysacking, and physical attacks.

Verbal Attacks

Verbal attacks include name calling, labeling, put-downs, and hostile gossip. Such verbal attacks are usually accompanied by negative nonverbal cues such as eye rolling or loud or sarcastic vocal tones.

Peanuts reprinted by permission of United Feature Syndicate.

Name-Calling

Name-calling is attacking another person using emotional terms such as idiot, geek, jerk, and stupid, and it can have devastating results. It almost always leads to an increase in the conflict. Negative references to racial or cultural heritage are especially offensive forms of name calling. Negative words can have incredible power to hurt others when people use them against one another to gain an advantage in a conflict.

Labeling

Labeling, which is closely related to name calling, occurs when one person gives a derogatory evaluation of another person. You say, "You're lazy" rather than "You did not clean up your part of the project," or you say, "You cheated" rather than "You accepted pay for Friday night from two people." The labeling creates anger and hostility, even when the other person agrees with the facts behind the accusation. Negative names and labels are not easily forgotten. They stick long after an issue is resolved.

Put-Downs

Put-downs are sarcastic verbal suggestions that someone is incompetent, such as "If you want it done right, don't ask John" or "Miss know-it-all thinks she can do the whole project better without us." Frequently, put-downs are made in a sarcastic tone of voice. They convey negative evaluations that are intended to hurt self-esteem.

Hostile Gossip

Hostile gossip is deliberately passing along lies or half-truths to hurt another person. The speaker uses a communication network of friends or co-workers to damage another person's reputation. Many teenagers have experienced the powerful and painful effects of hostile gossip. It also damages workplace relations. Most workplaces strongly discourage hostile gossip. People who engage in this behavior hurt the productivity of their co-workers and hurt their own chances for promotion. Workplaces experience high employee turnover rates when hostile gossip is not stopped.

Gunnysacking

Gunnysacking means storing up your anger at someone and dumping it all at once when the other person does one more annoying thing. For example, three months of stored-up anger finally spills out all at once when a friend forgets to call you about weekend plans. Often the other person has a gunnysack too. He or she informs you that you borrowed five dollars and didn't pay it back or you blew off the movie plans. Suddenly you find yourself in a huge fight that seemed to start over something very small.

Physical Attacks

Sadly enough, verbal messages are not the only way to deal with conflict. Today, more and more people seem to be turning to fists or even guns to deal with problems rather than negotiations. In our society, more people are physically hurt by someone they know than by a stranger. This is true in general life and on the job. As a result, many places of business, both government workplaces and private companies, have instituted security measures to make their offices, factories, and stores safer places for both their employees and their customers. For example, some companies now require their employees to carry identification badges at all times. In addition, there may be security guards at entrances and doors that must be unlocked with special keys before entering. Companies may also require that job applicants undergo background checks before being hired, and employees may be required to undergo counseling if there are problems on the job. Physical attacks are an extreme example of destructive conflict strategies. Competent communicators find ways to avoid such strategies at all costs and to teach others to do so also.

Constructive Conflict Strategies

There are many ways to become more skilled at managing conflict. These include active listening, reversing roles, and following fair-fighting rules. Let's look more closely at each one.

Active Listening

Essentially, active listening involves understanding and being able to paraphrase the other person's point of view before offering your comments or presenting other ideas. It requires you to listen carefully to the other person's words and feelings. You learned and practiced this as you worked through Chapters 4, 5, and 6. When you use active listening effectively, many issues are resolved more quickly because both parties make the effort to understand the other person's point of view.

Reversing Roles

Sometimes the only way to really understand where someone else is coming from is to walk in his or her shoes. Reversing roles means deliberately taking the other person's point of view to try to understand that person's position. Both people role-play the other person for 5 or 10 minutes. For example, in a disagreement over curfew rules, you and your mother might reverse roles for a 10-minute discussion. A restaurant manager might ask an employee to reverse roles in a dispute over giving free food to friends. Reversing roles allows both individuals to experience the conflict from the other's point of view and often leads to a more reasonable resolution to a conflict.

Fair Fighting

Fair fighting involves using agreed-upon rules to reduce the use of destructive tactics. It is an attempt to avoid repeating the hurts of previous disagreements. Both people need to follow the rules of fair fighting, or this strategy won't work. Rules include the following:

1. *Stick to the present.* This rule keeps the disagreement focused on the current issue. The goal is to avoid bringing up previous disputes—for exam-

Kimberly Heard
Fire Department Paramedic

Serving as a doctor's eyes and ears in a medical emergency is a major challenge, but Kimberly Heard thrives on it. She holds the title Paramedic in Charge for the Chicago Fire Department and works at the Northside Headquarters for Emergency Medical Service. A former journalism major who changed careers, Ms. Heard spends a significant amount of time in ambulances and hospitals. Her main responsibility is patient care, which involves administering appropriate treatment in the ambulance and maintaining radio communication with the hospital during the ride, as well as reporting medical information to the hospital once the patient has arrived.

This position involves many communication challenges. According to Ms. Heard, "The hardest part is dealing with the patient's family." In her efforts to gather background information from family members, she sometimes encounters conflict. Family members are understandably upset in crisis situations, and they can become frustrated and impatient with questions that seem insignificant. Ms. Heard recognizes that "It's an emotional time" and family members can react in unpredictable ways. On occasion the paramedic team encounters cross-cultural communication problems when they try to treat a patient whose family does not speak English. Misunderstandings occur when the paramedics cannot explain what they are doing and when they can't get necessary medical information from the patient or family.

Sometimes people have expectations about how a paramedic should act based on watching television shows such as *ER* or *Chicago Hope*. When Ms. Heard and her partner follow steps according to their training, some family members tell them they are doing the wrong thing. She says that the communication skills needed to do her job include "knowing how to talk to people, knowing the right words to say, making sure you are accurate in what you are saying, and not being afraid to ask for help."

Often a patient's life depends on the medical and communication skills of a paramedic. Paramedics are in constant contact with doctors on the radio. Ms. Heard says that it is her responsibility to "paint a proper picture" of the

patient's condition so that the doctor can provide the greatest assistance possible. "If I paint an incorrect picture, the doctor may send me to the wrong hospital or give the wrong medication."

Many rewards come from being a paramedic. Ms. Heard very much enjoys the camaraderie with her co-workers. She has the feeling that "people are always there to help each other." Colleagues always know when someone has had a rough time, and they provide important support. She also values the role she plays in helping people survive life-and-death situations.

The World of Work

ple, "Two months ago you reported the wrong cash register figures." Bringing up past issues raises tension levels and makes solving the current problem almost impossible.

2. *Negotiate time and place.* This rule requires people to pay attention to their surroundings. Comments such as "We'll talk about that when we get home" or "See me after the meeting" are ways to avoid fighting in public. A boss may make it a policy never to yell at an employee in front of a customer.

3. *Describe, don't label or engage in name-calling.* This rule is the flip side of the destructive strategy of labeling. Friends or co-workers try to describe the behavior that makes them angry rather than calling someone "lazy," "careless," or "gearhead."

4. *Avoid pushing buttons.* People who know each other well know how to push one another's buttons. They know the words, phrases, or nonverbal cues that create tension in the other person. You may say, "Doesn't matter to me" to person A and it's fine. If you say the same thing to your father, he might explode because the words and your tone carry a specific meaning. Words such as "Fine," "Yeah," or "Whatever" or phrases such as "No big deal," "Isn't dinner ready yet?" "You're crazy like your sister," or "I'm sure you know best" can start verbal wars instantly.

When you are involved in a conflict, avoid destructive tactics such as bringing up past grievances, name-calling, and pushing buttons.

Career Communication *Family Therapist*

Unlike others in the helping professions who counsel one person at a time, the family therapist usually works with two or more people at a time. The therapist sees all members of a family together, at least part of the time. Family therapists may be clinical or counseling psychologists, social workers, or clinically trained religious leaders. They meet with clients to try to help them solve painful relationship problems.

Because they see whole families, these therapists try to get the family members to "do their number," or play out their unhealthy communication patterns during a session. This helps to demonstrate the family dynamics in action. For example, angry teenagers are encouraged to talk about their feelings in front of other family members. Frequently an acting-out teenager is seen as a sign that the family has problems, not just that the teenager has a problem. All family members are coached to talk with one another during a session. Sometimes sessions are filled with conflicts and anger and other times with silences or sadness. The goal is to find ways for family members to create a nurturing and healthy environment for each individual.

Family therapists must be highly skilled listeners because they hear many different versions of the same events. They try to draw out the nontalkers and to pay attention to the nonverbal clues of silent members. Many therapists teach conflict resolution skills to family members to help them fight fairly.

Negotiation, Mediation, and Group Consensus Building

Two formal processes for dealing with significant problems are negotiation and mediation. Each will be described briefly in this section. In addition, group consensus building will be discussed.

Negotiation

Sometimes conflicts get so complicated that people agree to negotiate their differences. **Negotiation** is a formal problem-solving process in which people voluntarily discuss their differences, work out a settlement, and come to an agreement. Both people must agree to the process. They must discuss their shared and opposing interests. True negotiation occurs in situations involving major ongoing issues that force people to find resolutions. Negotiation is commonly used to help deal with workplace problems. There are many models for nego-

Conflict and Conflict Management

tiation. The following model, created by D. W. Johnson and R. T. Johnson, includes six steps: (1) State what you want. (2) State how you feel. (3) State the reasons for your wants and feelings. (4) State your understanding of the other person's position. (5) Create some plans to resolve the conflict. (6) Choose one of the plans.

Let's look at how these steps work with a real issue. Imagine that you told your boss months ago that you would be leaving your summer job at the amusement park one week before the start of school so that you could go on a vacation with your family. Now your boss says you have to work that last week because other co-workers have quit. The following steps show how you might negotiate a solution with your boss:

1. *State what you want.* "I want to leave work the third week in August."
2. *State how you are feeling.* "I am really frustrated."
3. *State the reasons for your wants and feelings.* "These plans were agreed to in May when I returned for the summer. My family made their vacation plans around my work schedule."
4. *State your understanding of the other person's position.* "I know you have a problem because Jody quit and you will be shorthanded."
5. *Create some plans to resolve the conflict.* "I can find you two friends to split my job for the week. They will require supervision. Or I can stay through the weekend, and our family can delay leaving until Sunday night instead of Saturday morning. The rest of that next week won't be busy. You won't really need me those days."
6. *Choose one* and agree to try it.

Check It Out

Read the following comments and rearrange them to match the appropriate order of the six negotiating steps.

- "You have been asking me to fill out and sign time sheets, to schedule workers, and to take money to the bank. I'm doing Sally's job but for a much lower salary."
- Choose one.
- "You could give me a raise until the position is filled. You could consider me for Sally's position. You could spread the work among all the employees."
- "I want to be paid at a higher level because you have been asking me to do manager-type work since Sally left."
- "I imagine that you are hoping to hire Sally's replacement soon, so you don't want to change things and you are frustrated with being shorthanded."
- "I am feeling unappreciated for my extra work."

Mediation

Mediation involves using an objective or neutral third person, called a mediator, to help others resolve their conflict. In school, many issues begin as "he said"/"she said" accusations. In some schools, students turn to mediation when they worry that what started as rumor or name calling is going to escalate. Peer mediation refers to using another student or co-worker as the mediator rather than a teacher or boss. Comments that might indicate the need for a peer mediator include

- "She's always making smart remarks about me in front of my friends."
- "He's always grabbing my wallet or hiding my stuff."
- "She's always talking behind my back and rolling her eyes when she sees me."
- "He's always putting me down in front of the other employees."

The mediator listens to each person's view, helps them talk with each other to clarify the problem, suggests solutions, and eventually creates a solution both agree to follow. This agreement becomes a contract kept by the mediator.

Group Consensus Building

Group consensus building provides a framework for creating a win/win solution that combines creative contributions from all group members. The goal of group consensus building is to satisfy as many interests as possible.

Many talented group leaders work before, during, and after group meetings to help members reach consensus or agreement on important issues. For example, representatives of a school community may address tough issues on how to respond to ethnic slurs painted on a school wall, what security measures to install in the school buildings, or whether to actively encourage international exchanges with other schools. Workplace concerns might include how to incorporate interns into private business negotiations, how to deal with sexual and gender discrimination complaints, or whether to merge two departments. As you might imagine, there would be great differences of opinion over how serious certain problems are, how to address them, and what will be needed to solve present problems and/or avoid future problems.

General steps used by leaders in group consensus building include the following:

- Define positions. Encourage the stating of diverse viewpoints in ways that encourage all members to speak.
- Listen for points of agreement.
- Listen for points of disagreement.

Eugene Watt, *Peer Mediator*

On any given day, a visitor to Loyola High School in New York City may come upon Eugene Watt sitting with two very angry students, trying to help them resolve their differences. As a peer mediator, Eugene is trained to listen and ask questions to resolve problems his peers are having. According to Eugene, "Students will listen to other students before they listen to teachers—so they take our advice . . . pretty much."

When asked about the kinds of disagreements he encounters, Eugene replies, "People say things they don't mean—they didn't really mean to hurt the other's feelings." He also notes that lack of respect is a common problem. Eugene views listening as the "number one communication skill." He also uses questioning techniques to get to the heart of a dispute. Sometimes he questions the two parties, and other times he questions other students to get a complete picture of what happened during an incident. His job is to see what is relevant to the issue, to try to understand both sides, and to make some assessments. He stresses the importance of active listening in his work, pointing out that each of the conflicting parties feels important when they know you are really listening to them, and it makes them more cooperative.

At all times, Eugene must be impartial. He must appear logical and nonbiased so that the students involved in the conflict will trust him. Sometimes he is forced to take a tough stand. For example, Eugene says he dealt with a situation in which two kids got into a fight at school over a basketball, and they got really mad at each other. He told them, "Either you guys play on the same team, or you don't play at all."

His experiences as a peer mediator have given Eugene an important set of communication and life skills that he will be able to use in college, in future jobs, and with his friends and family. In addition to his work as a mediator, Eugene is active in church activities and in sports. He is a very busy and talented communicator.

Student Worker Profile

- Ask members what must be included or what must happen for an agreement to be reached.
- Seek agreement from the group that they will honor those elements (what must happen or what must be included) as criteria for a solution.
- Brainstorm possible solutions.
- Evaluate ideas in light of the agreed-upon criteria.
- Make an agreement that satisfies as many people as possible.
- Continue discussion until everyone is able to buy in to the agreement, even if some are less satisfied than others.

As you conclude this chapter, remember this thought from Deborah Tannen, author of *The Argument Culture*: "Cooperation isn't the absence of conflict but a means of managing conflict."

 **Chapter 9** *Summary*

In this chapter, you learned about conflict and conflict management. Conflict occurs when two people feel that their beliefs or desires are incompatible with one another or when individuals within a group feel that their beliefs or desires are incompatible. Conflict is normal and it can be managed.

Conflict styles include competing, compromising, collaborating, giving in, and avoiding. Gender, culture, and workplace culture influence how a person chooses to manage conflict. Conflicts can have win/lose outcomes or win/win outcomes. Out-of-the-box thinking can help achieve a win/win outcome that is satisfying to both parties in a dispute.

Ongoing conflicts progress through five stages: triggering conditions, frustration building, active conflict, solution or nonsolution, and follow-up. Destructive conflict strategies include verbal attacks such as name calling, labeling, put-downs, and hostile gossip; gunnysacking; and physical attacks. Constructive conflict strategies include active listening, reversing roles, and fair fighting.

Some conflicts become so serious that they require formal negotiation or mediation in order to be resolved. When conflict occurs in group situations, effective group leaders use consensus building to reach a collective agreement that is satisfying to as many interests as possible.

Review Questions

1. What is conflict?
2. Describe the common styles used for handling conflict.
3. What are the five stages of an ongoing conflict?
4. Explain the difference between a solution and a nonsolution.
5. Name three destructive conflict strategies and give an example of each.
6. What are three constructive conflict strategies?
7. How might reversing roles help resolve a conflict?
8. What are the "fair fighting" rules?
9. What is negotiation? How does mediation differ from negotiation?
10. What is group consensus building?

Critical Thinking Activities

Speaking/Doing

1. Find an article in a magazine or newspaper that describes a negotiation in progress. It might be about two countries trying to settle a dispute, two businesses in conflict over products, lawmakers trying to reach agreement on proposed legislation, teachers negotiating a new contract with their school, or a community group protesting a city council proposal. Use the information in the article to complete the steps in a negotiation process for both parties: What does each party want? How does each party feel? What are the reasons of each? What is the understanding of each person's or group's position? What plans have been offered so far, if any? If no plans have been offered, create options and choose one. If plans have been offered, choose the one you believe is the best and defend your choice. Prepare a one- to three-minute report on the conflict and what is being done to resolve it.

2. Interview a parent, a relative, or a friend about a conflict with a person of the opposite gender or of another culture. What conflict styles were used? Did the person you interviewed adapt his or her behavior to accommodate the other person's style? Prepare a one- to three-minute oral report explaining what conclusions you might draw from the incident. What role did gender or culture play in the incident? If you wish, use

examples from your own personal experiences as well.

Writing

1. In one or two paragraphs, discuss the nature of conflict. Why is it normal? When can it become destructive? Make a chart that shows examples of conflict that have been handled constructively and examples that have been handled destructively. Find the examples for your chart in your local newspaper and in popular current-events magazines.

2. Select any three of the five conflict styles and describe a time when you used that particular style. Why did you choose that style for that situation? Write a three-paragraph essay, devoting one paragraph to each of the situations you describe.

Group Activities

1. In a small discussion group, let each member tell about a time when he or she was ridiculed or put down. What were the circumstances? As a group, discuss what strategies might have been used in each situation either to avoid the destructive behavior or to bring about a positive solution to the conflict. How might each situation have been handled more constructively?

2. Pair up with a partner. Have one person air a complaint. Perhaps there has been an issue at home over curfew or problems with a co-worker not performing a fair share of duties at work. What bothers him or her about the situation? Then have the listener repeat the complaint to the speaker. How accurately did the listener perceive the problem? How can conflicts escalate when messages are not decoded accurately? Switch roles and repeat the process.

Practical Application: Case Challenge

Jeremy says to Joaquin, "Hey Quin, I need you to pitch in for gas money."

Joaquin responds, "Out of my face, dude!" as he shuts the car door.

Jeremy, still upset about the gas money, finds Joaquin's ex-girlfriend Dawn, and says, "Has Quin always been such a tightwad? I'm sick of giving him rides everywhere."

Joaquin, when he hears from Dawn what Jeremy called him, decides that he will get back at Jeremy.

Jeremy gets into his car the next morning and realizes he's almost out of gas again. He's upset and confused. He just filled the tank a few days ago. Later he talks with Dustin, a mutual friend, and finds out that Joaquin took his gas. Now Jeremy decides to get even too.

That weekend Jeremy and Joaquin go to a party together out in the suburbs. Jeremy goes home without telling Joaquin, leaving him stranded without a ride late at night. Joaquin has to call a taxi to get home.

How could this conflict have been avoided? What are some steps Jeremy and Joaquin could have taken to prevent the destructive turn that their differences took?

Work It Out!

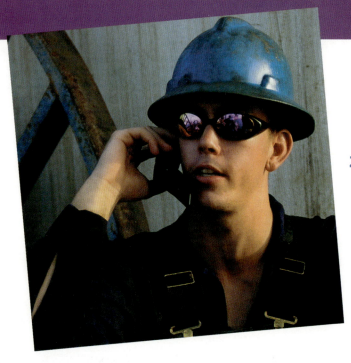

Let's Talk About It

In groups of six, discuss the following interpersonal situations. Each represents a problem you could encounter someday on the job. Brainstorm several solutions and choose the one that you think would be most effective.

1. The petroleum company Leroy works for rewards employees who show initiative. Leroy does extra work and reports ideas he has for improving efficiency at drilling sites. His boss likes him and has told him so, but when he reports on his team's progress, he takes all the credit for Leroy's extra work, and he presents Leroy's ideas as his own. Leroy doesn't say anything, but inside he gets very upset. He is finding it difficult to motivate himself to work hard. (What short-term solutions can you think of to help Leroy? What long-term solutions?)

2. Corky has a new job. This Friday is his birthday. He plans to bring cake and ice cream to share with his co-workers. At his previous job he always brought cake and ice cream on his birthday. Last week a co-worker brought homemade brownies. Everyone enjoyed them, but Corky overheard his boss confide to someone, "What's she up to? Trying to impress us?" The other person nodded knowingly. Now Corky feels uncomfortable. Should he bring the cake and ice cream or not? He's got four days to decide. (How can Corky help himself make the right decision?)

3. Lucinda works for a trucking firm. Every day she reads the newspaper before starting her work. Before lunch, she takes a break to play solitaire on her computer. Lately, she hasn't had time for either. She is constantly being interrupted by truckers who need dispatches signed, employees who want their checks, and supervisors who give her letters to type. She is totally stressed out. She thinks her co-workers are jerks. She doesn't have a clue what to do. She's thinking of looking for a new job. (Will a new job solve Lucinda's problem? What advice would you give her?)

How to Avoid Striking Out in a Job Interview

If you don't already have a part-time job, you probably will be looking for one at some point while you are still in school. Use this activity to help you find the right job for you. The practice you gain can help you later when you look for a career job. You may need to adapt some steps, depending on whether this activity is done in class or is assigned as homework.

1. Decide what kind of job you want. Make a list of jobs you can do. Choose one that you would enjoy. Get ideas from newspaper want ads, magazine advertisements, and classmates. If a computer is handy, check out the Internet. Be creative. Think about things that interest you.

2. Prepare a résumé. Take this step very seriously. You may be looking for "just" a part-time job, but practicing how to prepare a good résumé now will be enormously helpful to you when you look for a career job. Study the sample résumé on page 168. Be realistic and honest.

3. Learn what the job requires. Make a list of questions you want answered and questions you think you will be asked. Use the sample questions on pages 170–173 to guide you. Rehearse answers for the questions.

4. Now work with a partner. Practice an actual interview. Take turns being the interviewer and the interviewee. Practice everything from walking in and shaking hands to thanking the interviewer and leaving. Your partner can use the questions you have prepared as prompts for conducting the interview. After the interview, write your interviewer a thank-you note. Exchange notes and evaluate them. Critique each other's interviews. Use the Interview Evaluation Form on page 183 to guide you. Then do your interview again, adapting it according to your partner's suggestions.

Do a Team Project

Work in groups of six. Elect a leader. Brainstorm a short-term team project. Choose something modest, such as planning and completing a poster campaign to advertise a coming school event. Adapt the scope to the time limits your teacher imposes. Use the six steps of problem solving on page 200 to guide your work. At least once during the project, take time to discuss ways you can improve team performance. Be supportive of one another and offer only constructive criticism. If disagreements occur, apply the constructive conflict strategies described on pages 229–232 and look for win/win solutions. When you have completed your project, you should have something concrete to show for it—for example, a product, a report, or a proposal. Use the group evaluation forms on pages 203 and 204 to analyze your performance.

Try Out Your Leadership Skills

You are the leader of a six-member work team. You are involved in a critically important project requiring the full cooperation of all members. Two members present problems. Alfred is an expert. He is bright and aggressive. He dominates team meetings, imposing his ideas on other members. Often his ideas are good, but he refuses to accept the ideas of others. When he doesn't get his way, he sulks. His behavior has led to serious disagreements. Dorothy is a shy supporter. She is on probation. Your superior has confided that you may have to fire Dorothy if her performance doesn't improve. Dorothy has potential, but her personal insecurities hold her back. She never contributes ideas and waits to be told what to do. Right now you need the full participation of both Alfred and Dorothy, but each of them is hurting the team. You don't want to upset Alfred. He's too valuable. You don't want to lose Dorothy. You genuinely believe she is capable of contributing. What can you do?

Presentations

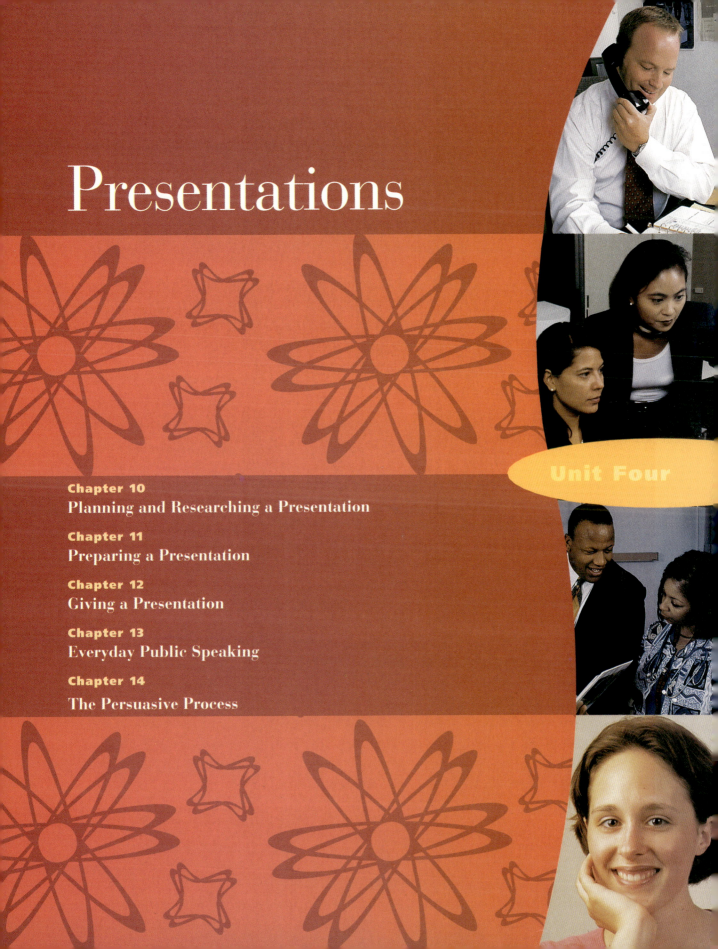

Unit Four

Planning and Researching a Presentation

Objectives

After completing this chapter, you will be able to

- define public speaking and its purposes
- give examples of public speaking in the workplace
- explain the public-speaking process
- demonstrate topic selection, audience analysis, and audience goals
- explain general principles for conducting research
- explain how to find and use sources of information
- demonstrate library, interview, and Internet research
- evaluate research materials

Key Terms

audience analysis

audience goal

cyberspace resources

fabrication

formal feedback

informal feedback

informative speech

persuasive speech

plagiarism

social-ritual speeches

training speech

> **❝** Thinking strategically about public speaking means abandoning the belief that there is an all-purpose, magic formula that will always produce a good speech. **❞**
>
> —DAVID ZAREFSKY, *Public Speaking: Strategies for Success*

Wrapping Up a Great Year

"I don't want to do this" moaned Ryan as he and Jordan finished arranging the chairs.

Cass laughed and said, "You should have thought of that when you became a group officer." She got a "Lay off!" from Ryan in response.

As the youth group senior leaders finished arranging chairs into 12-person concentric circles, the adult leaders, Cindy and Paul, set up a slide projector. Ryan called to them, "I hope you're going to run that thing tonight."

Case Study

"No way," Cindy replied. "This is your night. I get to sit back and grin."

"We're in deep trouble now," muttered Cass.

By now 25 adults were standing around the room. More group members filed in, bringing with them piles of brownies and chips. When everyone had arrived, Jordan called the group together, saying, "OK. Make it good."

Heads nodded as Ryan walked to the podium to welcome the parents. He began, "It's great all of you were willing to come out for our annual Youth Night Program. We are really pleased to see you and want to thank you for your support. Tonight we will begin with our traditional opening exercise, and then you'll hear from a number of members."

Cass walked to the podium and addressed the audience, "Listen up. Everyone get in groups of 12—6 parents and 6 teens to each group. No relatives together in a group. Pick a circle of chairs. Adults sit in the inner circle with the chairs facing out. Teens sit in the outer circle with the chairs facing in." She waited as people scattered around the room. "Now, everyone should be facing a nonrelative of a different generation."

There was some last-minute scrambling and trading of seats. "In the next half hour I will ask three questions, one every 15 minutes. When I yell 'Question!' I want the teens to all shift one seat to the right, introduce themselves, and discuss the question with the adult who is facing them. Parents do not have to move. After 45 minutes we'll all know each other better. Question one: What are two things that teenagers worry about—now or in the past? Start talking."

After 45 minutes, the discussion was over and the second half of the program began. Ryan, Jordan, and four other seniors sat at a table in front.

Ryan began, "As many of you parents know, the spring cleanup/campout was our big farewell event for seniors. We spent all day cleaning up the retreat center camp to get ready for summer. Each evening we sat around and told stories, discussed problems, ate a lot of junk food, and laughed. Paul took pictures all weekend, so we thought we'd share some with you. Jordan, you run the projector."

As the image of a group huddled around a campfire appeared on the screen, Ryan described the scene: "This is a shot of Liz, Cass, and Jodie roasting hot dogs on the first day of the cleanup. That's Cass in the middle, laughing. She's burning her hot dog to a crisp."

After a half hour of slides, some of which were upside down, and 15 minutes of announcements about plans for next year, Cass invited the adult leaders to the podium. "Our final act as seniors is to honor Paul and Cindy with these flowers and a signed picture of the group. You are the greatest."

Paul and Cindy walked forward to great applause from the audience and a standing ovation from the group members. One of the mothers rose and gave a short, spontaneous speech praising Cindy and Paul.

Fifteen minutes later the room had emptied. Ryan and Jordan started taking down the chairs and discussing life after graduation.

What observations can you make about the workplace culture of this group? What examples of speechmaking occurred in this case study?

The Public-Speaking Process

When police officers arrive for a shift, they hear announcements and updates on crimes in their area delivered by their watch commander. High school seniors coaching novice soccer players hold team meetings to review information, rules, and skills. Some offices hold weekly meetings at which employees give short talks on current projects. These are only a few of the countless workplace examples of public speaking in action.

Frequently people say, "Not me. I'm never going to give a public speech!" What most of them mean is, "I don't see myself giving 15- to 30-minute formal speeches to large audiences." What they don't think about are all the other kinds of public presentations that are part of everyday life—making announcements, giving awards, explaining a skill to a group of co-workers, reporting on a project to a boss, defending a position at a union meeting, and many more.

You will listen to countless presentations each year, and there will be other times when you will have to stand up and talk to a group of listeners just like yourself. Many of these talks will be given on the job. The more knowledge you have about the speaking process and the more practice you have, the easier it will be for you to participate confidently in these speaking situations. This chapter introduces the public-speaking process and discusses finding information for your presentations. Because of the workplace focus of this book, the emphasis will be on short, practical speeches related to everyday public-speaking situations.

There are countless workplace examples of public-speaking situations. You may need to explain a skill to co-workers, report on a team project, or give a major presentation for clients.

Elements of Public Speaking

Public speaking occurs when one person addresses a group of listeners for a specific purpose. The key elements in the public-speaking process may be diagrammed in the following way:

Situation

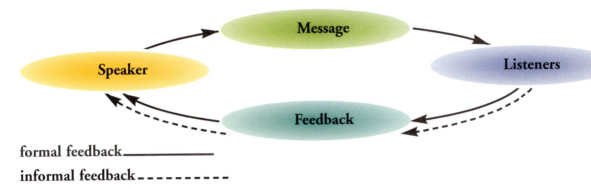

formal feedback _____

informal feedback - - - - - - - - -

One person has a reason to send a message to a group using verbal and non-verbal symbols. The message is created for these specific listeners. The listeners decode or interpret the message and provide feedback to the speaker, who then adjusts the message. All this occurs within a specific situation.

Although this is similar to the communication process described in Chapter 1, public speaking differs from conversation. Generally, public speakers use more formal language, louder volume, and larger gestures. Also, they speak to a group for a period of time without being interrupted. The speech is planned ahead of time, but the speaker does respond to feedback and makes adjustments during the presentation. Let's look at the five major elements of public speaking.

Speaker

Most speakers have specialized knowledge and skills to share with a group, or they may hold positions of leadership. Speakers may stand or sit, and they may use visual supports or a microphone. They develop a message targeted for a

Most speakers have specialized knowledge and skills to share with their audience.

particular group of listeners. The speaker decodes the listeners' feedback to adjust the presentation or to plan the next speech.

Message

The speaker's message is developed according to the purpose of the speech, the particular listeners, and the situation. The message is developed based on an audience analysis. The speaker's purpose may be to inform, instruct, or persuade the listeners. Most speeches follow a pattern and contain main points and supporting information.

Listeners

Listeners may be voluntary audience members, or they may be required to attend. The effectiveness of a speech depends partly on the speaker's skill and partly on the listeners' effort. Audience feedback should affect the speaker's presentation; if the speaker adapts to ongoing feedback from the listeners, the listeners will be more satisfied.

Feedback

Listeners give informal or formal feedback to a speaker. **Informal feedback** consists of verbal or nonverbal messages given spontaneously to the speaker during or after the speech. Listeners' frowns or blank stares tell a speaker the audience is confused. Sometimes a comment after a speech influences the speaker's next presentation. The comment "I found the graph you included useful" may encourage a speaker to use visuals again. "Where can I learn more about magic?" tells the speaker the audience member was interested in the topic. **Formal feedback,** also called a critique, consists of planned written or oral comments that evaluate the speech. Competent speakers pay close attention to listener feedback, formal or informal, using both to become better speakers.

Situation

The context in which a speech is given influences the entire process. Factors such as the occasion (why everyone is there) and the setting (place and time) affect the speaker and the message. A context that works against a speaker, such as an overcrowded room or a broken slide projector, limits a speaker's effectiveness.

These five factors influence each other as parts of the public-speaking process. It's important to remember the quotation at the beginning of this chapter. There is no magic formula that always produces a good speech. The same message can be presented many different ways. Note the following example:

> At Southwest Airlines the employees are encouraged to show their personalities when dealing with customers. Therefore, their public presentations are usually different from standard airline announcements. For example, instead of "Please pass your cups to the center aisle where the attendant will collect them," a passenger on Southwest might hear, "Please pass all plastic cups to the center aisle so we can wash them and use them with the next customers." Comments like this one usually get the passengers' attention!

> **Remember!**
>
> The key elements in the public-speaking process are
>
> ▶ speaker
> ▶ message
> ▶ listeners
> ▶ feedback
> ▶ situation

Purposes of Public Speaking

The main purposes for public speaking are to inform, to train, to persuade, and to participate in social rituals. Other reasons to give speeches are to entertain and to inspire. Although social-ritual speeches are discussed in Chapter 13, the primary focus of this text is on the three main purposes—informing, training, and persuading.

Informative Speeches

The goal of an **informative speech** is to increase listeners' knowledge of a subject. The most common types are speeches that describe, define, or demonstrate. You might give a report describing the problems your organization is having raising money. A nutrition expert might define differences among

Michelle Meyer, *Puppeteer*

A few times a month the elementary school students in Easton, Pennsylvania, are treated to a puppet show put on by local high school students in the Beginning Alcohol Addiction Studies program. One of those puppeteers is Michelle Meyer, a high school senior and president of the Key Club dedicated to community service. The puppet show addresses serious issues such as alcohol abuse, drugs, and self-image. When the puppeteers finish the show, they sing songs with the children and handle a question-and-answer period on serious topics raised by the audience members.

Michelle is aware that because her audience is made up of children, she must be careful about how she presents herself when she performs her puppet shows. She knows that the children look up to her as a role model. She says, "In dealing with such serious subjects, my attitude and position have to be serious as well, especially since I deal with children. I have to use simple language and simple concepts. Yet, I have to communicate the intensity and complexity of the harsh consequences that come with drugs and alcohol. I talk about warning signs, coping skills, and other relevant information."

In her role as president of the Key Club, Michelle and the other officers often give short informative speeches summarizing the projects they have completed and proposing new ones. While Michelle is often the one talking, she also knows she must listen carefully to the contributions of all members during meetings. "I cannot deny or ignore their opinions. We would not be a unified group if I did."

Because the Easton Area High School Key Club is large and is part of a much more complex network of clubs, Michelle spends five to ten hours a week organizing, planning, and communicating with various officers, members, the adviser, and others. In addition, Michelle is a serious dancer, who practices and performs regularly.

Michelle lives a very busy life but, clearly, she thrives on the pace.

Student Worker Profile

semivegetarians, vegetarians, and vegans. The holder of a black belt in karate might demonstrate a roundhouse kick and a one-two punch.

Training Speeches

The goal of a **training speech** is to teach specific information, procedures, or skills. You might diagram football plays to the freshman squad or teach a flamenco dance to the senior dance troupe. Training speeches are sometimes called instructional speeches.

Persuasive Speeches

The goal of a **persuasive speech** is to change the beliefs or behavior of listeners. Persuasive speeches range from slightly controversial to highly controversial. You might want to encourage friends to eat a healthier diet (slightly controversial) or to argue for tax increases (highly controversial).

Social-Ritual Speeches

Social-ritual speeches, also called ceremonial speeches, have specific functions and follow a short, predictable pattern. These functions include making announcements, giving welcomes, introducing a speaker, accepting an award, nominating a candidate, and others. Each type of social-ritual speech has a very specific goal. That goal varies with each type.

Topic Selection

Although you need to select topics to use during classroom speeches, in most workplace situations you do not look for a topic. Whether you are introducing performers at a talent show, explaining the ingredients in daily specials to a staff of servers, or persuading your co-workers to wear a new uniform, the topic reflects a current need or concern. When you choose a classroom speech topic, use the following guidelines: (1) select a topic that interests you, and (2) select a topic that will interest your audience.

Personal Interests

If you are not excited about a topic, it will be hard for you to get your audience interested. If you are bored, you will put your listeners to sleep. (There's nothing more contagious than boredom in a speaker!) If you are excited, your audience will pick up that feeling. But not every topic that fascinates you will excite your listeners.

Audience Interests

Ask yourself if your listeners will find your subject important, enjoyable, or useful. After you identify two or three topics that interest you, think about how your audience might react to them. Select the one that has the greatest

Planning and Researching a Presentation

Dilbert reprinted by permission of United Feature Syndicate, Inc.

appeal for all persons involved, one that you know something about, one that interests your audience, and one that is timely and important.

As you learn more about workplace speaking, you will recognize that in workplace situations topics are usually tied to an event or a specific need. For example, during an awards ceremony to honor her top saleswomen, Mary Kay of Mary Kay Cosmetics gave an opening speech on motivation. In it she explained the significance of the diamond bumblebee pin that each saleswoman was given:

> "Aerodynamically, the bumblebee cannot fly. Its wings are too weak, and its body is too heavy. But the bumblebee doesn't know it, and it goes right on flying anyway. It's a symbol of women who didn't know they couldn't fly, but they did anyway."

Talking about successful women made sense in this context because the topic was tied to the situation—an awards ceremony honoring successful saleswomen.

 Eye-to-Eye

With a partner, brainstorm 10 topics that meet the criteria of (1) being interesting to you and (2) being interesting to a class audience. Share your lists in groups of six, comparing areas that overlap.

Audience Analysis

Who will be listening to your speech? If your topic is computers, would you give the same speech to a group of elementary students that you would to employees at Dell Computers? Of course not. Would you want to address the issue of tax increases with a group of angry citizens and with a group of legislators using the same speech? Probably not.

A good speaker always considers how to connect the audience to the message. Here Allied Supreme Commander General Dwight D. Eisenhower gives last-minute orders to Allied paratroopers about to leave for Normandy, France, on D-Day, June 6, 1944. He told them, "Full victory—nothing else."

A good speaker always considers how to connect the audience and the message. **Audience analysis** refers to the process of identifying any information about an audience that helps the speaker tailor the message to that particular group. Audience analysis is part of the process a speaker uses to create a message appropriate for a specific audience.

In speaking situations outside class, you talk to many different audiences that you don't know very well. You will need to learn something about each audience in order to connect and communicate effectively. Audience analysis involves considering basic data, beliefs and attitudes, knowledge of the subject, expectations, and the setting.

Basic Data

The basic data about your listeners—such as age, gender, occupation, race, educational level, and income level—is useful. It helps you select appropriate references, such as movies, music, or sports. It tells you what type of humor to include, what vocabulary to use, and the right level of technical language. The more you know about your audience, the more ways you will find to connect them to your topic. Use examples and language that the audience will understand and identify with. What assumptions about the audience did the following band director make in motivating band members before a fund-raising drive?

"Okay, let's go all the way this year. No short yardage. Right to the end zone. The other schools' bands are going door-to-door with their holiday gift booklets. We're taking ours straight to the marketplace—companies and grocery stores— and we will score a touchdown. No field goals for us."

Planning and Researching a Presentation

Beliefs and Attitudes

It is important to know whether most audience members hold specific beliefs and attitudes related to your topic. Being sensitive to an audience's political views or religious beliefs can help speakers avoid offending an audience by accident. For example, telling the parents of your karate class that "We're going out to kill those guys" may not sit well with many of them.

It is also important to know what opinions the majority of your listeners might have about your topic so that you know how to develop your speech. This does not mean you have to tell the listeners what they want to hear. You can hold a different position on gun control than most of your listeners, but, when dealing with a sensitive topic like this one, you need to select speaking strategies that will keep your audience involved and that will not offend them.

Knowledge of the Subject

It is important to ask yourself, "Am I introducing this audience to a new subject, or are most people familiar with it?" If you plan to talk about a topic that is new to most audience members, you need to start with the basics. You may have to define words or terms, discuss unfamiliar ideas, or explain in exact detail how something works.

Expectations

At a community drama club dinner, what would you expect the main speaker to talk about? What would you expect from a speaker at an awards banquet? Audience members expect a speaker to do or say certain things, depending on the occasion and on their knowledge of the speaker. The speaker needs to pay attention to these expectations.

Audience expectations affect your choice of topic and how you talk about your topic. An audience that expects a movie star to tell stories about film experiences may be surprised to hear a speech on kicking the cigarette habit. Listeners who expect you to give a short welcome speech may be disappointed if you give a long one. As a speaker, you don't have to do exactly what the audience expects, as long as you have a reason for your choice. But, if you are going to do something quite different, you may wish to prepare your audience. If you fail to connect with your audience, no matter how brilliant the speech, you have failed as a communicator.

Setting

Analyzing the setting also helps you prepare for a successful speaking event. You should ask the following questions to analyze the possibilities and the limitations you will face. Knowing the answers to them will help you plan what to say and how to say it.

- What time of day is the speech? What are my time limits?
- What will be the size of the room? size of the audience? seating arrangement?

Audience expectations affect your choice of topic and how you talk about your topic. These doctors expect the speaker to provide detailed, technical medical information.

- What audiovisual equipment is available? Will I need a podium and/or a microphone? a laptop computer?
- Will I be the only speaker? If there are others, what will be their subjects and the order of appearance? Will there be a question period at the end?

Audience Goal

When you give a presentation, you need a clear audience goal. An **audience goal** describes what the listeners should be able to *do* after your speech is completed. Suppose you are giving a treasurer's report on a charity walk, and your funds are low. Your audience goal might be, "I want my listeners to each donate two more hours of time to fund-raising." An audience goal is always worded in terms of what the listeners should do, *not* what the speaker will do. Which of the following statements are stated as audience goals?

1. Listeners will list three suggested selling strategies to use with customers.
2. Listeners will hear about the group's philosophy and founder.
3. Listeners will use hotel guests' names when talking with them.
4. I will give four reasons for wearing uniforms in school.

Numbers 1 and 3 are correctly stated audience goals. They describe what the audience members should be able to do after listening to the speech.

An audience goal helps a speaker decide what content to include and what should be given the most attention. For example, if you are giving a speech to tourists on camping rules, your audience goal might be stated, "My listeners will be able to list four ways to clean up a campsite before leaving." With this goal, your speech will focus on ways to clean a campsite rather than on making fires or picking flowers.

Planning and Researching a Presentation

Phil Zepeda, *Director of Media Relations*

If you listen to the news in the Midwest, you are likely to hear Phil Zepeda periodically describing how the Red Cross is helping individuals and communities deal with a disaster. As the Director of Media Relations and Internal Communications for the American Red Cross of Greater Chicago, he is at the center of a critical communications network that involves people within his organization as well as across the nation and around the world.

His primary responsibilities include acting as chief organiza-

tional spokesperson before, during, and after national disasters; coordinating communications among Red Cross employees through monthly publications and e-mail; and providing media training for all employees so that they can deal with television, radio, and print journalists. He also gives talks to donors who support Red Cross programs in order to "tell everyone what we do with every penny of a donated dollar."

This position needs someone who is very flexible and able to juggle multiple tasks. When Mr. Zepeda talks about his responsibilities, he says,

"Because of the unpredictable nature of disasters, I must be able to stop on a dime and head in another direction at full speed." At one moment he may be working on an article for an internal newsletter, and at the next moment he may grab his coat and head to a disaster scene. He believes strong self-confidence is needed because "I may find myself talking to a local newspaper columnist from a small North Carolina town at one point, and the next moment I'm speaking with Katie Couric on *The Today Show*."

At most disaster sites Mr. Zepeda has to host news conferences to provide information and to answer reporters' questions. As a spokesman for the Red Cross, he must appear comfortable, confident, knowledgeable, and prepared.

On occasion, he gives persuasive talks in order to help maintain and increase donations. He says, "We have to constantly provide stories and images to the American public about what we are doing. It takes a concerted effort to bring the Red Cross down to a very local, personal level." He loves his work. It is challenging and varied, and it provides him with a sense of personal satisfaction and the ability to use all his highly developed communication skills.

Researching Your Presentation

A committee of the French Academy writing the Academy Dictionary defined the word *crab* as follows: *"Crab:* a small red fish which walks backwards." Commenting on this definition, the famous naturalist Cuvier said, "Your definition, gentlemen, would be perfect, only for three exceptions. The crab is not a fish, it is not red, and it does not walk backwards." It's amazing how much misinformation you read or hear every day because someone thought he or she knew the subject. Every competent and ethical speaker uses good research skills to prepare accurate and interesting presentations. But where do you find this information, and how do you know which information is the most accurate?

You have already done research assignments in the library. Oftentimes this can be very frustrating; you spend a great deal of time just trying to figure out what to look up and where to find it. It will help if you complete two steps before beginning your search: (1) assess what you already know and (2) make brief notes on some ideas. Write down the key facts that you do know. What is your audience likely to know? What is the purpose of your presentation? What is your time limit? Answering these questions will help you narrow your research process.

Accurate audience analysis helps you decide what facts might be most interesting to them, what might motivate them to act, what might offend them, and what will change their minds about a controversial issue. The more you know about your audience before you do your research, the less time you will have to spend looking through information.

Make brief notes that focus on the purpose of your presentation. What three or four ideas best support your purpose and audience goal? Knowing these ideas will help you limit the scope of your research. When you are already familiar with your topic, this approach to research works well.

If you choose a topic that you are less familiar with personally, you may have to do more general research to gather some ideas. Perhaps you are interested in learning about special effects in movies, but you haven't read anything about them. You might look for a book on special effects or rent a video on special effects to get some general background.

By knowing how long you have to speak, you can decide how much information you will need to make your presentation meet the time limits. You do want to look up more information than you need so that you can pick and choose the best pieces, but there's no point in researching too much information that is not

Accurate information is essential to successful speaking, and researching that information can be very frustrating. You may spend a great deal of time trying to figure out what to look up and where to find it.

relevant to your presentation. In the workplace, this is extremely important. For example, some bosses are famous for saying things like "If the report is more than one typed page, or the speech is more than two minutes, forget it."

Sources of Information

Samuel Johnson, the famous 18th-century scholar, once said, "Knowledge is of two kinds. We know a subject ourselves, or we know where we can find information upon it." To gather information, you may turn to your own personal experience, to expert interviews, to print materials, to electronic media resources, or to cyberspace resources.

Personal Experience

Competent public speakers begin their research by using their own experiences. They start with the connections they already have to a subject and then move on to other sources for information and ideas. If you are talking about the need for a teen drop-in center, you can rely on the experiences you and your friends have had on nights when you had nowhere to go. If you are reporting on the need for a teen job hot line or web site, you can recall your own experiences trying to find a job.

Expert Interviews

Interviewing an expert is one good way to obtain information for a topic. You can call an expert in your own community. A good interview does not just happen. An interviewer must prepare ahead of time to be successful in obtaining useful information. The best way to get what you need is to rely on the 5 W's and H discussed earlier in Chapter 3: *who, what, when, where, why,* and *how*. You can apply them to the interview process in the following way:

- *Why* are you asking questions? What information do you hope to learn? You must have a clear sense of purpose before determining whom to interview and what to ask.
- *Who* would be the best source? You need to select an expert in the field. For example, if your purpose is to help others understand the process of applying for college, you might interview a college admissions director. If you want your audience to know more about the health-care profession, you could interview a doctor or a paramedic. Begin the process early. If you wait until the last minute, you may not be able to find someone to interview. Successful people are busy people.

Interviewing an expert is one good way to obtain information for a topic. The school nurse might be an excellent source of information for topics relating to illness, diseases, injuries, and other medical issues.

- *When* and *where* will the interview take place? Be careful in selecting a time and place for the interview. Have some idea of a specific time and place that you could meet—a place where you will not be interrupted. Be on time and stick to the time limits you agreed to.
- *What* do you need from this expert? Do your homework. You should look up information about the expert before you prepare questions for the interview. Talk show hosts read biographies about their guests or make a point of knowing their work. They don't just recite a list of prepared questions. By knowing something about the person, you can prepare appropriate questions and keep from appearing confused.
- *How* will the interview be conducted? Decide the best method of conducting and recording your interview. If the person lives out of town, you might conduct the interview over the phone or through the Internet. Remember that if you plan to record phone conversations, you must first obtain the expert's permission to be recorded. If you are taking notes, use some kind of shorthand so that you don't look down at your notebook for the whole interview.

Questioning

It is important to keep your purpose in mind when you prepare questions for an interview. Write your questions in advance; otherwise, the interview can become unfocused. During the interview, keep your questions brief and to the point. Ask only one question at a time and listen carefully to the answer. It may provide information for a follow-up question.

It is also important to ask a variety of types of questions. Open-ended questions allow the subject to respond freely. Asking the district attorney, "What is your stand on capital punishment?" would be an open-ended question. If you

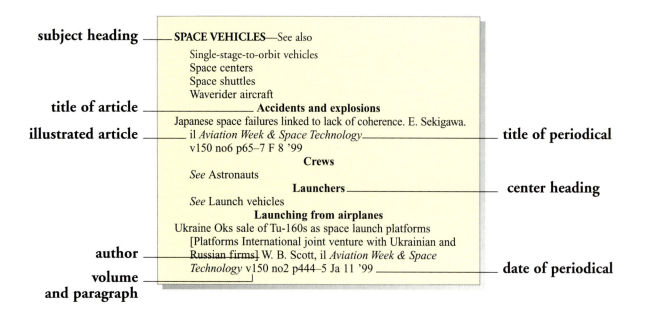

subject heading — **SPACE VEHICLES**—See also

Single-stage-to-orbit vehicles
Space centers
Space shuttles
Waverider aircraft

title of article — **Accidents and explosions**
Japanese space failures linked to lack of coherence. E. Sekigawa.
illustrated article — il *Aviation Week & Space Technology* — title of periodical
v150 no6 p65–7 F 8 '99

Crews
See Astronauts

Launchers — center heading
See Launch vehicles

Launching from airplanes
Ukraine Oks sale of Tu-160s as space launch platforms
[Platforms International joint venture with Ukrainian and
author — Russian firms] W. B. Scott, il *Aviation Week & Space*
volume — *Technology* v150 no2 p444–5 Ja 11 '99 — date of periodical
and paragraph

Electronic Media Resources

Electronic media resources include radio, television, video, and audiotapes. When you use information from radio and television, be sure to identify the name of the program, the name of the speaker, and the date on which you heard the information. For example, if you were discussing football "greats," you might say, "On July 28, 1999, WBBM news reported, 'Football star Barry Sanders is retiring 1,458 yards away from breaking Walter Payton's record of 16,726 career yards.'"

Radio and television information cannot be checked easily unless you can replay the program, so you have to take careful notes. Because radio and television information is difficult to recheck, many speakers use it for general stories, examples, and background information only. They turn to other sources for direct quotations, facts, and figures. Often researchers try to find a second source to verify a fact or figure. Occasionally printed copies or transcripts of radio and television programs are made available upon written request.

Many stores and libraries stock videotapes and audiotapes. If you use information from these kinds of sources in a presentation, be sure to identify both the title and the publication data of the tape.

Cyberspace Resources

The Internet provides you with an extraordinarily wide range of resources, sometimes referred to as **cyberspace resources.** Since the Internet is actually thousands of connected computers that you can access, much of the information it contains is global, current, and convenient.Unfortunately, some of the

information on the Internet can also be time-consuming to locate, unreliable, and even misleading.

If you learn some basic concepts for finding and evaluating sources on the Internet, you will find useful information on many topics. At times you may receive specific URLs (web site addresses) from your teacher or from a directory. In these cases, you can go directly to sites that have relevant information on your topic. Other times, you may need to use a search engine to find sites. Search engines such as Yahoo! and Alta Vista are indexes you can use to search thousands of sites by subject. Most of the major search engines will have some or all of the following searching capabilities:

- *Key Word* searches allow you to locate significant words that describe your topic. For example, if you wanted to look up information on Star Wars special effects, you might look up "Star Wars" or "special effects."
- *Boolean* searches allow you to combine words using "and," "or," or "not." "And" combines search words so that both words must be included. For example, "modern and art" would locate sources containing both words. The words might be together ("modern art") or they might be separated ("modern technology" and "art schools"). "Or" allows you to search for synonyms or word variations in the same search. For example, "car" or "automobile" would get results containing either "car" or "automobile." "Not" excludes words that might result in misleading connections. For example, if your topic were Cherokee Indians, you might try "Cherokee not Jeep."
- *Truncation* searches involve shortening the key word to its basic root and adding a special character such as ?, *, or # after it to tell the computer to search for variations on the word. For example, "music*" will also give you "musical" and "musician."
- *String* searches locate words or characters in the exact order you specify with no words or characters intervening. Use quotation marks to enclose the phrase.

Planning and Researching a Presentation

- *Adjacency* searches allow you to search for words that are next to or near each other.
- *Parentheses* searches combine concepts and techniques. The search engine will search for what's grouped inside the parentheses first.

Consider the Source

Although the Internet can be an extremely valuable source of information, it is often as reliable as a stranger standing next to you at a bus stop. Anyone can create a web site. Ask yourself these questions before using any information you find on the Internet: Is the web site source credible? (a government or university site, for example) What are the credentials of the person who developed this particular site? Has the site been updated recently? Can I verify the information in another way? Here are some examples of reliable sources:

- *Nonprofit, government, or educational organizations.* Their Internet addresses end in .edu, .org, .gov, or a country abbreviation such as .UK.
- *Expert authors.* They have academic degrees and relevant experience in their field that makes the information reliable.
- *Documented sources.* They cite their sources and have bibliographies.
- *Reliable print sources.* On-line copies of *Newsweek, Time,* and other high-profile magazines from the publisher or in a full-text index are just as reliable as the print versions.

The following sources of information should be questioned before being used:

- Commercial organizations that may be advertising to sell a product. Their Internet addresses usually end in .com.
- Anonymous authors or authors without identifiable credentials. The reader doesn't know them or their motivations.
- Undocumented sources. Where did they get their information?
- Lengthy quotations reprinted from reliable sources. They may be edited in a biased or inaccurate way. Check the original source.

Remember!

When you gather information for a presentation, you can use the following resources:

▶ **personal experience**

▶ **expert interviews**

▶ **print materials**

▶ **electronic media resources**

▶ **cyberspace resources**

Computer Search

To learn more about evaluating web-site resources, go to one of the following sites on the Internet. List three guidelines for research that are given on that web site.

http://gaskell.library.ucla.edu/libraries/college/instruct/web/critical.htm

http://milton.mse.jhu.edu/research/education/net.html

http://milton.mse.jhu.edu/research/education/practical.html

Jump Start reprinted by permission of United Feature Syndicate, Inc..

Taking Notes

Taking notes is a convenient way to gather information. An important factor to consider in taking notes is to record your source. Giving proper credit for original ideas or unusual facts, statistics, studies, and quotes is an essential part of ethical and accurate research.

Use 3″ x 5″ or 4″ x 6″ index cards or a computer program to record information. Cards are easy to sort, file, and organize. Keep your cards in a file box with dividers and arrange them according to areas of information. Put stories, problems, solutions, quotations, and so on, into separate categories.

Most research cards contain either direct quotations or specific information such as facts or examples. Information summary cards contain a short summary, in your own words, of the main ideas of an article or section of material. Direct quotation cards give the exact words of an author, which are put in quotation marks. Cards that contain specific facts or examples may simply list the important facts that will help you make your points in your speech. Look at the examples on page 268 to see what kind of information is contained on each type of research card.

Careful researchers also record the data they find from electronic sources such as on-line discussion groups, bulletin boards, and e-mail. Sometimes you may need to refer to a specific Internet site, such as the one for the Junior Great Books program. You would identify it as ***http://www.greatbooks.org*** on your note card. You might also record an e-mail interview with a university professor by indicating the person's e-mail address, his or her name and title, and the date of the interview.

Perhaps you have access to computerized note-card programs in which you can enter the same information. These note cards are not portable, but you can search for information from them more easily—using a search feature—than you can search through written note cards. Another advantage is that you do

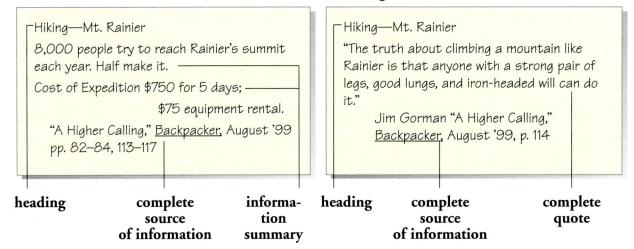

Information Card

Hiking—Mt. Rainier

8,000 people try to reach Rainier's summit each year. Half make it.

Cost of Expedition $750 for 5 days;

$75 equipment rental.

"A Higher Calling," <u>Backpacker,</u> August '99 pp. 82–84, 113–117

heading   complete source of information   information summary

Direct Quotation Card

Hiking—Mt. Rainier

"The truth about climbing a mountain like Rainier is that anyone with a strong pair of legs, good lungs, and iron-headed will can do it."

Jim Gorman "A Higher Calling," <u>Backpacker,</u> August '99, p. 114

heading   complete source of information   complete quote

not need to retype a quotation into your speech manuscript or outline. Instead you can transfer it by "cutting and pasting" it into your speech electronically.

Ethics of Research

As a researcher you have a responsibility to work with integrity. You work within a personal code of honesty to do the most accurate research possible and to give proper credit when you refer to the work or ideas of others. Unethical communicators deliberately fabricate information or commit plagiarism.

Fabrication involves making up information as part of the research process. Although you might be tired or frustrated in your search for appropriate information, as an honest researcher you must not make up an interview quotation or article title.

Plagiarism involves representing the words or ideas of others as your own. The most obvious case is handing in or performing work written by someone else and claiming that you wrote it. Sometimes students who do not take careful notes run the risk of plagiarism by carelessness. This can happen when you take notes from a source but you don't record the title, author, or date and just use the notes as your own or when you forget to put experts' statements in quotation marks. You are committing plagiarism even when you pretend you thought of a great idea when you actually heard about it during a newscast.

These ethical concerns are based on the belief that the works created by a person belong to that person. People have legal ownership over what they create, and others must obtain permission to use these creations. There are copyright laws that explain how one may legally use the work of others. Those laws are intended to protect creators such as writers, artists, musicians, and scientists.

Career Communication *Webmaster*

For someone who enjoys working on the computer and developing new skills, a webmaster is a great job. Less than a decade old, the position of webmaster does not have one entry point. Many current webmasters were doing very different kinds of work five years ago. Webmasters must have excellent computer skills, a creative streak, and fine communication skills.

Webmasters take printed copy such as information about a company, its statement of culture, its hiring practices, a list of its position openings, and names of the company officers and put that information into an electronic format for a web site. The webmaster must make the information easy to find on the site. Some web sites have hyperlinks, or direct connections to other related web sites. Most webmasters know the HTML computer language. In order to present all the information in an attractive and functional manner, the webmaster uses graphics and images to create a visually interesting web site that reflects a competent image of the organization. A skateboard company will not want the same image for its web site as a chain of hardware stores. A very formal organization will be visually portrayed in more subdued tones and with more classic images than a casual company, which may have more humor and vibrant colors on its web site. In order to create a web site that accurately reflects the organization, a webmaster must interview numerous employees of the organization to develop a sense of how to best represent its workplace culture. When a web site is "under construction," the webmaster receives feedback from numerous company members about the design of the site. In addition the webmaster has to talk with employees about adding and removing information.

Chapter 10 *Summary*

In this chapter, you learned about the main purposes for public speaking: to inform, to train, to persuade, and to participate in ceremonial events. In the workplace, speech topics are usually tied to a specific event or a specific need.

Effective speakers do an analysis of their audience in order to connect the audience with their message. They learn the following information about their listeners: basic data, beliefs and attitudes, knowledge of the topic, expectations, and the setting. Effective speakers also establish a clear audience goal to help them decide what content to include and emphasize in their presentations.

Speakers use a variety of sources to research information, including personal experience, expert interviews, print material, electronic media resources, and cyberspace resources. Taking notes is a common way to gather and organize the information found through research. Most research note cards fall into two types: direct quotation cards and information cards. Responsible researchers are careful not to fabricate or plagiarize information during the research process.

Review Questions

1. How is public speaking different from everyday conversation?
2. What are the general purposes of public speaking? Give specific examples of each.
3. What are the criteria for selecting a good speech topic?
4. What factors should be considered when analyzing your audience?
5. Why is it important to have an audience goal before you prepare a speech?
6. What are some typical resources for researching topics?
7. What information do you need to gather before seeking an expert interview?
8. What rules of etiquette should you follow when you interview someone?
9. What problem might you encounter if you use undocumented information from a website on the Internet?
10. What is plagiarism and how can you avoid it?

Critical Thinking Activities

Speaking/Doing

1. Look up a newspaper that was published on the day you were born. Prepare a two- to three-minute news broadcast of the headline stories. Also note the prices of merchandise—cars, houses, clothing. How has the world changed and how is it still the same? Present your news broadcast in front of the class. After your talk, compare information with classmates on how you located the newspaper. Did you use library resources? Was the newspaper on microfiche film? Did you find the newspaper on the Internet? How easy was it to find the particular issue you needed? Discuss with classmates what types of information you might want to find in old newspapers.
2. Bring to class a collection of articles, pamphlets, books, editorials, etc. Highlight some facts of interest from each of the sources you bring. Share these facts and the sources you got them from with your class. Discuss whether the data is from a reliable source or a biased source. How do you know?

Writing

1. Why is it important to have an audience goal *before* you prepare a speech? Select a topic that interests you and select an audience that might be interested in your topic. Write a goal statement that will specifically state what it

is that you would like for your audience to know, to believe, or to do at the end of your presentation. Make a brief topic outline of three main ideas that support that goal for that specific audience. Next, select a new audience and repeat the process.

2. Discuss in one or two paragraphs how you would determine if research material is reliable or not. Include at least three types of research sources in your discussion.

Group Activities

1. Work in groups of six to eight students. Prepare a segment for a news magazine show like *20/20* or *60 Minutes*. The segment should feature information about a social problem, a disease, a new scientific discovery, a human interest story, a business scam, or the like. Each team member should take one aspect of the story to research. Present your show to your classmates. Projects can be videotaped or performed live. Members of the group can also role-play the various characters—the victims, the experts, the reporters, etc.

2. With a partner or in a small group, look up *plagiarism* in the library. Find magazine articles or newspaper articles that discuss cases of plagiarism, especially those that have landed in court. What were the details and what were the consequences? Prepare a group report on your findings.

Practical Application: Case Challenge

Mr. Ware, chair of the Art Department, asked two graduates, Albert and Mingmee, to come back and speak to juniors and seniors about what opportunities were available for art students on their college campuses. Albert and Mingmee were each asked to give a five- to seven-minute speech. Mingmee gave the first presentation, describing her experiences as a photo major at State U. and her plans to study abroad in Florence, Italy, for her junior year. She briefly listed the other art majors that were available at State U. Albert described his experience at a small conservatory where he majored in painting. He described in detail the other art majors in sculpture and graphic design.

When a student asked Mingmee if all majors required an application portfolio she said she did not know. She did talk about developing her portfolio. Another questioner asked how much more it cost to major in film and, again, she was unsure. When Albert was asked about his school's study-abroad program, he had little to say. A junior said the web site at State U. listed a surface pattern major but she could not figure out what that was. She asked Mingmee to explain the major. Once again, Mingmee was stumped.

What problems do you recognize in this situation? What should these two college students have done before speaking to Mr. Ware's art students?

Chapter Eleven

Preparing a Presentation

Objectives

After reading this chapter, you will be able to

- define a purpose statement and give an example
- describe the main organizational patterns for speeches
- create a sentence outline and a word outline
- describe and use various supporting materials
- explain ways to evaluate supporting material
- list the characteristics of language that help get meaning across
- identify and give examples of figures of speech
- develop introductions, conclusions, and transitions for speeches

Key Terms

alliteration

chronological order

hyperbole

irony

metaphor

personification

purpose statement

simile

source credibility

supporting material

tone

transitions

> **"** If you don't know where you're going, any road will take you there. If you do know where you're going, only a few roads will take you there. **"**
> —OLD SAYING

273

Preparing for the Big Presentation

It was 2 A.M. on Thursday. Bianca, Charlie, and Megan were struggling with their presentation to the Westend Community College Board meeting, scheduled for the following Monday evening. What had started as a class project had grown much more complicated. Megan had been part of a rock-climbing group in high school and recently had taken Bianca and Charlie on a day-long expedition. The three had also visited a sports center that had a climbing wall. All three had gotten into the sport in a big way. As part of a class speech assignment, they talked about their experiences. The class was really excited by their talk, and so the three friends decided to get the college involved. They wanted to convince the school administrators to sponsor a rock-climbing club on campus.

"This seems like a no-brainer," said Bianca. "These clubs exist all over the country and it's a hot sport. What's not to like? We can turn out lots of students. You know how they are always looking for something new and exciting to do. This could become very popular on campus. The college is always looking for popular activities. The Board will really like this."

"You and I think it's great," replied Megan, "but the question is—what about people who don't know much about this? How will we convince them? They probably will look at our proposal very skeptically. They'll worry we're taking the students off to an emergency room."

"Meaning what?" questioned Bianca.

Megan continued, "Think about it. The students in the audience will want to hear about the challenges; the administrators will want to know about the dangers and the insurance costs. They'll also want to know whether or not the college will have to take on any additional responsibilities if the club is approved. And on top of that, they'll want to know about how other schools do it."

"Yuck," groaned Bianca. "So what do we put into this presentation? We have 15 minutes."

"Let's use some of your stories about pushing your limits and talk about the teamwork involved. They'll like that," suggested Charlie.

"Well, Megan sure knows about pushing your limits!" Bianca thought for a moment. "So how should this play out? Charlie can talk about how clubs work. He'll be good at that. He can draw on his experiences working on the events committee of the campus running club. I can talk about the background of the sport and how it is so popular. PBS broadcast a special last month that's available on video. I'll bet I can get some ideas from it. Megan, you can talk about bouldering and rope climbing."

"Do we want to use some visuals?" asked Megan.

"Something to show them what rock climbing looks like? Maybe a colorful opening slide that says, Going Vertical."

"I heard a great quote we can use. It's something like 'Don't follow where the path leads. Go to where there is no path and leave your own trail'—something like that," said Bianca.

Charlie stood up and yawned. "I have to work at the hospital admitting room at 8 tomorrow. I'm outta here to get some sleep."

"My brain is mush," added Meg. "We're done for tonight. Let's get together Saturday morning."

What will this group need to accomplish over the weekend to make sure they are prepared for Monday night? What important things have they not considered well or not considered at all?

Just as you only get one chance to make a first impression, so also you only get one chance to make your points in a presentation. Whether you are giving a formal speech or an informal talk, you have to present clear and organized ideas or your listeners will get confused. This chapter discusses six important tasks that will help you prepare clear and organized ideas: (1) creating a purpose statement, (2) selecting the right organizational pattern, (3) outlining the main ideas, (4) using appropriate supporting material, (5) choosing your language, and (6) creating introductions, conclusions, and transitions. These six tasks will be discussed in relation to preparing a formal speech or report, but it is important to keep in mind that they can be applied to informal speaking situations as well.

Purpose Statements

You have to know where you are going to reach a goal. The first step in preparing a speech is to write a purpose statement. A **purpose statement** summarizes the main ideas and goal of your speech. In a general way it is related to the overall speech purpose, such as persuading or informing. A purpose statement in a speech is similar to the thesis statement in an essay. Some speakers use one carefully worded sentence as a purpose statement, while others use two or three sentences. Purpose statements are included in the introduction to a speech.

A good purpose statement indicates the topic, provides a guide to the organization and main points, and contains the audience goal—for example, "Because I believe Penny's shoe store is not attracting youthful buyers, I am going to suggest three things you can do to bring in teenage customers: (1) change the window displays, (2) take out an ad in the high school paper, and (3) hire some younger staff."

The audience goal can be stated in the following way: listeners will be able to explain three ways to increase the number of teenage customers at Penny's shoe store. When it is well written, the purpose statement indicates the pattern of organization or the logical progression of ideas. Listeners will use this pattern to help them identify your main ideas as you present them.

Check It Out

Write three possible purpose statements for one of the following topics:
• ways to decrease drunk driving
• making senior year optional
• assessing the workplace culture of (choose a business)

FOX TROT

Patterns of Organization

Most formal informative and persuasive speeches have a general three-part structure—an introduction, a body, and a conclusion. This structure is similar to that of a composition. The introduction gains the audience's attention, tells them about your topic and purpose, and connects you to your listeners. The body contains the main points. The conclusion summarizes the main points and ends the speech in an interesting way. This standard structure illustrates the famous speaker's rule: "Tell them what you're going to tell them. Tell them. Tell them what you told them."

The body of a speech is built around main points that follow a particular organizational pattern. There are a number of common organizational patterns speakers can use. These include time order, spatial order, topical order, process order, cause-effect order, and problem-solution order.

Time, or Chronological, Order

Time order, also called **chronological order,** is a method of organizing the points of a speech by placing them in the order in which they happen. The speaker might organize information in terms of the past, present, and future. The speaker might discuss historical events in sequence. The speaker might talk about activities scheduled for this morning, afternoon, and evening or work that needs to be done at 9:00 A.M., 10:00 A.M., and 11:00 A.M. Often a story or narrative follows a time-order pattern. Events are presented in the order in which they happened. The following topics might use a time-order organization: my first day on the job, grandma's arrival in the United States, and my brother's famous speeding ticket.

Spatial Order

Spatial order is a method of organizing the points of a speech based on the physical relationship of people, places, or objects. One way to understand spatial order is to think of a map and imagine north to south or east to west. A speaker may talk about experiences or people in one place (New England, for example) and then move on to other places (the Midwest, then the Plains, then the West). Another way is to think in terms of top to bottom or front to back. For example, a speaker might discuss repairs needed on a house that students are renovating by dealing first with the exterior of the building, then the rooms on the first floor, and finally the rooms on the second floor. Some topics that might be organized according to space include visiting the Statue of Liberty, eating in New York's ethnic neighborhoods, and following the wagon trail routes to California.

Topical Order

Topical order is a method of organizing a speech by dividing the topic into its natural parts. There is no required specific sequence. Any point could be first or last. Yet together these points will tell the listeners a great deal about the entire topic. If you are describing three types of rock formations, it may not matter which you discuss first; if you are comparing two contemporary artists, it may not matter whose works you analyze first. Some subjects that might be organized by topic are types of video games, four challenges of the landscaping business, and American cars versus Japanese cars.

Process Order

Process order is a method of organizing the points of a speech based on the way something works or the way something is made. Workplace training speeches often use this pattern. The speaker explains the steps in a process from beginning to end. A process speech describes the steps that the listener needs to understand in order to use the information. Some topics that might be organized in terms of process include steps in screening your own T-shirts, training for a marathon, roping a calf, or transferring a phone call. Here is an example of a purpose statement for a process-order speech: "There are five easy steps to taking great pictures with a 35mm camera, which you will do in the next half hour."

Cause-Effect Order

Cause-effect order is a method of organizing the points of a speech based on a reasoning pattern that suggests that one event produces a second one—for example, riding without seatbelts results in a high number of automobile deaths, or reduced government spending causes an increase in hungry and homeless people. This order is used frequently by persuasive speakers who are advocating a change. Here is an example of a purpose statement for a cause-effect speech: "After hearing about the changes in the arts curriculum at our neighboring schools, you will recognize why our art students' portfolios are judged inferior in college admissions applications."

Problem-Solution Order

Similar to cause-effect order, problem-solution order is a method of organizing the points of a speech based on two major areas: the problem (or set of problems) and the possible solutions. This order is often used in persuasive speeches, when speakers are trying to persuade listeners to believe something or do something. Examples of speech topics that might use a problem-solution order are world hunger, global warming, and school overcrowding. A specific purpose statement might express the following idea: "Students in this district are standing at bus stops before sunrise in order to make their 7:15 classes. A more humane 8:30 start time would reduce family stress and increase first-period alertness."

Eye-to-Eye

With a partner, create three purpose statements for one topic area—for example, vegetarianism, extreme sports, current fashions, or job interviewing. Identify the organizational pattern that is implied in each purpose statement you create.

Remember!

There are six common organizational patterns that speakers use:

▶ time order

▶ spatial order

▶ topical order

▶ process order

▶ cause-effect order

▶ problem-solution order

Outlining

Think of outlining as putting up a scaffolding or framing a house. The outline identifies major points and supporting points of a speech. An outline is useful both in preparing and in presenting a speech that listeners can easily follow. A good outline provides the speaker with a map. If you follow the map, you won't get lost during the speech; and of equal importance, your listeners won't get lost either.

Types of Outlines

There are two basic types of outlines: (1) A sentence outline shows the relationship of information and the development of arguments or ideas. (2) A key-word outline lists only words for major ideas and divisions or headings.

A sentence outline is more detailed than a key-word outline. It forces you to think about each main point and supporting point and their relationship. Preparing a sentence outline helps you develop more confidence in your topic. After you have practiced your speech and gained confidence, you may wish to

Preparing a Presentation

use a word outline while actually delivering the speech. Word outlines permit you to have greater eye contact with your audience. Each type of outline is separate and distinct. They should not be combined.

Full-Sentence Outline

I. Teenagers suffer from lack of sleep.
    A. Sleep patterns change in adolescence.
        1. Your biological clock moves forward.
            a. You fall asleep later.
            b. You wake up later.
        2. Social patterns involve evening activities.
    B. School schedules work against the teenage sleep-wake cycle.
II. Learning is reduced.

Key-Word Outline

I. Teens' lack of sleep
    A. Changing patterns
        1. Biological clock
            a. Later bedtime
            b. Later rising time
    B. School schedule vs. biological clock
II. Reduced learning

A key-word outline lists only words or phrases. This speaker displays the key words of his outline for his audience to read and follow.

If you use overheads or PowerPoint to display outline points, your audience can view your outline during your presentation. This can be helpful in keep-

ing you and your listeners on track. It can be a problem, however, if you keep staring at the outline instead of talking to your listeners.

Guidelines for Outlining

Most outlines follow the format illustrated in these examples. They use numbers and letters to show the importance of each idea. Roman numerals (I, II, III) indicate the main points. Capital letters (A, B, C) indicate subpoints. Arabic numerals (1, 2, 3) indicate specific details about, or support for, the subpoints; and small letters (a, b, c) indicate support for, or information about, those specific details.

You need to remember that the type of symbol you use (I, A, 1, a) shows the level of importance of an idea. I, for example, is more important than A, because A is a subpoint under I. The Arabic numeral 1 is included under A because it is a subpoint under A, and so on throughout the outline. If there are subpoints, every main idea must be divided into at least two subpoints, and every subpoint must be divided into at least two supporting details. No idea in your outline should have just one subpoint under it.

Sometimes you might use a web-style outline to get your ideas on paper. Eventually, however, you will want to create a linear outline in order to organize your ideas in an order that you and your listeners can follow. A web-style outline looks like this:

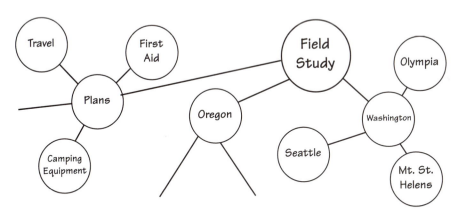

Computer Search

Use one of the search facilities on the Internet to find information about one of the following sports: rock climbing, snowboarding, parasailing, skateboarding, bungee jumping, or skydiving. Based on what you learn, develop a purpose statement and three main points you would use to develop a speech on the sport you selected.

Supporting Material

Once you have a structure for your speech, you can fill in the pieces. Effective speeches are built on a foundation of solid ideas and supporting information. Main points are explained or defended with additional information called supporting material. **Supporting material** develops the main points. As you prepare your speech, you will look for information that explains, illustrates, or defends the main points of your outline.

Types of Support

Effective speakers select the type of supporting material that is appropriate to the purpose of the speech, and they use a variety of types in order to reach all their listeners and to keep them involved. Supporting materials include definitions, quotations, examples, statistics and numbers, personal experiences, stories, and visual supports.

Definitions

Often you need to provide accurate descriptions of your meanings for certain terms you are using. A speaker may define and distinguish between *anorexia* and *bulimia* when discussing eating disorders. The workplace is filled with technical terms that need to be explained to newcomers. In addition, speakers may need to explain what they mean by words that represent abstract concepts such as *courage, risk,* or *failure.*

Quotations

When you use quotations, you are presenting another person's words on a subject. Usually, you quote persons who are experts in a topic area—for example, "According to Professor Mary Carskadon, Brown University sleep researcher, 'Kids are waking up and going to school at a time when their brains are still in the nighttime mode.'"

Sometimes speakers paraphrase certain ideas from a direct quotation. You may paraphrase what a source says as long as you tell your listeners you are doing so. When you use quotations, be sure to double-check your information. Be careful not to put your own words or point of view into someone else's mouth.

Examples

Examples help an audience remember the main point and make the speech come alive. They help listeners picture what the speaker is discussing. Examples make the speech more interesting and memorable—for example, "Edina, a suburb of Minneapolis, moved its school start time from 7:20 to 8:30 A.M. Faculty and students agree life is much better. In addition, students seem to be scoring much better on tests."

Media aids such as pictures, charts, video clips, and computerized art can provide interesting and lively visual support for a presentation.

Statistics and Numbers

Statistical information or numbers can be used to support a point. Statistics help show the importance of a topic or the size of a problem—for example, "A study on sleep schedules and grades shows that students with mostly A grades averaged 7 hours and 22 minutes of sleep a night. Students with mostly C's averaged 7 hours and 4 minutes." Statistical information summarizes and analyzes large amounts of numerical data. A good guideline for using statistical information is to keep it simple. Listeners can drown in lists of figures and lose sight of the issue or topic.

Personal Experiences

Using personal experience in a speech can provide a special kind of support, because it shows a personal connection to a topic. It indicates that you have knowledge of the topic based on firsthand experience. For example, if you are talking about sleep schedules, you could talk about two schools you attended that had different start times: "What a difference an hour makes! At my old school, I arrived somewhat alert at 8:15. You all see me dragging in here at 7:15 with my eyes shut."

Stories

You may tell made-up stories or stories based on fact to engage your listeners. Many businesses emphasize the rags-to-riches stories of company founders who started in a garage or with a $1,000 loan. You may tell a story of a mistake your brother made that taught you a great deal: ". . . so Mark ended up taking four gym classes the spring semester of his senior year."

Visual Supports

In addition to using verbal supporting material, a speaker can use nonverbal materials, such as pictures, charts or graphs, video clips, or objects. For exam-

ple, you might use a graph to show the link between grades and sleep schedules or the sleeping-waking cycle. You could display the graph using a poster,
an overhead transparency, or a computerized graphics program.

Evaluating Supporting Material

When evaluating supporting material, competent communicators look at five
factors: (1) the type of evidence, (2) whether it is from a believable source, (3)
whether it is current, (4) whether it is relevant to the goal of the speech, and
(5) whether it is a valid example.

Type of Evidence

When you evaluate supporting evidence such as quotes, numerical information, or examples, you need to determine if the evidence is fact or opinion. You
learned in Chapter 5 that a fact is information that can be proved or disproved.
Statements of fact are either true or false statements. An opinion is a judgment
based on beliefs or feelings. It cannot be proved.

Facts and opinions are both useful as supporting material. Neither is necessarily better than the other, but both should be used responsibly. Listeners
need to carefully evaluate claims that are based only on opinion and be especially wary of speakers who try to pass off opinions as facts. Effective speakers
identify facts and opinions clearly.

Credibility

How do you decide whether to believe a speaker? Another way to evaluate the
evidence is to examine the source. Does the speaker's evidence come from a
credible source? **Source credibility** means the source is trustworthy and
believable. For example, when speaking to business owners, you might quote
Tom Peters, a well-known business author and speaker who studies organizations that provide unusually good service. You won't quote the local television
intern as an expert on organizations that provide good service.

Many magazines and newspapers give an author's name and, occasionally, his
or her experience or titles at the end of an article. Books may provide biographical information. On a radio or television talk show, the host usually states a guest's
title, background, and experience in a field. This information helps you decide if
the writer or speaker can be believed on the topic being discussed. Sometimes
famous people, such as actors or athletes, will speak out for a cause that is unrelated to their area of success. These individuals may have sound opinions, but
they should not be regarded as experts. Celebrity status does not make a person a
believable source on auto safety or the dangers of smoking cigarettes.

Information found on the Internet has created concern about source credibility. As you learned in Chapter 10, the Internet includes material provided

ZITS

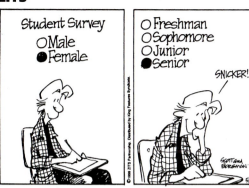

by any individual wishing to post a home page. Sometimes you will find material for which you have little or no source information. You should be very careful how you use such information. You don't want to build an argument in your speech based entirely on such information.

Current Status

Is a particular bit of information recent or up-to-date? If, for example, you are using statistics on numbers of stepfamilies, you don't want to quote figures from 1992. If you are quoting an expert, be certain the person still has the same title and holds the same opinion today as he or she did when making the statement. Politicians change political parties; breakthroughs in medical research make some treatments outdated; world events and personal experience alter opinions.

Relevance

Is the information related to the topic? Whatever your evidence, it should connect directly to your points. If, for example, you are talking about appropriate dress for an interview, don't go off on current trends in hairstyles.

It's easy to get off-track when doing research, especially when using the Internet. While researching material on Special Olympics volunteers, for instance, you can get sidetracked describing the competitors and events or recounting the history of the organization. Keep asking yourself, "Am I staying close to my topic?"

Validity

Is this a representative example? Do you have reason to believe people took this survey seriously? Be careful not to describe a very unusual situation as a typical example. If you are discussing the problem of taggers and graffiti and use a photo of the only wall in town covered with graffiti, your example is an exception. Be sure your supporting material reflects a majority of cases. Try to learn if a questionnaire was given to individuals who had the time and willingness to respond honestly and carefully.

Remember!

When you evaluate supporting material, ask yourself these questions:

▶ Is it fact or opinion?
▶ Is it believable?
▶ Is it current?
▶ Is it relevant?
▶ Is it valid?

Language

Wonderful words do not just flow spontaneously from speakers' mouths. Effective speakers carefully craft the key language of their talks. They pay attention to word choice, figures of speech, and tone to help them achieve the impact they want to have.

Word Choice

To make sure the audience understands the message, speakers try to use language that is accurate, clear, appropriate, and original.

Accuracy

As you learned earlier, people interpret messages differently. Words such as *bat, charity, peace,* and *attractive* mean different things to different people. Your audience will understand your message more accurately if you use words that are concrete and specific, rather than abstract and general.

Clarity

Lee Iacocca, former head of the Chrysler Corporation, reported that the secret of his success is talking "plain and simple." Words with four or five syllables or words that are less frequently used are not automatically better than one- or two-syllable ones, even though some speakers seem to think they are. Look at the difference in clarity between the following two examples:

> "He noted, by way of illustration, that this was figuratively a sinkhole. He made an application to the Council of Directors at the beginning of the year for a sufficient amount of funds, preferably from the appropriated budget, to make a purchase of three state-of-the-art computers."

> "He said, for example, that he had applied to the Council in January for funds to buy three good computers."

Technical words and words that are unusual or unfamiliar need to be defined. For example, students in the opening case study will have to define

rock-climbing terms such as *bouldering, rappelling,* and *abseiling* when they speak to the school board.

In business, vague terms are sometimes used to make something sound less harsh. When people lose their jobs, for example, they may be *downsized, out-sourced, reengineered,* or *selected out.* Such terms are misleading. None of them is as clear as *laid off, let go,* or *fired.*

Clarity is also affected by the way you pronounce words and the way you construct the sentences you speak. Whether your language is formal or informal, your speech gives you an opportunity to practice both correct grammar and good articulation. When you mispronounce words or speak with grammatical errors, the audience members lose their focus because your speech patterns distract them.

Lee Iacocca, former head of the Chrysler Corporation, is an accomplished motivational speaker who emphasizes the value of talking "plain and simple." In this photo, taken in the fall of 1987 in Detroit, he is introducing the 1988 line of Chrysler Corporation cars.

Appropriateness

Speakers must use language that is appropriate to the topic, the listeners, and the occasion. The statement "Hi Y'all. I sure am glad you could stop by to see us in our fancy threads" is not the best way for a speaker to address an audience at the National Honor Society induction ceremony. Select your language to suit the occasion. Your language should be formal and dignified when the occasion is formal, such as an honors ceremony, an important business meeting, or a sales presentation. It should be informal when the occasion is casual—for example, a company picnic, an employee's birthday party, or a club banquet.

Originality

Competent communicators find original ways to say something familiar. They are creative without being unclear. The more effort you put into finding original ways to express yourself, the greater your chance of reaching your audience goal.

Preparing a Presentation

Career Communication *Real Estate Agent*

Real estate agents are sometimes compared to matchmakers: they are expected to bring together buyers and sellers of land and buildings. Some real estate agents specialize in large pieces of open land, others deal in corporate buildings, and many focus on residences or homes. No matter what their specialty is, the agents need to be able to inform and persuade their clients.

A residential real estate agent helps clients sell their homes. He or she will explain how to prepare the property for sale, will attempt to find buyers for the property, and will take the client through the closing process. At other times the

agent will help a client find a new home. This involves reviewing possible interesting properties, taking the clients through countless available homes, and guiding them through the closing of the one that is finally selected. Agents ask questions and listen actively to learn exactly what a client wants.

Often they make presentations to clients and to fellow realtors, describing their properties. Successful agents spend a significant amount of time preparing a presentation, familiarizing themselves with the selling points of a particular property, and then crafting descriptions of those selling points that will engage and impress their clients.

Agents need to know a great deal about home values, home design, and financing options. Because real estate agents work in response to client needs and market factors, they must be flexible, patient, diplomatic, and skilled.

Figures of Speech

Figures of speech help a speech come alive. They appeal to listeners' imaginations and help them remember what was said. Figures of speech are ways of making language more imaginative and more memorable. Five commonly used figures of speech are *similes, metaphors, personifications, hyperbole,* and *irony. Alliteration,* though not a figure of speech, is another useful language tool.

Similes

A **simile** is a comparison of two things that are not alike. A simile includes the word *like* or *as*. For example, a speaker might say "Interviewing for that job with Mr. Abbot was like going through the toughest audition of my life," or "Listening to that salesperson's voice was like having someone stick sharp pins in my ears."

Metaphors

A **metaphor** is also a comparison of two things that are not alike. The comparison is implied. The words *like* and *as* are not used. For example, a speaker might say, "My group is a rock; they make me feel secure," or "I work with a bunch of corporate drones."

Whether you know it or not, you use metaphors every time you talk about "surfing the Net" or "riding the information superhighway." Sports metaphors and similes are used commonly in business. Success is often talked about in terms of "scoring a touchdown" or "winning the gold." Business competitors may "take the field," "go to the mat," or "play hardball."

Personification

A figure of speech that gives human characteristics to nonhuman things is called **personification**—for example, "The letters on the screen were dancing before my eyes," "That computer doesn't like me," and "That idea really grabbed me." As you know, letters can't dance, computers don't have feelings, and ideas can't literally grab a person. All of these expressions are merely colorful ways of getting a point across. They "grab" your listeners' attention.

Hyperbole

An intentional exaggeration is called **hyperbole**. For example, a speaker might say, "By doing my report for me, this intern saved my life!" (The intern may have saved his job but not his life.) "It is the sale of a lifetime." (There will probably be more sales just as big.)

Irony

Irony is the use of words to convey a meaning that is the opposite of the literal meaning: "It was the usual great dorm food—cold hot dogs and cold pizza." "This chair is really comfortable, especially if you're a small cat." Speakers often use irony as a form of sarcasm to emphasize a point they are making.

Alliteration

The repetition of initial sounds in closely connected words is **alliteration**. This language device is often found in poetry. It catches the attention of listeners and helps make a point more memorable. "The Big Bang" and "the terrible twos" are examples of alliteration. Comments such as "Your report should be clear, concise, and concrete" or "Analyzing a family means looking at rules, roles, and relationships" also contain alliteration.

Check It Out

Read the following workplace comments and identify the figures of speech.

- The sleek silver convertible called my name as I walked into the showroom.
- She hit that ball to the moon!
- Careful. Don't spend the whole 20-cent raise in one place.
- Let's get this show on the road.
- That sale was just like an easy layup.

Delle Chatman, *Screenwriter, Actor, Director*

It's difficult to capture the great range of artistic endeavors Delle Chatman has pursued over the past decade. This multitalented artist has worked as a screenwriter, actor, film and video director, photographer, and teacher of screenwriting. She wrote her first film script at the age of 12, studied acting in college and graduate school, and returned to writing when she found there was a shortage of roles for African American actresses.

She is especially proud of her script for *Free of Eden,* star-

ring Sidney Poitier and his daughter Sydney Poitier, which played on network television and is now available in video rental stores. Because of its focus on mentoring, this film has found a "life beyond its air date" because many educational institutions bring Ms. Chatman in to screen the movie and discuss its script. She is also proud of creating the role of an African American cowboy for *The Young Riders,* a television series about the Pony Express riders.

When asked for her advice to young artists, she says, "If you find over the course of a

month that the dates you made with yourself to write, paint, or shoot pictures have been broken, you haven't got much desire. The things you really want, you make time for." In order to make time for her work, she goes to bed quite early, gets up at 2 or 3 A.M., writes for a few hours, and then catches one last hour of sleep.

Delle Chatman finds working with words a constantly rewarding experience. Creating fresh images and making a script come alive for actors and audiences is an artistic challenge she relishes. "The right word," she says, "gives life to a character, inspires an image for the cinematographer, and fashions a plot out of a random event. Its power is enormous. Change one word and everything changes."

When she began her career, she held the "misguided

notion" that artists did not need to be actually involved in business activities such as marketing. Now she knows she has to persuade others to pay attention to her work and specifically "convince people you have something they need and want." She approaches a meeting in which she has to "pitch," or sell, a script with the attitude that it is a storytelling opportunity. Producers want to hear the story before they read the script. She carefully prepares what she is going to say in advance and presents the story as if she were giving a performance. She knows she is talking to the first audience for her work.

Delle Chatman loves the opportunity to create art in many forms. For her, screenwriting "is an opportunity to beat life into a shape that makes sense to me—from fade in to fade out."

Tone

Tone is the style or manner of expression in speaking. There are many ways to say the same thing. Depending on your workplace, your presentations and reports may be funny or serious, formal or informal, lengthy and detailed, or breezy and brief.

In some schools, announcements are made in a matter-of-fact manner—formal and direct. In other schools, announcement time becomes a comedy session. In some organizations, group reports are regularly interrupted with questions and jokes; in others, no one speaks until the presentation is completed. When you prepare a speech, take time to consider the context and circumstances, and adopt a tone that is appropriate to both.

Introductions, Conclusions, and Transitions

Much of the effect of a speech depends on how well you greet the audience, how well you leave the audience, and how well your speech hangs together. It is important, therefore, to put time and effort into introductions, conclusions, and transitions.

Introductions

In the introduction to a speech addressing the problems of pollution, Mike Bowlen, CEO of ARCO, grabbed the attention of his audience with this description of London in 1952:

> "I want you to imagine this scene: it's a damp morning during the Christmas season in London. The city awakes to see streets with a thick gray mist. But this is no ordinary London fog. As the clouds roll through the streets and seep into the houses, men, women, and children are gasping for breath. Within hours, hospital emergency rooms are crammed with people complaining of stinging lungs. When the fog finally lifts, five days later, thousands are dead."

An introduction should serve three purposes:

1. *Gain attention.* This is your big moment! Find a way to make people say "This is going to be good!"
2. *Introduce your topic and purpose.* Before your introduction is completed, your audience should know what your topic is and the purpose of your speech. Your introduction should also preview your main points.

3. *Connect with your audience.* You should come across as a person who is interested in the topic and in your listeners.

The following sections discuss some common types of introductions.

Startling Statement

A startling statement presents information that surprises the audience—for example, "If you start saving $2,000 a year in an IRA at 18, you are likely to have more than $2,000,000 by the time you retire."

Rhetorical Question

A rhetorical question is one requiring no answer from the audience. It challenges the audience to think. It should not be answerable by a simple yes or no—for example, "If you had the chance to meet any living famous person, whom would you choose?"

Humor

A joke or funny statement serves to relax an audience. The humor should also relate to the topic—for example, "When it comes to dealing with my heart, I'm like Woody Allen, who said, 'I'm not afraid to die. I just don't want to be there when it happens.'"

Quotation

A quotation from a famous person grabs the attention of the audience and lends authority to your ideas—for example, "'No leader can create a successful team alone, no matter how gifted he is.' These words, spoken by Phil Jackson, former NBA player and Chicago Bulls basketball coach, capture the essence of good leadership."

Story

A brief story, well told, can involve the audience in your topic right from the start—for example, "Let me tell you a story about Jose. Jose had bad grades and poor attendance until his sophomore history teacher recognized that his humor and arguments were signs of intelligence. That history teacher asked him to audition for the school's mock-trial team. Four years later Jose became a star scholarship student at Indiana University."

Personal Experience

A personal experience gets the listeners' attention and helps the audience connect with the speaker—for example, "Last week I left Sudan, where rain never comes but famine does. In the past six months I have seen children struggling . . . ."

Example

An example presents a vivid illustration of the topic—for example, "To be successful in business, you need to adopt a variety of winning business practices.

Debbie Fields, founder of Mrs. Fields cookies, has followed this advice very successfully. Among other things, if her cookies are not sold within two hours, she donates them to charity."

Reference to the Occasion, Audience, or Topic

A reference to the reason for your speech focuses your listeners' attention on what is going on, why they are there, and why they are listening to you—for example, "Welcome to Cheerleading Camp. This group is one-in-a-million. Well, actually you are one part of 3.3 million cheerleaders in the United States."

Effective speakers know the value of a strong introduction. They use startling statements, rhetorical questions, humor, personal experiences, and other devices to grab the attention of their audience immediately.

Conclusions

In the conclusion of your speech, you need to remind your listeners what you told them and give them a final thought. A conclusion has three purposes:

1. *Summarize your main points.* Listeners can forget your main points; therefore, you need to remind them.
2. *Repeat your main goal.* Motivate your listeners to reach your audience goal.
3. *Provide a clear ending.* Don't leave your listeners wondering whether the speech is over.

There are many types of conclusions. Some of the most common are summaries, quotations, appeals to the audience to act, and stories. One very helpful technique is to connect the conclusion to your introduction. This approach helps reinforce your purpose and gives your speech a sense of balance.

Sarah Roberts, *Library Page*

If you were looking for Sarah Roberts, the first place to check would be the local library. While most of the kids in the Iowa farm community where she grew up were learning to ride tractors and playing basketball in their parents' barns, Sarah was traveling to the worlds of her favorite fictional characters. Once she turned 16, she was able to turn her passion for books into a way to earn money, working as a library page at Ericson Public Library in Boone, Iowa.

The job of a library page essentially involves locating books and reference materials for library patrons and reshelving the books once the patrons have finished using them. Pages also help patrons use the equipment in the library, such as computers and microfiches. Sarah likes meeting new people and being surrounded by books all day. She also enjoys helping people find the information they need. Sometimes she locates reference materials for students working on an upcoming paper or presentation, or she guides parents in choosing good books for their children. Often people will ask her to recommend a book for them to read, and Sarah says that she enjoys that aspect of her job most of all. "To make a good recommendation, I talk to the person to discover a little about his or her personality and interests, and then I make a suggestion that fits with what I've learned. I'm not right about their tastes 100 percent of the time, but it's very satisfying when patrons come back to tell me how much they enjoyed the books."

After graduating from high school, Sarah attended the Des Moines Area Community College for two years before transferring to the University of Iowa in Iowa City, where she majored in history. At both schools she worked as a library page. Sarah thinks that she has gained a broad base of experience by working in libraries in different settings, and that she is well prepared for the career she would eventually like to pursue—that of librarian. "No one I know was surprised when I told them I wanted to be a librarian," Sarah says with a smile. She is already investigating graduate schools that offer master's programs in library science. Perhaps the biggest question for Sarah will be what to do with her pet hedgehog, Spike, if she attends graduate school out of state. As far as her future is concerned, though, Sarah has no need to worry. Her experience and enthusiasm should take her as far as she wants to go.

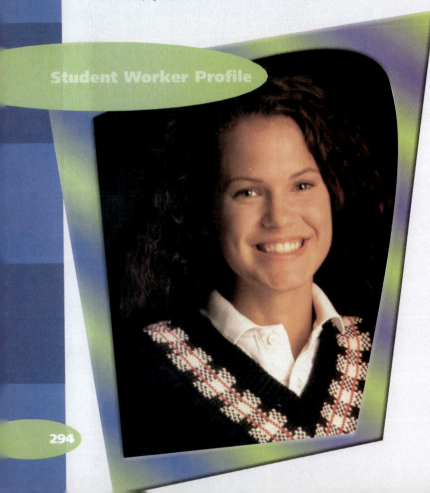

Student Worker Profile

294

When you are giving short reports or training speeches, the introductions and conclusions should be very brief. If your workplace report is three minutes long, you will not spend two minutes introducing it and one minute concluding it. You should be businesslike and get to the point quickly.

Linking Ideas Through Transitions

Transitions are words, phrases, or sentences that form links between ideas. You have probably noticed the key sentences that move a speaker from point to point or from introduction to main body to conclusion. Such statements connect the parts of a speech and help listeners follow the flow of ideas. They serve as verbal signals that the speaker is moving from one point to the next.

There are many transition words or phrases. The following ones are typical: *first, second, also, next, as a result, in addition to, another point, on the other hand, furthermore,* and *finally.*

 *Summary*

In this chapter, you learned how to prepare a presentation. First, you create a purpose statement that indicates the topic, provides a guide to the organization and the main ideas, and contains an audience goal.

You should organize your speech in a way that reflects its purpose. Six common patterns of organization are time order, spatial order, topical order, process order, cause-effect order, and problem-solution order.

An outline identifies major points and supporting points of a speech. The two basic types of outlines are the sentence outline and the key-word outline.

Supporting material explains, illustrates, or defends your main points. Seven common types of supporting material are definitions, quotations, examples, numbers, personal experiences, stories, and visual supports. Evaluate supporting material on the basis of what type it is (fact or opinion), whether it is from a credible source, whether it is relevant, whether it is current, and whether it is a valid example.

Use language that is accurate, clear, appropriate, and original. Make use of figurative language to add interest and variety to your speech. Adopt a tone that is appropriate to the audience and occasion.

Common types of introductions include startling statements, rhetorical questions, humor, quotations, stories, personal experiences, examples, and references to the occasion, audience, or topic. Many of these types can also be used for your conclusion. You should use transitions within the body of your speech to connect your ideas in a way that the audience can follow.

Review Questions

1. What should a purpose statement do?
2. What are the common organizational patterns speakers can use?
3. Using the broad topic "transportation," write five titles for a speech that would be organized using time order, space order, topic order, process order, and problem-solution order.
4. What does a speech outline identify?
5. What type of outline would be best to use while delivering a demonstration? Why?
6. Name the types of supporting material good speakers often use.
7. Name five ways to evaluate supporting material.
8. Name some figures of speech and give an example of each.
9. What are the purposes of an introduction? a conclusion?
10. What purpose do transitions serve in a speech?

Critical Thinking Activities

Speaking/Doing

1. Write an introduction on a topic of your choice. It should include an attention-getting device and your purpose statement. Rehearse it and perform it in front of the class without notes. At the end of the introduction, ask members of the audience to give you feedback: Was your attention-getting device effective? What is your topic? What is your purpose? What main points will be covered in your presentation? Would classmates be interested in hearing the whole speech?
2. Find an inspirational quotation that has meaning for you. Create a small poster featuring the quotation and illustrate it. Present the poster to the class, explain why the quotation has significance for you, and suggest topics it could be used with in a speech.

Writing

1. Write a key-word outline for one of the titles that you made up for Review Question 3. Be sure to use the appropriate numbers and letters for each subdivision.
2. In one paragraph, explain why Lee Iacocca might agree with the advice, "Don't use fifty-cent words when a nickel word will do!"
3. Select a topic and write an outline for a three- to four-minute speech. Turn in a key-word outline of your speech.

Group Activities

1. Pair up with a partner. Select a professionally written speech, such as Martin Luther King's "I Have a Dream" speech. Make a copy of the script. Using highlighters, create a key for the various figures of speech that the speaker uses. For example, metaphors might be blue, similes might be pink, etc. Go through the speech and color-code any figures of speech that you find. Share your results with the class, and read aloud a portion of the speech to illustrate the richness of its language.

2. Divide the class into groups of six to eight students. Have one person begin by challenging another group member to create a figure of speech on a particular topic. For example, Bob might challenge Sung Li to create a metaphor about ice cream. The group member being challenged can either create a metaphor and take the lead away from the challenger, or he or she can dare the challenger to do it. If the challenger can do it, he or she remains the challenger. All answers are to be judged by a consensus of the group. All group members should be given an opportunity to participate.

Practical Application: Case Challenge

Bryan is a college intern at a sports marketing company. His workplace is best characterized as a "work hard/play hard" environment. Employees interact in a casual and friendly manner. Bryan has been asked to give his first four-minute presentation on future marketing strategies for the Abbott soccer ball account, which his supervisor manages. Bryan was asked to rehearse his speech with his supervisor and another intern before the actual presentation. He arrived and began in the following manner:

"Ladies and Gentlemen, it is my pleasure to talk with you today about the Abbott soccer ball account. Please hold any questions because I may answer them along the way. As the famous saying goes, 'The opera ain't over till the fat lady sings.' Today I will talk about the history of the account, the current status, and our future plans.

"As you know, Super Sports Marketing has had the Abbott account since 1988. At that time we concentrated on basketballs and paid only slight attention to soccer. This was a time when U.S. TV did not broadcast soccer and few schoolchildren played it. Those who did were boys. These were the dark days of U.S. soccer. By 1992 . . . ."

If you were listening to this rehearsal, what feedback would you give Bryan about his presentation to help him make it better?

Chapter Twelve

Giving a Presentation

Objectives

After completing this chapter, you will be able to

- define *delivery* and explain the four methods of delivery
- demonstrate nonverbal components of personal delivery style
- explain how to rehearse a speech
- describe ways of developing speech confidence and managing stage fright
- demonstrate how to adapt to distractions during a presentation
- demonstrate how to handle question-and-answer periods and team presentations
- follow guidelines for using media aids

Key Terms

clarity
extemporaneous speech
impromptu speech
manuscript speech
memorized speech
Q&A
stage fright
visualizing
voiced pauses

> 66 Every child, woman, and man should possess license to speak or sing in his or her true voice. 99
>
> —JOYCE MAYNARD, *At Home in the World*

Adapting to Unpredictable Situations

After participating in a statewide conference on distributive education, seniors Terry and Leslie decided Royal Ridge High School needed a senior internship program to provide valuable work experience for students before they enter the workplace full-time or go to work during their college years. They persuaded Ms. Nobles, the community teen job coordinator, to invite local employers to an evening meeting where they could present their proposal to community business leaders.

On the day of the meeting, Terry and Leslie got together to go over the agenda for the evening.

"We'll want to be sure that we cover all the advantages of the internship program," said Leslie.

"No problem," Terry replied. I already know what I want to talk about. I'll focus on the student talent pool and put together some slides to illustrate my points. You can focus on your firsthand experiences as an intern. What's to worry about? We've got it covered."

That evening, at 7 P.M., 19 business leaders appeared to hear the students' ideas. Forty to fifty participants had been expected, so Terry and Leslie had prepared for a large group.

As the evening opened, Terry welcomed the business leaders, thanked them for coming, and outlined a one-hour program. He stood behind the lectern using a microphone because the group had spread themselves throughout the 100-seat auditorium. Terry had prepared a slide presentation but had not been able to practice in the auditorium. Due to difficulties with electrical outlets, the slides had to be coordi-

nated by Ms. Nobles in the back of the auditorium. Terry had to say "Next slide" every time he needed one. Occasionally slides and comments were not well coordinated. Nevertheless, he made a good case for creating a student talent pool that employers could draw on for help in exchange for providing meaningful work experiences.

Midway through the talk Max Gibson, manager of the local supermarket, began to ask specific questions. Terry stopped and tried to answer them. By the fourth question Leslie was looking very anxious because Terry was discussing topics she planned to cover, but she did not know how to break into the discussion tactfully. Finally Ms. Nobles suggested that all questions be held until both presentations were over, predicting that some questions would be answered by Leslie's remarks. Although Terry presented good information about the talent pool available and the need for internship experiences, after about 12 minutes members of the audience were looking restless or bored. When he concluded, three listeners slid out the back door.

As Leslie began her presentation, she stood at the front of

the auditorium and invited those in the back to move up. All but one person did so. She opened with a story about her successful internship and then indicated the topics she planned to cover. Then Leslie asked the audience if there were any specific issues they hoped she would cover. One woman asked her to address work during school hours and the level of supervision expected. A man requested she discuss how students would be matched to the employers. Leslie thanked them, made a few notes, and proceeded to talk about the expected relationships among the school, the student interns, and the employers. When answering a listener's question, she nodded to the person as if to say, "There's your information." In order to hold the listeners' attention, Leslie moved across the front of the auditorium and walked up the center aisle on occasion. She spoke loudly enough to be heard throughout the large auditorium. Terry held up a large poster-board visual that detailed the employer-intern matching process. It was a bit difficult to see beyond the tenth row, but listeners paid attention as Leslie went through each step listed on the poster board.

What are three things that appear to be working well in this dual presentation? What suggestions for improvements would you recommend to Terry and Leslie for the next time they give such a presentation?

The delivery of a message is as vital to the success of a presentation as the message itself. Delivery refers to the manner in which you convey the message—your verbal and nonverbal style of communicating. Sometimes it is called the package in which you wrap your message. How you say something can determine if your message is really understood.

Every individual has his or her own unique style. Your style is influenced by your skills and your personality. Ann Richards, the former governor of Texas, has a very distinct style of speaking, and it is very different from the powerful style of Reverend Jesse Jackson. Both are popular speakers and dynamic leaders. Though their styles of delivery differ, they are equally effective.

Effective delivery can make or break a sales presentation. In less than a minute, customers will decide whether or not they are interested in your idea or product. Television has taught audiences to expect quick sound bites of information on the news and complete product messages in 30-second commercials. Without a dynamic delivery, you will lose an audience's interest and attention. To ensure that you present your ideas well, it is important that you understand some basic principles related to giving a presentation.

Methods of Delivery

Different situations call for different methods of delivery. There are four basic methods that speakers use: extemporaneous, impromptu, manuscript, and memorized. Each of these methods has different strengths and weaknesses.

Extemporaneous Method

The most common form of delivery is the extemporaneous style. For an **extemporaneous speech,** speakers use a prepared outline but do not plan or write out each sentence. Time is spent organizing thoughts and ideas and rehearsing from a key-word outline. The emphasis is on communicating with the audience, receiving feedback during the speech, and adapting spontaneously to the audience's needs or reactions.

Speakers usually write the speech outline on note cards or a single sheet of paper, using key words or phrases. The notes contain references to supporting material, names of people, statistics, or descriptive words to help speakers remember an example or story. That way, while they are talking, they can hold the card in one hand and refer to it easily.

Good extemporaneous speakers often memorize their opening and closing remarks, knowing that a strong beginning and a strong ending will impress their listeners. They also practice delivering the body of the speech aloud in order to polish key phrases and ideas.

Ann Richards, former governor of Texas, has a distinct down-to-earth style of speaking that captivates audiences. In this photo, taken in Austin, Texas, she is announcing her candidacy for the governorship.

Extemporaneous speakers write the speech outline on note cards that they can refer to easily when they deliver the speech. Here, George W. Bush, another Texas governor, uses note cards effectively.

Advantages The speaker is very organized in thought, rarely forgets what to say, appears confident and poised, and can be flexible to adjust to anything that might occur during the speech. It's easier to adapt this type of speech to different audiences or respond to audience feedback than with other types of speeches. You can rephrase or repeat ideas if necessary.

Disadvantages Speakers may stumble over words or forget the next main idea. These problems are not likely to happen if you have rehearsed the speech several times, but keep in mind that you can't polish every phrase. The extemporaneous method may give you false confidence. Many beginning speakers think that they will not have to prepare very carefully or rehearse very much because grand ideas will come as they talk. If you believe this, you may be in for an unpleasant surprise!

Impromptu Method

An **impromptu speech** is one delivered with little or no preparation. It's presented "off the top of your head." In real-life situations, people are often called upon unexpectedly to say a few words. A religious leader may ask you to lead a prayer. A teacher may ask you to talk briefly about an upcoming event. Conversations and arguments are basically a series of impromptu speeches. A question-and-answer period after a presentation is another example of an impromptu style of speaking. When you use this approach, you must always be thinking on your feet. The bottom line is "Don't speak before you think."

Speaking effectively in an impromptu style calls for a quick wit and a confident attitude. You should be yourself. It's best to pause briefly before speaking and think of two ideas that you would like to address. Next, decide what two bits of information would support those ideas and how they relate to this particular audience. Within 15 to 20 seconds, you have a structure for your speech. The rest will flow naturally.

Learning to deliver impromptu speeches confidently is one of the greatest assets you can acquire. It is very impressive in a business meeting when someone spontaneously interjects a brief argument or idea with confidence and organization or when the boss says, "Maria, anything to add?" and Maria presents a well-developed idea in 60 seconds.

Advantages Impromptu speaking sounds natural, and it builds organizational skills under pressure. Impromptu speakers learn to think very quickly on their feet.

Disadvantages You have no notes to rely on, so if you become nervous and lose your train of thought, you have nothing to fall back on. Also, it's easier to stumble over words, looking for the "right" expression. Finally, your success may depend more on appearing confident than on a well-thought-out idea.

Manuscript Method

A **manuscript speech** is written out entirely and delivered word-for-word from a typed or handwritten paper. It is important to use this method of delivery when you need to say exactly what you mean, when you have very detailed information to present, or when you have a very tight time limit. Politicians use manuscript speeches when they speak at political conventions or at major diplomatic events. Corporate executives use them when they address stockholders or all-company meetings. Educators, business leaders, and artists often use them when they speak at conferences and banquets.

You will usually deliver a manuscript speech from behind a podium on which you place the written speech. Place the speech slightly off center on the podium so that you can slide the pages to the side rather than picking them up and turning them or placing them on the bottom. Don't grip or hide behind the podium. It is there to hold the script, not you!

Advantages Using a manuscript allows a speaker to carefully choose the wording and phrasing of a speech. Ideas are fully developed. Manuscript speeches are useful to people who can't afford to say something by mistake that might

Terry Harrell, *Sales Representative*

Mr. Harrell relies on good organizational skills to make sure that he is on time for all of his appointments, knowing that doctors and nurses have little time in their busy schedules to spend with him.

He says, "I like the fact that I can actually measure my success." He knows that if he can convince doctors to believe in his products, he will be successful. He also appreciates the opportunity to go into surgery with a medical team to answer questions such as "Is the incision long enough?" or "Where should the implant go?"

Terry Harrell is an orthopedic clinical specialist. He works for the Genzyme Tissue Repair company, selling cartilage implants to replace cartilage in the knee. In the course of doing his job, he has found himself in operating rooms during surgery, in medical offices calling on physicians, and in seminar rooms teaching physicians and nurses about Genzyme's products. In his words, "I sell to physicians one-on-one, and I educate health care professionals in group and one-on-one settings."

To do his job successfully, he has to display excellent impromptu speaking skills and the ability to think quickly on his feet. He prepares for an appointment by knowing his products thoroughly, organizing in his mind what he wants to emphasize, and preparing answers for questions doctors might ask. He has to be able to explain what a product does without being able to demonstrate it because the demonstration would require actual surgery. "I have to be able to paint a picture with words." He also depends heavily on his listening skills since "I have to understand clearly what doctors need." He criticizes the image of a salesperson as "jabbering" or talking all the time. He says that a good salesperson asks questions and listens carefully to the questions a doctor asks.

His workplace frustrations come from dealing with doctors who refuse to consider new techniques and are "stuck in the past." Sometimes he has to work hard to "counter sell" the claims of competitors who are pushing products that he believes are inferior.

As a former college football player, Terry Harrell encountered many fellow athletes with knee problems during his playing days. Little did he know that one day he would become an expert on treating knee problems.

damage or ruin their careers and to people who give many speeches and don't have a lot of time to rehearse or memorize a text.

Disadvantages Using a manuscript may encourage beginning speakers to read the speech without looking up. The audience will quickly lose interest if you do that. It's difficult to get feedback if you don't look up, and it's difficult to use gestures and movements to help convey your ideas. Also, people sometimes read too fast or in a monotone.

FYI *Stages of Manuscript Development*

Creating a manuscript speech is similar to creating a fine essay. A first draft is written and then edited. A speech may go through three or four drafts before the speaker is satisfied that the language captures the appropriate mood and tone and "sounds like me." Look at the following three drafts of one paragraph of Katie's speech on her volunteer work in Paraguay. This paragraph accompanied a large slide of Katie immunizing a child.

Draft 1

In the photograph, I am giving a shot to a young boy, Diego, who doesn't want it because he thinks it will be painful. Before giving a shot, I would explain to Diego what it was for and that it didn't hurt too badly. I explained to Diego that if he didn't have the immunization, he could become very ill and might need many shots, which would hurt much more.

Draft 2

In the photograph, I am giving a shot to a young boy, Diego. He is scared because he thinks it will be painful. Before giving the shot, I explained what it was for and that it didn't hurt too badly. I explained to Diego that if he didn't have the immunization he could become very ill and might need many shots.

Draft 3

I am immunizing Diego in this photograph. He is frightened of the pain. I explained that the shot would keep him from getting very sick and that it wouldn't hurt for long.

These three drafts illustrate the value of evaluating and revising what you have written. Katie's third draft is clearer and more focused than the first two. It eliminates unnecessary words and phrases and speaks more directly to her listeners.

Career Communication *Tour Guide*

Some people make a career out of giving public presentations. Among those careers, tour guide ranks high on the list. There are many kinds of group guides, including museum or art gallery docents, travel guides, and lecturers. One special type is the college tour guide.

Most campus guides are current students at the school. Some are volunteers. The goal of the tour guide presentation is to inform prospective students and their parents about the school and to persuade them that it is a fine place. These guides are credible sources of information because they are enrolled at the school.

Tour guides meet their groups—ranging from 3 to 60

visitors, depending on the school—and deliver a short informative speech on the school's history. Then they lead the group on a walking or bus tour of the campus. They joke that an important job skill is being able to give a speech while walking backwards.

Tour guides work without notes. They memorize the main points they want to make about the locations and build-

ings they describe. The guide stops at different points on campus and discusses the location: "This is the Ashford Science Center, where many undergraduates work with professors in their labs." or "This is the university theater, where students from all majors perform in 10 shows a year." Tour guides must be prepared to answer questions, including "How's the food?" "How important are fraternities and sororities on this campus?" and "Will the faculty help you find summer internships?" Students who volunteer to serve as tour guides enjoy meeting new students and introducing them to the various facilities that will become their campus home.

Memorized Method

A **memorized speech** requires you to learn the speech and deliver it word-for-word without notes or a manuscript. Some professional speakers and politicians who travel around the country speaking to groups memorize certain speeches. Sometimes they will personalize a speech by leaving blanks in it to insert local names and references, but the basic message is performed over and over again.

The keys to performing a memorized speech are in the organization and in the delivery. To deliver a memorized speech successfully, you need to memorize your outline thoroughly so that if you forget sentences you can improvise ideas by remembering where you are in the outline. Plus, you will adapt your delivery each time you give the speech so that it sounds spontaneous.

Advantages A memorized speech can be carefully crafted. Each word and phrase can be polished to ensure that the ideas are presented as clearly and creatively as possible.

Remember!

The four basic methods for delivering a speech are

▶ Extemporaneous

▶ Impromptu

▶ Manuscript

▶ Memorized

Gestures are a natural part of communication. Your hands and arms can serve as a visual punctuation to your words. President Theodore Roosevelt, shown here delivering a campaign speech, was a forceful speaker noted for his use of gestures and movement.

Disadvantages It's very easy to forget a line when you are nervous. You can be left standing there with nothing to say. Also, speakers sometimes talk too fast or in a monotone. This is particularly true when the same speech is used again and again.

Personal Delivery Style

Personal delivery refers to the nonverbal messages you communicate during a speech—your appearance, voice, eye contact, facial expression, gestures, and body movements. Your nonverbal messages may support your spoken message, or they may keep listeners from getting your message. There are three main categories of personal delivery style: body language, eye contact and facial expression, and voice. You can use the acronym BEV to remember these categories.

Body Language

Speaker body language includes gestures, movement, posture, and appearance.

Gestures

Gestures are movements of the head, shoulders, hands, or arms that speakers use to describe or emphasize a point. A speaker may describe how to shoot a basketball by going through the motions of shooting or place emphasis on an idea by pounding on the lectern.

Gestures are a natural part of communication. Your hands can serve as a visual punctuation to your words and sentences. For example, how might a speaker gesture while saying the following statements?

- "There are three—only three—major issues in this campaign."
- "We've made terrific gains against our competition. Last year our sales records were only this far apart. This year we have outsold them in every product line and we are this far out in front."

To be effective, gestures must be large enough to be seen and understood by the audience. Hand gestures should be made above the waist and move out and away from the body. In general, the larger the audience, the larger the gesture needs to be. You may hold note cards in one hand as you move around. You can still gesture with small note cards, but you don't want to wave large sheets of paper at your listeners. As you rehearse a speech, you need to plan your gestures. Rehearse in front of a mirror or, even better, record yourself on video and watch your performance without sound.

Remember that the things that feel like basketballs at the end of your arms do not look that way to your audience! Let your hands hang easily at your side or hold your note cards in one hand and let the other hand stay near your side until you gesture.

Movement and Posture

New speakers often ask, "How do I stand?" and "Should I walk around?" If you are in a situation where it is appropriate to stand, you need to appear comfortable and confident. Place your feet slightly apart, and evenly balance your weight on both feet. Don't try to put your feet too close together, or you might sway. Try to avoid locking your knees so that you don't stop circulation and cause dizziness. Also, avoid shifting your weight onto one leg and then the other. Listeners will think you are nervous or uncomfortable. Also avoid putting your hands in your pockets and playing with loose change or keys.

Good speakers use movement to make their message clearer to the audience. Here are three simple guidelines for using movement: (1) Take a few steps during the major transitions in a speech. (2) When you move, face in the same direction you are moving. (3) Stand balanced on both feet.

How you walk to and from the front of the room before and after your speech is part of your performance too. Don't send mixed messages or confusing messages to your listeners. Don't slouch down and then stand tall. Don't leave the front before you have finished the last sentence of your speech.

Not all workplace presentations are made standing up. Often reports are given around a conference table. The way you sit is part of your nonverbal delivery. If you sit forward in your chair, leaning in toward the table and toward other members of the group, you convey interest and leadership. When you fall back or slump into the chair, with arms on the armrests, you appear more passive. Your posture sends a clear message about how you feel about yourself, the others, and the issues being addressed in the meeting.

Giving a Presentation

Appearance

Appearance matters when you are giving a speech! Remember, you are communicating with your audience from the moment you enter a room or rise from your seat. The audience forms an initial impression of you based on your clothes, hair, and jewelry. Your appearance should suit the occasion and support your message. Avoid excessive jewelry or outrageous styles that may distract your listeners.

Eye Contact and Facial Expression

Because most speeches you deliver will be to small- or moderate-sized audiences, listeners will be able to focus on your eyes and facial expressions.

Eye contact

It is very important that you look the audience in the eye. There are many myths about where to look to avoid getting nervous, including the suggestion that you should look at the rear wall over the audience's head. If you do this, you will lose your listeners' attention and respect. Your goal is to give each and every audience member the sense that you have connected with him or her.

Choose one person to direct your comments toward, maintain eye contact for five to ten seconds, and then turn your eyes to someone else for the same

Your facial expression should match the tone of your speech. The expression on this speaker's face communicates warmth, support, and helpfulness.

amount of time. If there is a small group around a table, you should focus on one individual, speak for 10 to 15 seconds, and then shift your attention to someone else and do the same thing. During the course of your speech or presentation, you should look at everyone.

Facial Expression

Your facial expression should match the tone of your speech. It should reflect the emotions you are asking your audience to feel. They look to you as a guide on how to react to your message. Nothing is more damaging to a speaker's effectiveness than having the nonverbal message contradict the verbal message. For a light, upbeat topic such as a motivational talk on team-building skills, you would want a smiling face. A speech on a more serious problem would call for a concerned and unsmiling expression on your face.

Voice

Your voice is like a musical instrument. It has the capacity for great variety. You should use that variety to your advantage. Varying your vocal qualities adds interest and meaning to your message. The vocal characteristics of rate, volume, pitch, tone, and clarity all affect a speaker's delivery.

Rate

Rate is the speed at which you speak. In the workplace, you need to consciously control your rate of speaking to be understood by all. Have you ever called a place of business only to have the receptionist answer and speak so quickly that you couldn't understand what was said?

There are several reasons why speakers deliver a message too quickly. In the case of the receptionist, it's probably familiarity and habit. He or she knows the greeting by heart and says it so often that it becomes automatic. A greeting such as "Austin North Hilton. How may I direct your call?" becomes "AustnNorthHiltnHowmydirecyourcall?" with the words running together, making them indistinguishable.

Nerves or fear will also cause a speaker to speed up. The adrenaline begins to pump into your system and gives you the extra energy to overcome the fear. You have to harness that energy and consciously control your voice when that occurs.

However, if you speak at the same rate throughout the entire speech, you are likely to bore your listeners. Use variations in your rate to call attention to certain points and to add variety. Slow down, for example, when presenting detailed, highly complex information. Reducing your rate of delivery is one way to ensure that your listeners will grasp your message.

Finally, pauses must be silent. **Voiced pauses**—verbal hesitations or interruptions such as "ah," "uh," "um," or "you know"—are distracting to listeners. When too many voiced pauses are used, listeners stop paying attention to the speaker's message. Sometimes listeners even start counting the "uhs" or "you knows."

Check It Out

The average rate of speaking is between 120 and 150 words per minute. Select a passage from a book. Count out the first 120 words and mark where the 120th word comes. Continue counting 30 more words and mark where the 150th word comes. Read the passage aloud and time yourself with a stopwatch. Stop reading after one minute. Are you within the range of 120 to 150 words? This exercise will give you a rough idea of the appropriate speaking rate for listeners to understand your ideas clearly.

Pitch

Pitch refers to the highs and lows of your vocal range. Changing your pitch will often change the meaning of a sentence. A speaker's pitch should help support the meaning of the message. For example, when speakers express pleasure or excitement, their pitch rises. When speakers express sadness or seriousness, their pitch tends to get lower.

Nervous speakers tense their vocal cords and speak in a high voice. This distracts an audience and makes the speaker sound boring. In everyday conversation, you change your pitch naturally. If you think of public speaking as a type of conversation and approach a speaking situation accordingly, your pitch will change naturally as you talk to your audience.

Volume

Volume refers to the loudness or softness of a voice. A speaker must adjust the volume of his or her speech to overcome outside interference or to compensate for the size of a room and audience. Problems occur when a speaker's voice is too soft to hear. This is common with speakers who are experiencing some stage fright. A very soft voice conveys insecurity and uncertainty. Also, the message may not be heard. A voice that is too loud will often connote aggression and hostility. To appear confident, a speaker needs to speak loudly enough for all of his or her audience to hear easily and comfortably.

You should vary your volume to emphasize and highlight main ideas. You can also use volume to regain an audience's attention. It "wakes them up" when you change volume—raising it, lowering it, or even becoming quiet.

If you are using a microphone to increase volume, be sure to test the microphone beforehand. Anticipate and fix static feedback from a speaker system before you give your speech. Don't blow or tap on the microphone in front of an audience. "Testing, testing" is not a good introduction to your message.

Remember the following guidelines for using a microphone: (1) Don't stand too close to the microphone. It magnifies each sound. (2) Don't yell when using a microphone. (3) Don't look at the microphone while speaking. Speak directly to your audience. (4) Don't let the microphone block your face.

Tone

When your boss or teacher addresses you by name, can you guess if you are "in trouble"? How do you know? It is the tone of a person's voice that lets us know the attitude or emotion underlying the message. Even very young children learn quickly to recognize differences in meaning just by the change in a speaker's tone. Anger, fear, sarcasm, irritation, joy, and puzzlement are just a few of the attitudes that we make clear by changing the tone of voice. The best way to know how your voice sounds to others is to record yourself on tape. You may be surprised by what you hear.

Clarity

Clarity refers to the clearness of a speaker's words. It includes articulation and pronunciation. A competent speaker tries to say words carefully and correctly. Slurred or mispronounced words—for example, "wader" for "water," "strenth" for "strength," or "dis" for "this"—distract listeners from focusing on the message.

Often speakers need to refer to names or places that are hard to pronounce. Take time to learn and practice the correct pronunciation of any difficult words. If you know you are going to have difficulty pronouncing a certain word, write its pronunciation on a note card. You can refer to it, if you need to, when you deliver your speech.

Often speakers need to refer to people and places that are hard to pronounce. Madeleine Albright, America's first female secretary of state, is frequently faced with having to speak in public about people and places whose names would be difficult for many of us to pronounce correctly.

Giving a Presentation

Rehearsing the Speech

Competent speechmaking requires practice. Rehearsing your speech is one of the most important parts of your preparation. In this section, you will examine ways to rehearse an extemporaneous speech, although many of the same techniques apply to other delivery methods. Rehearsing involves ordering the ideas in your mind and polishing your delivery.

Ordering the Speech in Your Mind

As you prepare to speak, imagine the main ideas in their correct order. The following simple steps will help:

1. Read over your outline silently two or three times. Go straight through without going back over any section.
2. Repeat step 1, but this time do it aloud.
3. Try to give your speech without looking at your outline or note cards. Stand up and practice gestures and movements. Even if you can't remember certain points, go through the entire speech without stopping.
4. Read your outline silently as in step 1.
5. Read your outline aloud as in step 2.
6. Try again to give the complete speech.
7. Continue steps 4 through 6 until you can complete your speech without any errors.

Polishing Your Delivery

After you are able to deliver the main ideas aloud in the correct order, you can pay attention to your delivery. Use the following steps to help you polish your delivery:

1. Imagine your audience in your mind. Set chairs in front of you or have one or two friends listen to you. If you are using visual aids, be sure to practice with them.
2. Try to connect with your real or imaginary audience. Be enthusiastic, both verbally and nonverbally.
3. If your audience is real rather than imaginary, adapt to your listeners. Watch for cues indicating that you need to change your delivery. Ask for feedback.
4. Give special attention to the introduction, conclusion, and any stories, examples, or jokes. Memorize these parts so that they will sound exactly as you want them to sound.

Christina Gómez, *Choir Director*

When parishioners stop after services at Our Lady of Angels Church to tell the children how well they sang, they are also complimenting the efforts of Christina Gómez, the co-director of the children's choir. She works at this Bronx, New York, church each week, finding great pleasure in the positive response of the children to the music.

In her line of work, Christina knows how critically important it is to concentrate on polishing your delivery. During rehearsals, Christina has the children go over the songs again and again to find just the right expression for each one and to make the songs come alive in performance. "Practice, practice, practice. That's what it's all about," she says.

Her various responsibilities include "picking out the music, teaching the children the songs, making sure they are behaving themselves during Mass, and helping to organize the performances." Christina thinks that the children are "wonderful" because they are so open to learning. Sometimes she finds it easier to work with them than with adults because she shares an ongoing sense of

mutual respect with the children. She tries to treat them as equal partners. Christina believes that if you build a partnership with the children, "they'll have more respect for you and will work with you rather than fighting you."

Unlike some instructors who may take their work too seriously, Christina says, "When I teach children to learn songs, it's very important to me that they have fun. To accomplish that, I choose upbeat songs and break down the parts for them. I make sure they understand

what the songs mean so that they can have a blast singing them."

Christina believes she manages two communication tasks in her work. The first is to relate to children in ways that allow her to get her message across without being condescending. At the same time she has to talk with parents, parishioners, and church staff when she needs help and direction. According to Christina, the role of a choir director is very significant because "When you sing, you pray twice."

Student Worker Profile

To help reduce stage fright and increase confidence, effective speakers rehearse their speeches aloud and, when possible, in front of an "audience"—real or imagined.

5. Spread your rehearsal time over three or four days. If you wait until the last minute, you will only increase your nervousness. Allow enough practice time so that you become comfortable with your speech.

Speaker Confidence and Stage Fright

Most people worry about delivering speeches. Business author and speechwriter Jeff Cook asked participants in his public-speaking workshops what they feared most about speechmaking. Here are some of the fears that participants reported: "I'll make a terrible mistake." "I'll freeze." "My voice will crack." "The audience will ask me something I don't know." "My speech will bore the audience."

Confident speakers are able to think on their feet. They know that if something goes wrong, they will adjust and make the best of it. If you are prepared, you will be able to cope with any problems that occur during your speech.

Stage Fright

Most people experience tension when they have to speak to a group. Some people experience real anxiety called stage fright. **Stage fright** is extreme nervousness when talking to an audience. Being nervous is common. Even experiencing stage fright is not unusual. The best speakers experience it sometimes.

What happens when you are nervous? People experience various symptoms. Some signs of nervousness while speaking include "butterflies" in the stomach, dry mouth, fast breathing, pounding heart, shaky legs, shifting from foot to foot, tense voice, and sweaty palms.

Although you may not like the way you feel when you are nervous, stage fright can have an advantage. If you can turn the nervous energy caused by stage fright into speaking energy, you can make your speech better. You can make your nervousness work for you rather than against you.

Most speakers feel more confident about their ability to handle stage fright when they keep in mind that stage fright becomes easier to control with practice. It's also reassuring to know that when you are experiencing stage fright you feel much worse than you look. Often, the audience can't tell just by looking at you that you are very nervous.

Many speakers use visualizing to reduce their nervousness. **Visualizing** is seeing a picture in your mind. Most athletes use visualizing as part of their regular training. Successful speakers visualize every step of delivering a speech, from walking up to the front through answering the last question.

FYI *Tips for Developing Confidence*

The following suggestions will help you use nervousness to your advantage:

1. *Prepare thoroughly.* The more prepared you are, the more self-confident you will feel.
2. *Rehearse aloud.* Visualize a successful speech as you rehearse.
3. *Breathe deeply.* Take a few deep breaths before you begin. This helps you relax.
4. *Start strong.* Have your first two or three sentences memorized.
5. *Reduce signs of nervousness.* Avoid playing with a pencil or with your hair.
6. *Display media aids effectively.* This will help use up some of your nervous energy.
7. *Read nonverbal feedback.* If you focus on your listeners, you will pay less attention to your nervousness.

Computer *Search*

Check out the following web sites to learn about organizations dedicated to speechmaking: ***http://www.toastmaster.org/*** and ***http://members.tripod.com/Speechmeisters/toastmas.htm***. Read the information provided at these sites. Would you enjoy becoming a member of one of these organizations? Take notes and share what you learn with your classmates.

Adapting to the Situation

Each speaker has to be prepared to adapt or improvise. When unexpected things occur, you can't just stop talking and quit. They may occur during a speech, during a question-and-answer session, or during a team presentation.

During the Speech

Look at the following situations. What would you do if one of them happened to you?

- You are giving your speech when an announcement comes over the loudspeaker.
- You stumble and nearly fall down on your way to the front of the room.
- Halfway through your speech, you realize that your remaining note cards are out of order.
- The computer program locks during your PowerPoint presentation.

If any of these situations ever happens to you, you must, above all else, remain calm. In the first situation, stop speaking, wait for the announcer to finish, and then continue your speech. In the second situation, stand up and continue walking to the podium. In the third situation, stop for a few seconds to put your note cards back in order. In the fourth situation, you might say, "My equipment is broken, so I'll explain the process on the board." Don't let surprises stop you. Competent speakers take surprises in stride. They may laugh at themselves, ask the audience for 20 seconds, or move to the next point.

Eye-to-Eye

With a partner, think of ways to handle these situations: (1) The audience bursts out laughing because you said "hoppiness" instead of "happiness." (2) You forget your next idea. (3) Your manuscript falls off the podium. (4) A friend keeps making faces at you.

Question-and-Answer Periods

"There will be a Q&A period after the reports." These words strike fear into the hearts of many speakers because they worry about being surprised or caught off guard. A **Q&A** period is a question-and-answer time following a presentation. If you take part in a Q&A period, you need to consider the following guidelines:

1. *Think before you speak.* Many speakers pause for 15 seconds to plan their responses, or they repeat the question to gain some extra time.
2. *Listen to the question.* A nervous speaker might hear a few words and start to plan the answer. Often this results in answering a question that was not asked. Sometimes it helps to work the question into your answer to ensure that you are sticking to the issue.

3. *Make sure that all listeners heard the question.* If the questioner speaks softly, you may ask the person to repeat the question loudly, or you may paraphrase it for the audience.
4. *Limit your answer.* Answer accurately but briefly.
5. *Avoid a debate.* Answer a question but don't engage in a five-minute argument with one listener while the others just sit there. Tell that person you can talk to him or her later.

Question-and-answer periods are very common in the workplace. Organizations often hold formal Q&A sessions with reporters or stockholders to discuss major announcements and talk about issues when a problem arises. Informal Q&A sessions are a routine part of company employee meetings and presentations.

Team Presentations

A team presentation is a speech or report given jointly by a group of people. Team reports are common in college classes and in the workplace.

Adapting to a team presentation involves several considerations. Team members must work to maintain a team image and to support each other. While one person is speaking, the entire team is frontstage. Nothing ruins a presentation faster than to have other team members engaging in backstage behavior—rolling their eyes, giggling, whispering to one another, or staring out the window—while one member speaks. Backstage behavior is unprofessional and out of place in front of an audience.

If one member makes a mistake, the whole team is responsible for managing the problem. If your teammate gives incorrect information, should you (1) leap to your feet and correct the person, (2) moan and put your head on the table, (3) try to work in a correction when you speak, or (4) send a note to the speaker, if it can be done easily? Numbers 1 and 2 will tell the listeners that this is *not* a team. Numbers 3 and 4 will convey a team image.

Here are three guidelines for good team delivery:

1. *Plan what each person will talk about and stick to it.* It's difficult when someone gives "your" talk or when someone does not cover key material.
2. *Watch your time.* If one team member takes too much time, the other members have to speed up or cut content.
3. *Pay attention to each other.* Look at your teammates as they speak. This will convey a team image to the listeners.

A Q&A period is a question-and-answer period that follows a speech or presentation. Here Lech Walesa, charismatic leader of the Solidarity movement in Poland, fields a question after a speech.

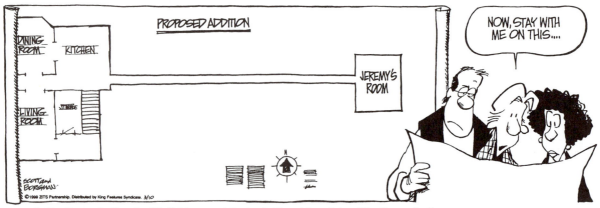

Using Media Aids

If you want your audience to remember your message, you may need to use media aids as part of your delivery. Media aids include anything the audience can see or hear, such as posters, transparencies, objects, slides, photos, videos, and audio recordings.

Reasons to Use Media Aids

Speakers use media aids for three reasons. First, such aids enhance understanding of the subject. Visual and auditory learners store images and sounds to help recall information.

A second reason for using media aids is to create the reality of what you are talking about. Volunteers who try to raise money for disaster victims find that listeners are truly affected by the visual images and recorded sounds. Photographs and taped recordings make the problems real in ways that talking about them seldom can.

A third reason for using media aids is to add variety to your message. It gives you confidence to have something concrete to illustrate your message, and it allows the audience to focus on something more than just the speaker. Remember that your audience has grown up with television, video games, and clever advertising. But always keep in mind that media aids are just tools to help the audience understand what you are talking about. They are *not* meant to replace the speech itself.

Media aids play an increasingly important role in business today. Businesses are competitive and rely on new customers to ensure income and profit. Their sales representatives must make presentations on a daily basis to potential clients. Today most of these presentations involve computer graphics or video material. Using media aids helps businesses communicate more clearly with their customers.

Types of Media Aids

A competent presenter needs to know the pros and cons of each type of media aid in order to select the right ones for his or her purpose. A good way to do this is to evaluate the media aid in terms of four factors: capabilities, area, purpose, and setting. You can remember these four factors by using the acronym CAPS.

Capabilities: The size of your budget may be a factor. A transparency costs less than a video, for example. You also need to determine whether the equipment is available and whether you have the expertise to use it.

Area: The size of the room and the layout of the seating will affect your choice. Everyone in the audience should be able to see a visual aid clearly. You can't use a detailed graph or an overhead transparency containing small print if you are meeting in a large hall.

Purpose: What do you hope to accomplish by the end of your speech? For example, you have been asked to give a presentation to group officers planning next year's budget. Will you be asking for a budget increase? Or will you be illustrating ways your group can save money? You probably wouldn't want to use a video to illustrate budget statistics, nor would you want to use a single poster board to describe projects that will save money.

Setting: Where will the presentation take place? If it is outdoors, you may have to rely on posters and flip charts rather than equipment that requires electrical outlets.

Here are some pros and cons associated with eight commonly used visual aids:

Chalkboard or Whiteboard *Pros*: Boards are best for casual presentations or when you want the audience involved with giving you ideas. This is an inexpensive aid. *Cons*: If your handwriting is sloppy or unattractive, some members of the audience may not be able to read what you've written.

Posters or Flip Charts *Pros:* They are easy, inexpensive, and reusable. *Cons:* They may be difficult for large audiences to see, and they take time and artistic skill to prepare.

Overhead Transparencies *Pros:* They are easy to make. Audiences can take notes from them. *Cons:* They are a poor choice for large audiences and can draw attention away from the speaker.

Handouts *Pros:* They are easy to make. Audiences can refer to them later. *Cons:* Like overhead transparencies, they can draw attention away from the speaker.

Dilbert reprinted by permission of United Feature Syndicate, Inc.

Objects and Models *Pros:* They can clarify demonstrations. Real objects illustrate certain points well. *Cons:* They can be distracting and awkward to handle.

35mm Slides *Pros:* They are useful for large audiences. They are easily carried. *Cons:* The order of slides limits speaker improvisation. The darkened room hides the speaker and limits note taking. They can be expensive.

Videos *Pros:* They are excellent for explaining complicated topics or processes. They usually maintain listener interest. They can be used with large groups. *Cons:* They are expensive. Showing parts of movies to groups may violate copyright laws. Projection equipment is not easily portable.

Computer Presentations *Pros:* Computer visuals can be customized for your needs. They look very professional. *Cons:* The projection equipment is expensive, and specialized training is needed to create these visuals.

Audiotapes and Other Recordings *Pros:* They are good for large audiences. They add authenticity to some presentations. *Cons:* Sound quality can vary depending on the equipment used to play them.

If you decide to use media aids in your presentation, be sure to practice, practice, practice! Media aids can get in the way and seriously interfere with your message if you don't use them carefully and well.

FYI *Tips for Using Media Aids*

Chalkboard: Write or print clearly. Use large lettering. Don't block the board when talking. Don't talk to the board. Keep it simple—use key words or phrases.

Posters/Flip Charts: Use dark ink; limit colors. Print in large, clear letters. Show posters only when ready to use them. Place them on an easel or hang them. Don't hold them.

Overhead Transparencies: Stick to the rule of six (six words per line; six lines per transparency). Add color selectively. Place transparencies in frames for easy handling. Show as you go—uncover parts as you refer to them. Turn off the projector light when not referring to transparencies.

Handouts: Have enough for everyone; make extra copies. Pass them out when needed, not before. Double-space material for easy reading.

Objects and Models: Be sure they are large enough for all to see. Don't pass them around; it's distracting. Keep models simple. Avoid live creatures or dangerous objects.

35mm Slides: Be sure that slides are in order and that the remote works. Number each slide. Mark your outline with slide numbers to keep on track.

Videos: Be sure you start at the right place. Make an edited version if using selected cuts from long videos. Don't let them take the place of your speech.

Computer Materials: Keep them simple. Don't attempt complicated demonstrations. Be sure you know how to use the computer well.

Audiotapes and Recordings: As with videos, be sure you start at the right place and make an edited version if using selected cuts. Test the sound quality of the equipment.

Chapter 12 *Summary*

In this chapter, you learned how to deliver a presentation. Different situations call for different methods of delivery, including extemporaneous, impromptu, manuscript, and memorized.

For an extemporaneous speech, speakers use a prepared outline on note cards that contain key words or phrases to remind them of the main points of their speech. Impromptu speeches are delivered with little or no preparation and without notes. Manuscript speeches are written out completely and read aloud. Memorized speeches are written out and delivered word-for-word without notes or a manuscript.

Your personal delivery style is determined by your body language, eye contact, and vocal qualities. You should dress appropriately, stand balanced on both feet, establish eye contact with the audience, and vary the rate, pitch, and volume of your voice to maintain the attention of the audience.

When you rehearse your speech, first order the main ideas in your mind. Then polish your delivery, paying special attention to your introduction, conclusion, and stories or anecdotes within the body of the speech. You can control stage fright by practicing your speech thoroughly and by using the technique of visualizing in your mind every step of your delivery. Remain calm if something unpredictable occurs during your speech or during a question-and-answer session.

Use visual aids wisely. Evaluate them on the basis of these four factors: capabilities, area, purpose, and setting.

Review Questions

1. What are the four methods of delivery? Briefly describe each.
2. How do you organize an impromptu speech?
3. When should you choose the manuscript method of speaking?
4. What is the key to successfully performing a memorized speech?
5. What factors are included in your personal delivery style?
6. How should you stand and move during a formal presentation?
7. Why is eye contact an important part of your delivery?
8. What can you do to control stage fright?
9. What are the guidelines for responding to questions from the audience?
10. How do you determine what media aids to select for a speech?

Critical Thinking Activities

Speaking/Doing

1. Select a short sample of writing. It can be a short story, an essay, or a brief speech. Perform this material on tape or video as you would normally speak. Then mark the piece for vocal variety. Highlight words that require extra emphasis. Mark places where you want to pause with a slash mark. Underline passages that might be delivered rapidly and put a wavy line under passages that should be delivered slowly. Use symbols to mark loud passages and soft passages. Perform the piece again, using the marks to guide your delivery. What differences do you notice?
2. Have your teacher write out 20 to 30 topics on pieces of paper and put them in a bowl. Select a topic and deliver a one- to three-minute impromptu speech based on it, taking only about 30 seconds to organize your ideas.

Writing

1. Discuss the advantages and disadvantages of each method of speaking discussed in this chapter. Describe a situation for which you would choose each method. Write one paragraph for each method you discuss.
2. Find two manuscript speeches in anthologies, magazines, or newspapers. Choose two speeches that are different from each other. For each speech, write a paragraph explaining what visual aids you could use to enhance delivery. Give reasons for your choices.

Group Activities

1. Form groups of six to eight students. Place a basket with slips of paper in it in the middle of each group. The first student will draw a piece of paper and read the statement printed on it, using the tone suggested. For example, the paper may read, "You're late again" [anger] or "Thanks a lot" [sarcasm]. The group is to guess the tone.

2. Divide into groups of four to six students. Imagine that you are representatives of a large corporation or government agency (for example, the Atlanta Centers for Disease Control, American Airlines, or McDonald's). Prepare a team presentation on a situation that involves your industry (for example, a recent outbreak of a disease, airline safety, or nutrition and fast foods). Use visual aids in the presentation. Include a Q&A period, with audience members playing stockholders or reporters.

Practical Application: Case Challenge

Veronica, a new member of the speech and debate team, walked and spoke with a sophisticated grace that was far beyond her years. The coach of the team, Ms. Kirkland, was sure that Veronica would be very successful.

Veronica had signed up to deliver an original speech at the next tournament. Ms. Kirkland had her hands full practicing with the varsity speakers and didn't get a chance to watch Veronica practice the speech. She asked her top senior, Jane, to give Veronica some tips on the way to the tournament.

Jane sat next to Veronica on the bus and volunteered to listen to her practice her delivery. "That's OK. I'll do it later," said Veronica.

"What? But you compete in two hours!"

"I know. Don't worry. I'll be fine."

At the tournament, Ms. Kirkland was busy with the varsity speakers and sent Jane to watch Veronica's performance. Jane was impressed by the poise Veronica communicated as she walked to the podium when it was her turn to speak.

Veronica spoke about her own experiences dieting. As she described her struggles, she began to raise her voice. Soon she was shouting. Suddenly she stopped. She had forgotten where she was. It took her 30 seconds to regain her composure. Jane was stunned. She focused on Veronica intently, trying to communicate as much positive feedback as she could muster. But inside she felt sick.

Later, the tournament results were posted. Veronica had placed eighth in a group of nine contestants. She was devastated.

When Ms. Kirkland read the speech, she discovered that it was well written. Ideas and examples were clear. There were interesting quotes and solid supporting material. So how could Veronica have placed so poorly?

What can Jane say to Ms. Kirkland and Veronica to explain Veronica's poor showing and to motivate her to work on her speech for the next tournament?

Chapter Thirteen

Everyday Public Speaking

After completing this chapter, you will be able to

- explain types and functions of social-ritual speeches
- create and deliver social-ritual speeches
- describe the purposes of an informative speech and a training speech
- prepare scripts or notes for informative and training presentations
- deliver a short informative speech and a training speech
- respond effectively to audience questions
- determine if audience members are learning what you intended to communicate
- critique social-ritual, informative, and training speeches

Key Terms

connected information
critique
demonstration
eulogy

> **66** Give me a fish and I eat for a day. Teach me to fish and I eat for a lifetime. **99**
>
> —CHINESE PROVERB

Adjusting to Alternative Strategies

Sabrina Erlinder, a college senior, is an entrepreneur and the president of Lines on Line, a new software company that encourages young artists to create designs on the computer. Sabrina has been invited to speak at a conference on new technology. Lines on Line is a young company, so Sabrina knows that this invitation is a wonderful opportunity to get the recognition that she's been wanting and to win new customers.

The room lights dimmed, and Sabrina began reading from her very carefully prepared script, while using her laptop to flash a series of attractive PowerPoint slides on a large screen. Unfortunately, after the first dozen slides, she accidentally pressed the "reverse" button instead of the "advance" button. The audience realized her mistake, but she was completely unaware of the problem and continued reading and punching the wrong button. Finally, she looked up and discovered that the picture on the screen had no relationship to the presentation. She fumbled with the remote control and accidentally pressed the review key, which created more confusion.

Sabrina became flustered and tongue-tied; she tried to continue without her slides but lost her place in the script. Within a minute, her wonderful presentation disintegrated into confusion and embarrassment. Somehow Sabrina finished her speech without any visuals and concluded with the remark, "Any questions?" When no one raised a hand, she asked, "Did anyone get lost along the way?"

Again, there was no audience response. The audience's unspoken reaction appeared to be "How can you trust a company that can't even operate a computer program?"

In another conference room down the hall, Charmaine Brown, a college junior and entrepreneur, also made a big presentation. She was attempting to attract new customers to Webbings, her web-design business.

After an introduction in which she described the development of her two-person company, Charmaine began to project her computer graphics to demonstrate her company's capability. She used a laser pointer to highlight certain key images.

Within two minutes the pointer failed because the laser light lost power. Charmaine jokingly said, "Everyone will really have to pay attention now," as she began to provide careful verbal descriptions to indicate which part of the image was important to the audience. She would say, "In the lower left-hand corner in lovely shades of blue and yellow is our client's company logo."

The audience followed Charmaine's directions easily. One audience member noted loudly, "This is like playing Where's Waldo?" Everyone, including Charmaine, laughed.

After 10 minutes, the presentation ended and Charmaine asked, "If you wanted to gain customer attention for your product, which three of the symbols we analyzed would be useful for you?" One respondent said the tree

because of the environmental focus. Others chimed in with opinions, and the question-and-answer session ran another 10 minutes. Half the audience stopped to get Charmaine's business card.

Describe two differences in the speakers' responses to their problems with technological equipment. How did Charmaine handle her situation more competently than Sabrina handled hers?

Basic Everyday Speaking

Although you may not be aware of it, you listen to countless basic public speeches every week. You probably deliver a number of them yourself each week. At work, school, community group meetings, and religious services, you regularly encounter short and simple speeches. In addition, you listen to longer speeches to inform or to instruct at school or at work. You may even deliver a few of these. Basic public speeches include (1) social-ritual speeches, which have a specific function and follow a short, predictable pattern; (2) informative speeches, intended to tell an audience about a topic; and (3) training speeches, intended to teach an audience new skills.

The success of each speech type depends on the speaker's ability to create a stimulating presentation that meets the audience goals. Speech effectiveness is determined by informal and formal listener feedback, ranging from spontaneous comments to careful critiques. Let's look at each type and the feedback appropriate to each.

Social-Ritual Speeches

A social-ritual speech, also called a ceremonial speech, is a special type of basic speech. It is short, follows a set formula or pattern, and has a very specific goal. You hear examples of social-ritual speeches when announcements of school events are made, when you sit at an awards ceremony, and when you attend a workplace meeting. These speaking rituals play an important part in our lives. They bring us together, often to celebrate good news and accomplishments. Speaking rituals are more meaningful when people are prepared to play their parts. The impact of a social-ritual speech is diminished or lost altogether when speakers try to "wing it" or make up what they are going to say as they go along. Some common social-ritual speeches include announcements, welcomes, award presentations, acceptances, introductions, nominations, storytelling, toasts, and eulogies.

Announcements

The goal of an announcement is to give an audience information that may be important or of interest to those present. In this following example, the goal is (1) to describe an upcoming event, (2) to encourage the audience to attend it, and (3) to inform the audience of the date, time, and place. Often an announcement is delivered in an impromptu manner.

Chapter Thirteen

PEANUTS

Panel 1: HAVE YOU HEARD ANY ANNOUNCEMENTS? I ALWAYS LIKE THE ANNOUNCEMENTS..

Panel 2: "THE ROLE OF SO AND SO WILL BE PLAYED TODAY BY SO AND SO...THE USE OF RECORDING DEVICES AND CAMERAS IS FORBIDDEN"

Panel 3: I LOVE THE ANNOUNCEMENTS.. / YOU'RE VERY WEIRD, SIR..

Peanuts reprinted by permission of United Feature Syndicate.

"The community center volleyball league will participate in the district finals next Wednesday night, October 26, at 7 P.M. in the Crown Center. Come see terrific men's and women's teams in action. No charge if you promise to cheer for your favorite team."

Sometimes an announcement involves telling good news. It can be as brief as "I am pleased to tell you that Elena Fernandez has been promoted to principal of Lakeland High."

Welcomes

The goal of a welcome speech is to make the audience feel appreciated and to prepare members for what will follow. Usually the speaker stands to welcome a large group.

"Good morning and welcome to Parkview Student City Council Day. There's a place for each of our special student participants, whether it is the mayor's chair or a seat at the city council desk. Your local political leaders are hoping you have some brilliant ideas they can use at the next city council meeting. Have a politically aware and thoughtful day."

On occasion, you will need to welcome a new member to a group because you are the chairperson or the person responsible for welcoming newcomers. If the group is sitting at a table, the chairperson usually welcomes the newcomer:

"Before we start, I'd like to welcome Beth Abbott to our sales team. Before coming to us, Beth was a sales representative for a major electronics firm in Los Angeles. We are pleased to have her ideas and energy on our team."

Everyday Public Speaking

The goal of an award presentation is to honor someone who has done something special or who has accomplished a major goal.

Award Presentations

The goal of an award presentation is to honor someone who has done something special or has accomplished a major goal. When giving an award, you must describe the award, tell why the winner deserves it, name the winner, and hand out the award. Usually, you stand and call the winner to the front of the room. Frequently, you shake hands to congratulate the winner. If the winner is a surprise, name the person at the end. If the audience knows who is going to receive the award, you can name the winner early in the speech.

> "The Citywide Scavenger Hunt Award goes to the Jersey High team for their dogged determination. In 12 hours, they completed 56 of 60 required tasks, including getting a $100 donation to the Special Olympics and finding a 1916 nickel. Please join me in saluting Annil, Dave, Ryan, and Leang. Come on up and receive your team trophy."

When there is an actual award, the winner accepts it with the left hand, while shaking the presenter's hand with the right hand. Sometimes an award presentation is similar to an announcement: "Njoki won a place in the All-State Orchestra. Let's hear it for Njoki!"

Acceptance Speeches

The goal of an acceptance speech is to express pleasure at receiving an award or recognition. When delivering an acceptance speech, you should first thank the person or organization who gave the award, tell why the award or honor is important to you, and express how you feel about receiving it. You should also thank anyone who helped you win the award, but remember, most award events are not the Academy Awards or the MTV Music-Video awards. Don't thank everyone you ever met!

"I am very pleased to accept the District Technology Innovation Award on behalf of our team, who dreamed and schemed to create a lightweight, fold-out grocery cart for senior citizens. Thanks to Ken Morris and Angie Rogers for the technical support. Now we are looking forward to marketing our product. Thank you."

When the award recognizes a lifetime of achievement, the speech is longer and often quite moving. For example, when Orlando Cepeda was inducted into the Baseball Hall of Fame, he told the following story as part of his acceptance speech:

"My father, he was great baseball player in Puerto Rico, and he taught me how to play. But he was black, so he couldn't come to the States to play, and they didn't pay the players anything in Puerto Rico—$30 a week. So we were very poor when I was growing up.

"From the time I came to the States to play, my goal was to make some money so I could help my mother take care of my family. I'm a very lucky man to be born with the skills to play baseball. I escaped poverty."

Politicians give acceptance speeches when they win an election. Here, actor Clint Eastwood is delivering an acceptance speech after voters elected him mayor of Carmel, California, in April of 1986.

333

Introductions

The goals of an introduction are to give the audience information about the speaker and to create a positive attitude about the speaker. When introducing a speaker, you need to give the speaker's name and title, tell something about the speaker's experience, and describe why the listeners will find the speech interesting or valuable.

> "One of the most critical skills any camp counselor can have is CPR. This year we are fortunate to have Seth Barnes as our CPR instructor. Seth is a certified CPR trainer and a paramedic on our local ambulance squad. Some of the counselors he has trained have helped save the lives of several campers. Seth, the floor is yours."

Nominations

The goal of a nominating speech is to support someone running for an elected office or position. The nominator tries to convince the listeners to vote for or support this person. When making a nomination, you must name the candidate and the position, describe the candidate's qualifications, and express your hope that the listeners will vote for this person.

> "I'd like to tell you why Kimber Marshall should be our chapter's representative to the Youth Against Hunger conference in Denver. Kimber chaired our town's committee last year and managed three food drives involving the college and the senior center. We should be proud to have her represent us in Denver. She is my choice; I hope she will be yours."

Self-Nominations The goal of a self-nomination speech is to explain why you are highly qualified for a particular office or position and to indicate your interest or motivation to serve in that role. This speech usually occurs after a person has been nominated for a position and the chairperson of the meeting asks the candidate to "stand and tell us a little bit about yourself."

> "Hi. As most of you know, I'm Amanda Modesta, and I've been a member of the Prairie View Drama League for three years. I've worked on the stage crew ever since I joined the League and have managed publicity for the last two shows. I'm good at details and can count! Therefore, I'd be a great treasurer."

Storytelling

The goal of personal storytelling is to illustrate a specific point, to make a specific point more memorable, or to entertain. This does not involve telling a piece of fiction; rather, it is telling a story about yourself or people you know.

The goal of a formal toast is to honor one or more people on a very special occasion and to wish them well. This photo, taken in January of 1963, shows President John F. Kennedy making a toast at an official dinner in the White House.

You may *choose* to tell the story, or you may have to respond to the request of another person to do so—for example, "Jackson, tell the story about the time you drove your father into the lake." Sometimes the stories are part of a spontaneous moment honoring another person.

> "My poor Dad tried so hard to be patient when he taught me to drive. (My mother wouldn't even get in the car with me.) As we got to the lake, my father thought I would slow down, but I just kept going. (This was because I couldn't find the brake.) Well, we were about 10 feet into the shallow end of the lake before my father yelled and shoved his foot on the brake. When I asked him later why he let me get so far, he said, "Until the water ran over my feet, I thought you knew what you were doing.""

Toasts

The goal of a formal toast is to honor one or more people on a very special occasion and to wish them well. The most common situation is a wedding toast to the bride and groom, but there are other occasions such as promotions or farewells. Toasts prepared in advance usually contain some positive statements, funny and serious, about the person being honored and a statement of congratulations or good wishes.

> "Here's to Fernando and Karla, who are beginning a whole new chapter of their lives. Fernando has been a great older brother—fun, kind, and compassionate—

Everyday Public Speaking

and our relatives are so pleased to welcome Karla to the family. May you have great happiness together in the years ahead."

Sometimes you are part of an informal toast—often impromptu and usually a "one-liner": "Here's to Jane. Congrats on being cast as the Wicked Witch of the West!" (followed by the clink of pop cans).

Eulogies

The goal of a **eulogy** is to honor and remember the life of a person who has died. Sadly enough, young people may be called upon to make some remarks not only upon the death of an older relative but also sometimes upon the death of a peer due to illness, accident, or violence. Many memorial services and funeral services include an opportunity for friends and family members to offer spontaneous, individual thoughts and remembrances of the deceased. Such comments are usually brief—a few sentences consisting of a single recollection or a simple anecdote. A full eulogy, prepared in advance and usually given by a close friend or family member, can be quite long. As part of his eulogy of his nephew John F. Kennedy, Jr., Senator Edward Kennedy said,

> "We dared to think, in that other Irish phrase, that this John Kennedy would live to comb gray hair, with his beloved Carolyn by his side. But, like his father, he had every gift but length of years."

When you do an informal critique or evaluation of a social-ritual speech, answer the following questions: (1) Did the speech meet its intended goal? (2) Did the speech contain the necessary parts? (3) Did the nonverbal messages support the tone of the speech—for example, funny, warm, excited, sad? (4) Was the speech well-adapted to the audience?

Knowing the structure of each type of social-ritual speech will make it easier to plan one ahead of time or to present one on the spot. When you give a social-ritual speech, remember the advice of President Franklin Roosevelt: "Be sincere. Be brief. Be seated."

Eye-to-Eye

Pair up with a partner in a group of eight. Have each member of a pair deliver an example of a social-ritual speech. If the speech needs another person (for example, for an introduction, an award, or a nomination), the partner should play the role of the other person. Allow time for each pair to practice. Then deliver the speeches to the entire group and critique one another.

Informative Speeches

The goal of an informative speech is to increase the listeners' knowledge. The speech may introduce the audience to a new subject, update them on an old subject, or present an in-depth look at a current issue. An informative speech needs to be accurate, fair, and objective. It's not intended to persuade listeners. Informative speeches are very common in the workplace. Travel guides, museum docents, park rangers, Scout leaders, and medical professionals are just a few examples of workers who are required to present such speeches regularly.

In a demonstration, a speaker explains how something works or how something is done. Some cooking demonstrations, especially those in culinary classes, are intended to teach an audience. Others, especially those on commercial television, are done to inform and entertain an audience.

Types of Informative Speeches

Sometimes you are called upon to give information—for example, reporting on a committee task at a town council meeting or presenting an oral report in class. In the workplace this responsibility occurs regularly in formal and informal ways. When the boss says, "What did you find out about the costs of installing new carpeting in the reception areas?" or "How are plans coming along for the spring fashion show?" employees are expected to give impromptu, informal reports on the spot. When the boss says, "On Tuesday, I want you to talk to the group about the three fund-raising practices you researched," you are expected to give a formal report. The following are the most common types of informative speeches:

Description

In a description speech, a speaker describes a person, place, thing, or experience. One person may describe what happens at a state track meet; another may describe her experience doing CPR for the first time. When Harley-

Career Communication *Video Store Manager*

Effective video store management depends on an individual's willingness to learn continuously, explain and describe over and over again the content and themes of the films in stock, deal with frustrated or confused customers, manage a high-turnover workforce, and keep good business records. This is no easy task. Whereas many people in sales have to learn about new products once or twice a year, those in video rental and sales update their knowledge of films, audiences, and ratings weekly.

A video store manager gives numerous impromptu informative talks every working day.

Truly successful managers are able to describe hundreds of films for customers. They also ask questions to determine what kind of films to recommend. When customers don't like the recommendations, the manager is likely to hear about it.

Because many students work in video rental stores, managers must cope with high turnover rates. High school students leave for college. College students go home for the summer. Some students switch shifts because of school commitments or move to other entry-level positions. Therefore, effective managers emphasize good training, and they work to create a supportive environment to reduce turnover.

Finally, they oversee many business functions such as tracking countless customer billings, deciding how many copies of particular videos to buy and when to sell them, managing promotions, and handling payrolls.

Davidson representatives go to schools to talk about careers, they describe a sample career ladder for motorcycle technician, including service staff, service technician, master service technician, shop foreman, and service manager. During the talk they describe each job level in detail.

Definition

In a definition speech, a speaker explains a word or concept in great detail. For example, a speaker may define what the term DVD means to the sales force of an electronics store. Civic groups often sponsor contests that require speakers to define terms such as *freedom* and *democracy*. You might explore the language of a topic important to you, such as genetic coding, sports medicine, Indian dance, or fly-fishing. In a speech about the band P.O.D.'s album *Fundamental Elements of South Town,* a music critic called it "a Molotov cocktail of molten metal and spiritual uplift that carries the band's message."

Demonstration

A speech in which a speaker explains or physically demonstrates how something works is called a **demonstration**. For a demonstration speech, a speaker may use a visual aid to explain or demonstrate a particular concept or thing. You may use a large poster of a motorcycle to explain a Harley-Davidson's parts, their names, and how they work. A medical technician may use a plastic model of a heart to demonstrate to patients how a heart valve works. The speaker is not instructing the listeners to do something, just to understand a product or process. For example, a speaker may do physical demonstrations to explain, not to teach, the art of kickboxing, dog training, or drumming.

Computer *Search*

Check out a web site that provides interesting information. After studying the information, prepare a one-minute informative report summarizing one topic presented on that web site.

Principles for Informing

When you speak to inform, you need to remember certain principles about sharing information. Audiences are more attentive and receive information better when (1) they have a need to know, (2) the information can be connected to something they already know, (3) the information is well organized, (4) the information is repeated, and (5) the information is tied to values or feelings.

The Need to Know People who feel a "need to know" receive information more easily than those who are indifferent. When your teacher tells you what to study for an important test, you listen closely. Your audience, too, will listen closely if they have a need to know your subject. If your boss asks you to attend a Chamber of Commerce session on downtown street construction plans, you may be indifferent. However, if the speaker connects the street construction plans to how they will affect customer access to your store, you will become interested. Thus, one of your first duties is to analyze your listeners' needs or interests. You can create a "need to know" for your listeners by explaining why this information will be useful to them.

Check It Out

Prepare a brief statement explaining what you might say about each of the following topics to create a "need to know" for two of the audiences listed.

Topics	Audiences
Internet travel services	parents group
recent diet research	friends
Navajo rug weaving	employee luncheon

Connected Information It is easier to understand something new if you can relate it to something you already know. **Connected information** is new information that is related to information the audience already knows. Competent speakers use information that connects to what listeners already know. You might relate information about new diet research to examples of older diet programs or connect the films of a new filmmaker to the work of Stanley Kubrick or Oliver Stone. Comments such as "If you have ever cut film on a flatbed, you will find the Mac editing system is a breeze" and "If you can write a spiderweb outline, you can build hyperlinks" are examples of ways that effective speakers relate their topics to something the audience already knows.

Organization Well-organized information is more easily understood than information that is disorganized. If you are describing a process, you must start at the beginning and discuss each step in sequence until you reach the end of the process. If you skip around instead of presenting the steps in order, your audience will become confused and may not understand you. Process, time, spatial, and topical order, which you learned about in Chapter 11, are organizational patterns that work well in informative speeches.

Repetition Repeated information is more easily understood and remembered than information that is given only once. But be careful not to overuse repetition. Too much repetition in a speech can become as tiresome as too many reruns of a television show. Competent speakers choose the most important ideas in their speech and use repetition to emphasize those points. Very often new employees in a large organization hear a speech about their company's history and values. Workplace themes such as "It's better to seek forgiveness than permission" may be repeated to drive home the point that their company values personal initiative and personal responsibility. When the Reverend Jesse Jackson ran for president, he gave a speech addressing poverty. One repeated phrase in that speech had a particularly powerful effect on listeners:

> "Most poor people are not on welfare. They work every day. They take the early bus. They work every day. They care for other people's babies, and they can't watch their own. They cook other people's food and carry leftovers home. They work every day."

Values and Feelings Information tied to feelings or values is more easily remembered than information that relies heavily on facts. Suppose you are expected to give a speech describing the contributions your workplace makes to the community. You may give the facts and figures, but when you talk about the difference the Parenting Center makes in the lives of young mothers or tell stories of the fathering program's success, you are more likely to have an impact.

Information tied to feelings or values is more easily remembered than information that relies heavily on facts. The speaker in this photo is appealing to feelings of patriotism in his audience.

Check it Out

Interview a worker about informative speeches he or she delivers. Ask him or her to give you three strategies to help listeners stay involved and remember the main points.

The Informative Speech and Your Audience Goal

The audience goal for an informative speech is to gain new knowledge. The audience may make use of the information they learn or make personal changes based on the information. The speaker's responsibility is to provide the information.

For example, Rochelle might give a report to her co-workers at a mall safety meeting because eight employees were robbed recently while walking to their cars after work. Her audience goal may be, "I want my colleagues to know at least two steps to protect themselves." After her speech, Rochelle would probably be very pleased if her listeners could list six to eight safety steps. On the other hand, if the next night Rochelle saw some co-workers leave in pairs, move their cars closer to the doors during evening break, carry a whistle to attract attention, or ask a night guard to walk them to their cars, she might be even more pleased, knowing that her co-workers had used the information she provided.

Reaching an audience goal is not always easy. Effective speakers know the importance of emphasizing and repeating the information they want their listeners to learn.

Josh Volinsky, *Soccer Coach and Ski Instructor*

Josh Volinsky of Concord, New Hampshire, is the athletic coach of some very special young people—members of the New Hampshire Special Olympics teams in soccer and skiing. Much of his work centers on the practice sessions that take place before the games. Josh's soccer team is made up of kids with a variety of talents and skills, as well as widely differing levels of patience and attention spans. During his training talks and practices, he focuses on the basic fundamentals of the game, such as passing and dribbling, and he places a strong emphasis on teamwork. Josh says, "The challenge is to meld these different personalities into a cohesive unit that will function together as a team."

Working with the skiing team presents an even greater challenge because the training program is "much more in-depth and strenuous on the athletes and coaches." Competitors and coaches live together for four days in a hotel, and the coaches are responsible for the participants at all times. For the first two days the coaches pair off with competitors and give them one-on-one instruction. On the third day the skiers compete. The fourth day is devoted to the fun of skiing together noncompetitively.

These experiences have taught Josh a number of communication lessons. He says that the most important rule when you are giving an instructional talk to young people is to use appropriate language. Young athletes "will pick out the inappropriate words and latch on to them." It is the coach's responsibility to behave in a mature fashion because "we are actually role models to the athletes, and our behavior, both on and off the practice field, has an effect on them and on what we expect of them."

Josh says that a competent communicator needs to have many communication strategies available in order to be effective. "Sometimes I give little inspirational speeches to encourage athletes to continue, even though at that particular moment they would rather do anything else." He has had to learn to be patient and understanding as a coach. "Staying calm and in control is important, especially when you get to the top of a steep hill with a kid who is absolutely convinced that she can't ski and she will never get down." Clearly there are surprises every day, and Josh has learned to be prepared for whatever happens.

Visual learners rely on demonstrations to help them learn. They watch someone else and memorize the steps. In this photo, children in Sibsagar, India, are watching a girl perform a yoga backbend posture.

Training Speeches

The goal of a training speech is to teach listeners how to do something. When do you find yourself in the role of an instructor or trainer? Do you ever find yourself explaining a dance step to friends, demonstrating a baseball swing for your teammates, helping classmates with algebra, or showing co-workers how to operate a particular computer software program? Although you may not think of it as a speech, you are making a type of public presentation in which you are instructing a group of people.

On occasion, you can tell others how do something only once, and they've got it. More likely, you will find yourself repeating your directions or finding new ways to explain your points because the first time was not enough. The most important thing to remember is that your listeners should be able to do something very specific when your presentation is completed, whether it's performing a new task on the computer, explaining new camera technology to a customer, making a skim latte coffee, or playing chords on the guitar.

Learning Styles

Do you learn best when someone talks through a process step-by-step a number of times? when you keep trying something and, based on feedback, get better at it?

Watching Some people learn well by observing—watching over and over until they get it. They are highly visual learners who rely on pictures and demonstrations to help them learn. You may learn to dance most effectively by watching someone else until you have most of the steps in your head. You can play the steps back in your mind, almost like a film.

Everyday Public Speaking

Doing Others learn well by doing—trying and trying, again and again. People who learn best by physically doing something are sometimes called kinesthetic learners. For example, these learners develop computer skills better by physically repeating each step over and over, rather than by listening to directions or watching the instructor.

Listening Some people learn best by listening. Their ears are their best learning tools. They listen, imagine, and remember well. These learners respond to vivid and memorable verbal phrases—for example, "Although MADD stands for Mothers Against Drunk Driving, I think of it as Mothers Against Death and Destruction. The death of one destroys the lives of many."

Everyone uses some of each style to learn something, but most prefer one of these styles over the others. As an instructor, you have to be prepared for many kinds of learners, and you may find the people who learn differently from you to be the most difficult to reach.

Eye-to-Eye

Imagine that you are expected to teach a small group to do one of the following tasks. Which teaching method (or methods) would you emphasize? Which learning style would be the most compatible with this method? Select a teaching method (or combination of methods) and a learning style for each task. Explain your choices in a class discussion.

Tasks	Learning Styles	Teaching Method
make beaded jewelry	watching	tell/repeat
install a motherboard	doing	demonstrate
train lifeguards	listening	give directions
write a film script		assign tasks

Checking on Your Audience Goal

If your purpose is to instruct your listeners, you need to find out if they can do what you set out to teach them. In other words, have you reached your audience goal? This means developing some criteria to determine how well you succeeded.

One simple and obvious way to check on whether your instruction is successful is to ask your audience questions to see if they remember what you attempted to emphasize. The following questions are examples of checking what your audience has learned: "What are the four steps to follow in making a caffe latte?" "After you do three turns, how do you end that dance sequence?" "What are two ways you could protect yourself while heading to the parking lot after work?" If you discover that most of your listeners cannot answer your questions correctly, you have more work to do!

Sanjay J. Patel, *Business Owner*

As founder and president of Career Development Advisory Services, The CDA Group, Sanjay Patel enjoys the excitement and satisfaction of owning his own company. Mr. Patel started the CDA Group to address some of the problems he experienced during his years in the corporate world. His eight years working in banking and consulting at large internationally recognized organizations have taught him a great deal about effective and ineffective workplace communication. He has firsthand experience with problems such as communication breakdowns between junior and senior employees and between customers and employees, as well as employee deficiencies in writing and speaking skills. His organization is dedicated to helping workers avoid these problems.

Mr. Patel has developed a wide range of professional training programs, which he offers to employees in large organizations, as well as to individuals who wish to improve specific skills. His classes include Conquering the Fear of Public Speaking, Contemporary Business Etiquette, Effective Communication Skills, and Crisis Management. He says that effective listening skills are an important part of his training programs because "they are the key to communication success on every level."

He encourages young people to start developing strong business communication skills while they are still in school, "a practice that will serve them well when looking for jobs later." Many young people enroll in his business etiquette course to learn the rules of protocol for relating in different professional settings. In this training program, students learn how to make positive first impressions, how to look and sound professional, and how to develop self-confidence. There are specific discussions of communication skills such as making introductions, handshakes, and telephone etiquette. There is even a section on dining etiquette, which addresses topics such as how to order, who pays, and how to tip. When asked why business etiquette is important, Mr. Patel replies, "When you are interviewing for a job, not only is your written résumé evaluated but your 'visual résumé' is evaluated."

The World of Work

Etiquette is especially important to companies when they are evaluating a job candidate for a position that involves dealing with customers or clients.

Sanjay Patel takes great satisfaction in reaching his audiences successfully. His goal is to always "exceed [his] listeners' expectations." He finds the positive feedback extremely rewarding. "When I get that positive reaction," he says, "it puts a smile on my face."

© 1999 by King Features Syndicate, Inc. World rights reserved. Reprinted with special permission of King Features Syndicate.

Another way to check what your audience has learned is to have them perform the skill or task. You can use this as a basis for determining what steps, if any, need to be reviewed or whether you need to go back and start over.

Eye-to-Eye

With a partner, pick a skill to teach and decide on specific audience goals for your instructional speech. Then list questions you would ask to check on whether or not those goals have been attained.

Critiquing Speeches

The formal feedback given by a critic is called a **critique**. A competent critic gives helpful, useful critiques of speeches, offering opinions on what was effective and suggestions for what could be improved.

There are three reasons for learning to be a competent critic. It will (1) help you become a better listener, (2) help you improve your own speaking, and (3) help others become better speakers.

A competent critic becomes a better listener. As you develop your ability to analyze and critique speeches, you will become a smarter consumer of speeches. You will listen to speeches more carefully in your everyday life.

You can improve your own speaking by observing the strengths and weaknesses of other speakers, as well as your own. Suppose you say to a classmate, "You never looked at us." This comment reminds you to work on eye contact in your own public speaking.

As you give feedback to speakers, you can help them improve their performances. If you are part of a team, doing this will help you also. You may make comments such as "I could not tell when you moved to the third point" or "I thought your gestures helped show what you thought was important." Your feedback tells the speaker what could be improved and what worked well.

Becoming a Constructive Critic

Constructive criticism tells the speaker what worked well, what could be improved, and how to improve. The following are some guidelines for giving constructive criticism:

Be specific. Don't say, "Your speech was good." Instead, tell the speaker exactly what was good—the evidence, the organization, the visual aids, or the delivery.

Establish some criteria. Consider the speaker's purpose. That will help you focus your comments. If the speech is a type of social-ritual speech, you can begin by asking yourself whether the speech contained the necessary parts.

Describe what you saw and heard. Don't jump in with comments such as "Your eye contact was great." Say instead, "You looked at everyone in the audience; it made me feel as if you were talking to me." Don't say, "The ending was bad." Say instead, "There was no conclusion. You need to remind us of the main points at the end."

Limit your points. Don't tell the speaker five things you liked, eight things you did not like, and six ways to improve. Select only the most important things.

Discuss both strengths and weaknesses. Critics too often focus on the negative. You also need to point out what worked. This tells the speaker to continue doing what worked. Avoid making someone leave feeling bad.

Recognize improvement. There's nothing better than having someone notice a positive change. If a speaker tried very hard to make eye contact with most of the audience, it's frustrating when the effort is not recognized. On the other hand, if a critic says, "It's clear that you made an effort to look at audience members. You included many more people than last time," the speaker will feel rewarded.

You can improve your speaking skills by observing the strengths of other speakers. Jot down specific things that impress you—solid evidence, clear organization, helpful visuals—and make a point to incorporate those strengths into your next presentation.

Everyday Public Speaking

Critiquing the Informative Speech and the Training Speech

Use the following form to critique an informative speech.

Evaluation Form: Informative Speech Feedback

Speaker's Name_____

Speaker's Topic_____

	Excellent	Good	Needs Improvement	Comments
1. Introduction:				
Gained attention	☐	☐	☐	_____
Was appropriate to audience and occasion	☐	☐	☐	_____
Contained clear purpose statement	☐	☐	☐	_____
2. Body:				
Main points well organized	☐	☐	☐	_____
Supporting materials varied	☐	☐	☐	_____
Transitions clear	☐	☐	☐	_____
Contents well researched	☐	☐	☐	_____
Information accurate and current	☐	☐	☐	_____
3. Delivery:				
Eye contact with audience	☐	☐	☐	_____
Movement and gestures that supported ideas	☐	☐	☐	_____
Voice clear and loud enough	☐	☐	☐	_____
Vocal variation and tone	☐	☐	☐	_____
4. Language:				
Difficult words explained	☐	☐	☐	_____
Appropriate use of repetition/ figures of speech	☐	☐	☐	_____
5. Conclusion:				
Summarized main ideas/ purpose	☐	☐	☐	_____
Held attention	☐	☐	☐	_____
6. Visual Aids:				
Supported purpose	☐	☐	☐	_____
Were appropriate for setting	☐	☐	☐	_____

Use the following form to critique a training speech.

Evaluation Form: Training Speech Feedback

Speaker's Name_____

Speaker's Topic_____

The parts of your speech that worked well were

The introduction got my attention.

The visuals help show the steps

The parts of your speech that did not work as well were

The speech ended with the last point. There was no conclusion.

The second point was covered very quickly. Hard to get.

In your next speech, I'd like you to

Tie your conclusion to the introduction.

Repeat steps more often.

Listeners would learn better if you would

Explain the whole process briefly at the beginning.

Stop after you tell people to try a move.

Chapter 13 *Summary*

In this chapter, you learned about the many everyday public-speaking opportunities that occur in school, in the workplace, and in social situations.

Social-ritual speeches include announcements, welcomes, award presentations, acceptance speeches, introductions, nominations, storytelling, toasts, and eulogies.

Informative speeches include presentations intended to describe, define, or demonstrate. A competent speaker is able to use principles of informing and a clear audience goal to ensure success.

Training speeches are intended to teach listeners how to do something. A competent instructor is able to adjust to listeners' learning styles to be effective.

In addition to speaking, a competent communicator provides careful critiques that evaluate others' speeches thoughtfully.

Review Questions

1. List three everyday speeches you have heard in the last three days.
2. Upon what does the success of each speech type depend?
3. Name four social-ritual speeches. Why are social-ritual speeches important?
4. What information must be included in an award presentation?
5. When introducing a speaker, why is it important to tell the audience about his or her qualifications or experience?
6. What can a speaker do to increase the chance that the audience will listen and remember the message given?
7. Give an example of how you would connect a new idea to an old concept for an audience.
8. How can you be certain that your audience has learned what you intended them to learn?
9. How can writing a critique of a peer's performance help you become a more competent speaker? How can your critiques help others?
10. What are the guidelines for constructive criticism?

Critical Thinking Activities

Speaking/Doing

Select one of the types of social-ritual speaking. Prepare a one-minute speech (approximately), following the standard pattern for that particular speech. Perform the speech in front of the class. Before performing the speech, write down (1) the type of speech selected, (2) the intended audience, and (3) the occasion for giving the speech.

Writing

1. The Student Council is holding elections for next year's officers. You wish to run for one of the offices. Write a self-nomination speech explaining your qualifications for that office and your reasons for running. Assume that you are finally elected. Write an acceptance speech. Be sure to use vivid, concrete language in both speeches.
2. In one paragraph, describe the three listener learning styles discussed in this chapter. In a second paragraph, describe how you learn best. Give an example of a time you learned a skill well and a time you had trouble learning a skill. How did your learning style influence both situations?

Group Activities

1. Work in groups of 8 to 10 students. Each student is to write a one- to two-minute speech on his or her favorite vacation spot or place to get away. Use very specific words to describe the location. There should be three reasons why this is your favorite spot or three features about the location that make it memorable. As each member speaks, group members should write a page of constructive criticism about the presentation. After all of the speeches are completed, each speaker should ask questions to check on how much of the presentation was remembered.

2. Work in groups of six students. Each student is to teach the other members of the group how to perform a specific skill. After the presentations, the speaker should check to see who can repeat the steps of the instruction. If fewer than four students remember the steps, repeat the assignment the next day.

Practical Application: Case Challenge

As Consuelo, Jeff, and Cameron walked in the door of the volunteers' orientation meeting at Madison Hospital, Myrna Hansen, the Director of Volunteers, had just finished introducing the hospital president, Dr. Peterson. Dr. Peterson began his talk by warmly welcoming the volunteers and adding, "I want to take just a few minutes to explain to you why your work here at Madison is so important to us."

He then quickly moved to a discussion of the new Madison Hospital extension facility being constructed on the other side of town. He remarked, "The new part of the hospital complex is a state-of-the-art facility with 200 patient rooms. The Emergency Department has an on-site x-ray suite with a CT scanner and an in-house laboratory. The registration procedures at the emergency room are mobile; that is, the admitting staff will come to the patients' bedsides rather than have sick patients stand in line in the waiting room to sign in." Then Dr. Peterson moved to a discussion of the new Health Learning Center, focusing on the portable computerized health-monitoring systems that are a special feature of the center.

Jeff looked at Cameron and shrugged. Cameron whispered, "Beats me," in return.

Dr. Peterson continued, "The Health Learning Center will link up with . . . ."

By now Consuelo was checking her daily appointment calendar. Fifteen minutes later, having finished talking about the Health Learning Center, Dr. Peterson wrapped up his welcome. Jeff was staring into space, Consuelo was making a list of things to buy for the swim-team party, and Cameron was doing math homework.

What went wrong with Dr. Peterson's speech? What could Dr. Peterson have done to make this a successful presentation?

Chapter Fourteen

The Persuasive Process

Objectives

After completing this chapter, you will be able to

- define *persuasion* and describe the persuasive process
- analyze listeners' needs and positions
- create logical, emotional, and credibility appeals
- demonstrate ethical standards
- identify false persuasive strategies
- construct and deliver a persuasive message
- evaluate persuasive messages
- discuss the ethics of persuasion

Key Terms

cause-effect reasoning
credibility
credibility appeals
deductive reasoning
emotional appeals
faulty appeals
hierarchy of human needs
inductive reasoning
logical appeals
persuasion

66 Knowing how to express a point of view so that a particular group of listeners will be moved to accept it is a skill acquired gradually, throughout a lifetime. 99
—JEFF SCOTT COOK, *The Elements of Speech Making and Public Speaking*

Moving Listeners to Action

Joe walked into the student-union conference room. He was neatly dressed and looking serious. He carried a bundle of handouts and three sheets of paper filled with notes for his presentation. Looking around the large conference table, he spotted a seat with his name in front of it and sat down there. A few of his friends tried to say hello but seemed to recognize that he did not want to get into a conversation.

Five minutes later, Gail, the co-chair of Dance-a-thon, opened the meeting, saying to the students and adults seated at the table, "This is the big night—the time we select the charity for this year's Dance-a-thon. As you know, last year this university raised over $300,000 for multiple sclerosis. Quite a chunk of change! Tonight we will have three presentations for very worthy causes, and then the student steering committee will go into closed session to select one."

The group looked at the three student presenters and their backup representatives from the three charities. After each 15-minute presentation, the steering committee would make a decision, and more than 4,500 students would begin months of fund-raising.

Joe was the third speaker, and he waited nervously for the other two speakers to finish their presentations. Finally his turn came. He gave Gail the bundle of handouts and asked her to distribute them. Then he took a deep breath to steady his nerves, adjusted the notes in front of him on the table, smiled at the student steering committee, and began.

"Hi. I'm Joseph Valdez, a freshman in engineering, and, as some of you know, I'm here to represent the Leukemia Research Foundation. I recognize that the other causes represented here tonight are very worthy. All I can do is explain my commitment to leukemia research. I want to suggest that if you accept the Leukemia Research Foundation, you can raise money and run a donor drive at the same time. That would be a first for Dance-a-thon. But the real question is 'Why this group?'"

Joe continued, "The Leukemia Research Foundation is a very important organization in my life because funds from this foundation contributed to the research that gave my older sister, Stephanie, a new lease on life. Most of my family and friends and I are bone marrow donors. I was fortunate enough to be a six-point match for Stephanie, so I was the actual donor for her. But leukemia has not touched only my family. Last year two sophomores left this university in winter term, and each died this summer. Some of you attended one of those funerals. Leukemia strikes all ages and has claimed many victims.

"There are many kinds of leukemia and many treatments. These include unrelated donor transplants, as well as autologous transplants—treatments in which a person's stem cells are treated and reintroduced into his or her body. Drug treatments include interferon and other drug trials with promising results . . . ."

Joe continued for another five minutes and concluded, saying, "I am passing around a handout with information about the Leukemia Research Foundation and the types of research it supports. Lahn Sung Park, the Foundation representative, and I will answer any questions. I realize you have a difficult decision ahead of you, but I hope you will consider this worthy cause because leukemia has already affected the lives of numerous students on this campus, and it needs to be understood and controlled. Thank you for giving me this opportunity to talk about leukemia research. Mr. Park and I will now try to answer any questions you might have."

As Joe gestured to the audience, inviting questions, he breathed a sigh of relief. There were smiles of approval around the table. He had performed well.

What are four ways in which Joe tried to reach his audience? In what ways did Joe try to present himself as a credible persuader? What are two questions you would have for Joe?

What Is Persuasion?

Persuasion is central to your life. Every day, you send and receive persuasive messages in conversations, reports, and speeches. You try to convince your father or mother to let you borrow the car or to allow you a later curfew. You try to persuade your boss to promote you or change your hours. You encounter persuasive messages through the media. Sometimes you send and receive persuasive messages simultaneously.

Persuasion is a complicated process. Some people are easily persuaded, while others are not. Some persuaders are fair and ethical, while others are not. Every citizen needs to understand the persuasive process—how verbal and nonverbal messages and feedback are used to influence others—and how this process functions in one-on-one, small-group, and public-speaking situations.

What does *persuasion* mean? **Persuasion** is a communication process with a goal of influencing other people. A persuasive message is a communication strategy designed to change a listener's beliefs or behavior or to move a listener to action. To accomplish this, the speaker must focus on the receivers of the persuasive message. As a persuader, you may use what you know about sharing information, but since you want to change your listeners' beliefs or behaviors, you need to do more than just inform or train them.

Some situations call for interpersonal persuasion, such as convincing your friends to see a certain movie or to order a pepperoni pizza instead of a hamburger pizza. Children learn quickly what strategies will work. You have developed most of these approaches through trial and error. However, in the world of one-to-group persuasion, advertising and marketing professionals have made a business out of researching what works.

There are many types of formal persuasive presentations in the workplace—for example, a public relations firm "pitching" an idea to a new corporate client or your principal asking the school board to budget funds for a new gymnasium.

A successful persuader tries to influence you by putting you in a mental state of conflict. Most people prefer to avoid mental conflict. They are more comfortable when their attitudes and beliefs are in agreement. Persuaders try to make you resolve the conflict in a specific way. They try to convince you that their ideas offer a way to resolve that conflict.

You know how you feel when you want to go to a party but your boss needs you to work. There is a conflict between what you really *want* to do and what you think you *should* do. Now imagine you are a persuader. You want your friend Kerry to go to the movies with you. Kerry says, "I promised Mrs. Dalton I'd help do inventory tonight." You might say, "You can go over and help after the movie. They'll still be working" or "The movie changes tomorrow, so this is your last chance" or "Mrs. Dalton will have more bodies than she will need at the inventory." Kerry will have to weigh your arguments against Mrs. Dalton's arguments. She might say, "You promised, and I'm counting on you," or "How can you say you're reliable and bail out to see a movie?" As a persuader, you try to convince Kerry to reduce his mental conflict by resolving the conflict your way or to your advantage.

Persuasion is a very powerful communication process. In its simplest form, you are making an *if* and *then* argument: *If* you do X, *then* good things will happen or bad things will be avoided. Or *if* you do Y, *then* you will be rewarded or you will avoid certain problems. There are two factors you have to consider as you develop your persuasive competence—ethics and impact.

There are many types of formal persuasive presentations in the workplace. The business professionals in this photo are participating in a video conference with a client in another part of the world.

357

Persuasive messages have a specific impact or effect. In 1963, U.S. Secretary of Defense Robert McNamara appeared before the U.S. Senate Foreign Relations Committee to defend the administration's $1.4 billion budget to assist countries opposed to communism.

The Ethics of Persuasion

Often a persuader is faced with ethical decisions related to questions of right and wrong. As persuaders attempt to change listeners' minds, they may be tempted to talk about only one side of a very controversial issue. Ethical persuaders do not ignore information that might weaken their positions. They consider both sides, acknowledge what might be important points on the opposing side, note why they disagree with some or all of those points, and try to convince their listeners why their positions are stronger.

In every step of the persuasive process, you will be faced with ethical questions. You will have to ask yourself whether you have looked at all sides of the issue and whether you have given your listeners all the information they need to make an informed decision.

The Impact of Persuasion

Persuasive messages are intended to have a specific impact or effect. You see examples of such intentions in local, national, and international situations. Military recruiters try to convince you to join the Army, Navy, Air Force, or Marines. Major speeches by the president of the United States and other world leaders are often intended to change policies or to gain support for new legislative programs. Leaders of Mothers Against Drunk Driving (MADD) meet with state legislators to convince them to vote to lower the legal blood-alcohol level for drivers to under 0.08 percent.

Your persuasive messages may not have an impact on large numbers of people, but they have the potential to significantly affect you and your listeners. Profiles of effective teenage persuasive speakers are found within this text.

Some speak on topics such as alcohol awareness or working with the Special Olympics. Others use persuasive strategies in the workplace—selling a product or convincing co-workers or bosses to make changes. In each situation their messages are intended to have an impact.

As you study persuasion, think in terms of some topics or issues that matter to you. You might consider some of the following general issues: legal rights of adopted children, animal rights, loss of forest land, neglect of the elderly, capital punishment, and race relations. You might also consider some of the following specific issues related to your everyday life: regulations on body piercing, work hours for teens, eating disorders, violence in schools, and medical benefits for part-time summer help.

Eye-to-Eye

In groups of four, brainstorm 15 persuasive topics that would be of interest to you and your classmates. Star any topics you believe are highly controversial. Underline ones with strong ethical implications. Share your results with one other group, noting similarities and differences. What topics are mentioned most often or seen as highly controversial?

Steps in the Persuasive Process

How do you persuade other people? You don't just start to talk, hoping to say or do the right thing. Effective persuaders use the following steps: (1) Decide on an audience goal. (2) Analyze the listeners. (3) Create logical, emotional, and credibility appeals. (4) Organize and deliver the persuasive message. (5) Evaluate your effectiveness.

Decide on an Audience Goal

You must carefully decide what you want your listeners to do after hearing your message and how you will know if you have been successful. As you learned in Chapter 10, your audience goal is the belief or behavior you want your listeners to adopt. For example, you may want your listeners to volunteer to work at a Halloween party for children who live in a homeless shelter. You want them to actually show up and help—not praise your idea or donate cookies. Your audience goal is to staff the event with 15 to 20 of your friends.

This step involves a clear declarative statement of what you want your listeners to do as a result of your persuasive message: for example, "I want my listeners to sign a petition" or "I want my listeners to recycle bottles and cans regularly."

Analyze the Listeners

How do you persuade someone to accept your point of view or behave as you suggest? The more you know about your listeners, the easier it is to find the most effective strategies. To become a competent persuader, you must analyze your listeners to identify (1) their needs and (2) their positions on your topic.

Listener Needs

Persuaders try to appeal to their listeners' needs. All human beings have similar needs. But some needs are more important than others at different times. According to psychologist Abraham Maslow, there are five basic types of human needs: physical, safety, belonging, self-esteem, and self-actualization. These needs range from the most basic (physical) to the least basic (self-actualization). People need to meet the most basic needs first. After they have satisfied them, they will focus on meeting the higher-level needs. Let's look more closely at Maslow's **hierarchy of human needs**.

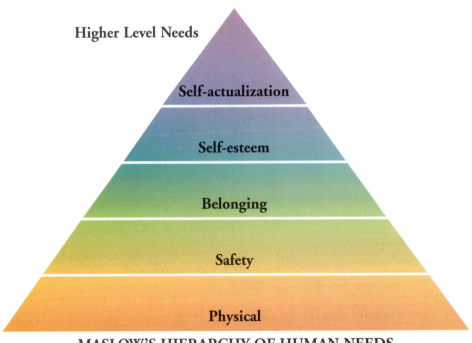

MASLOW'S HIERARCHY OF HUMAN NEEDS

Physical Needs People need basic things such as food, drink, shelter, and medical care for survival. If these needs are not met, life becomes uncomfortable and frightening.

Safety and Security Needs People need to feel safe and protected from threats and danger. When people feel attacked or live in unsafe school or work situations, life feels insecure. Lack of money or security makes life insecure.

Belonging Needs People need warmth and affection and a sense of being part of personal groups or community relationships. The alternative is loneliness and isolation.

Self-esteem Needs People need to feel valued. They need to feel that they have freedom, competence in certain areas, respect, recognition, and appreciation.

Self-actualization Needs People need to do what fulfills them and makes them feel good about themselves. They want to explore their potential and challenge themselves.

Maslow arranges these needs on a scale from basic to higher-level needs because he believes that the lower-level needs must be fulfilled before the other needs become important. If you are frightened about your security, you will not be very concerned about your self-esteem. However, if you have fulfilled most of your physical, safety, and belonging needs, you will be able to focus on your self-esteem and self-actualization needs.

Effective persuaders know listeners' current needs and try to show their listeners how the suggested change will help them satisfy their needs while at the same time accomplishing the persuader's goal.

Imagine that you wish to convince some friends to work at the homeless shelter's Halloween party. Think about a specific friend who might be willing to help out. Which message would be most successful in convincing that person to volunteer?

- You'll have fun because Judy, Dawn, and Tiffany will be there also.
- It will be the best thing you have done in a long time.
- You'll be better off in the shelter than on the streets that crazy night.

Belonging needs are the third level of Maslow's hierarchy. People need warmth and affection and a sense of being part of personal groups.

Any of these might work, depending on the needs of the person you are trying to convince.

Listener Position

All listeners are unique, but you can group audiences in general according to how they view your topic. The term *listener position* refers to the attitude that a listener brings to a speaker's topic or ideas. Listener positions can be broken down into four basic categories: supportive, uncommitted, indifferent, and opposed. In some audiences, all the listeners may have the same attitude toward the speaker's topic. Other audiences might include listeners that have several different attitudes. Effective speakers adapt their persuasive strategies to take into account the attitudes of their listeners.

Supportive Listeners Because supportive listeners agree with your ideas, they are the easiest to persuade. Your task is to reinforce those beliefs and convince listeners to become more involved. When a Republican nominee for the presidency addresses the Republican National Convention, he or she has a supportive audience. When the captain of the boys' varsity football team addresses students at a pep rally, he has a supportive audience.

In some cases you need to educate your supportive listeners. For example, your listeners may support your cause to help save a historic site, but they don't know much about the situation, so you may have to inform them of the need to act quickly before wrecking crews destroy the landmark.

Uncommitted Listeners If asked how they feel about your topic, uncommitted listeners may answer "I don't know" or "Prove it to me." Because they have no set opinion about your ideas, you have a chance to help them decide what to believe and how to act. You must adapt your message to make it relevant to their lives in terms they can understand. For example, the city council may be holding open hearings on where to build a new park in town. Members don't have a set location in mind; they are open for suggestions. It is up to you to persuade them that your idea is best. Look at the problem from their viewpoint. What will they be most interested in? Safety and money will probably be issues. Sufficient accessible and available land will be a requirement. How can you address those issues in convincing the council that your location meets their needs?

Indifferent Listeners News commentator Andy Rooney would often start his segments with "Have you ever wondered . . . ?" Indifferent listeners, who have little or no interest in your topic, would respond with "No, and I don't care." This makes the persuader's job tougher. How do you make someone "care" about your topic? What does it have to do with them? Time, distance, and apathy often make it difficult to reach audiences. When environmentalists argue that industries must stop cutting down our rain forests or face an environmental collapse, listeners think, "The rain forests are thousands of miles away, and the catastrophe is 100 years away. Why should I care now?" or "I'm just one person. What can I do?" The speaker is challenged with finding material that will make the audience listen and care. Give them a solution that will help solve the problem. Maybe they can't save the whole forest, but they can plant a tree.

Opposed Listeners will be openly hostile to your topic or ideas. The level of controversy is high. Today, telemarketers often face hostile listeners. Controversial issues such as gun control and prayer in schools often polarize people. One strategy that can reduce hostile tensions is to show a willingness to find a compromise or to find a middle ground to satisfy all needs. Another strategy is to suggest that you might be wrong and are willing to listen to other views as well. Avoid direct confrontation. Confrontation only escalates hostilities and puts the members of the audience in a defensive mood.

Create Logical, Emotional, and Credibility Appeals

Once you have a sense of what your listeners' needs are, you next have to consider how to appeal to those listeners. The Greek philosopher Aristotle first prescribed the three strategies for persuasive speaking. He called them *logos, pathos,* and *ethos.* Today they are referred to as logical appeals *(logos),* emotional appeals *(pathos),* and credibility appeals *(ethos).* Most persuaders use a combination of these strategies to influence their listeners.

Logical Appeals

Logical appeals make use of solid evidence and sound reasoning. To make a strong argument, you will need to find valid evidence to support your ideas. You can test the evidence you find with the following questions: (1) Is it a fact

The four basic listener positions are supportive, uncommitted, indifferent, and opposed. Are the listeners in this photo supportive? indifferent? uncommitted? Do some appear to be more supportive than others?

363

Aleli Estrada Scerba, *Software Trainer*

As a member of Spencer Stuart Consultants, Aleli Estrada Scerba holds the title Regional Trainer and Coordinator—Americas. She instructs members of business organizations to use new software applications. This position allows her to use her education in economics, business administration, and communication. Her main tasks involve communicating technical and software language in laymen's terms, persuading people to adjust to changes in their office operations, and coordinating and notifying people of schedule

with five to eight employees, and then she may work one-on-one with individuals who need extra help.

She often finds herself using persuasion skills because she encounters many people who, as she puts it, "know how to do their jobs with their eyes closed and their hands tied behind their backs, and then we tell them to change that." As part of that persuasive process, she says she does an audience analysis of her listeners to find the best ways to talk with them. She tries to build rapport with the clients and read their nonverbal feedback to under-

stand how much of the new information they are really able to take in at one time.

One of her greatest challenges is training older employees who believe they do not need to learn this new technology to do their work well. She has to persuade them that the software is "new, better, and more efficient."

Aleli Scerba finds great pleasure in her work, saying, "It is rewarding when people have learned and can make immediate applications of the software." She enjoys meeting new people and the opportunity to continue her own learning.

changes. It also involves continuous personal education, since she is constantly learning new software applications and processes.

Ms. Scerba finds herself in airports with great regularity. In the last year her travel schedule included Mexico City, Bogotá, Toronto, Montreal, New York City, San Francisco, Sydney, and Melbourne.

Consultants for Spencer Stuart usually remain at a business site for a week while they train an entire office in new software applications. During that week, Ms. Scerba does "rollout training"—introducing new software—in a classroom

or an opinion? (2) Is it current? (3) Is the source credible? (4) Is it relevant? (5) Is it valid or representative?

Logical appeals are built on solid evidence such as definitions, facts, statistics, examples, and expert testimony. For example, if you say, "Kids in 8th grade are making bad choices, and it's dangerous," you have expressed an opinion, but you haven't backed it up with any solid evidence. If you say, "According to the last Forum on Child and Family Statistics report, 9 percent of 8th graders smoked daily, and 12 percent used illegal drugs last month," you are making a case based on current and valid evidence.

A speaker uses reasoning to show listeners the logical connection between ideas. When you use reasoning, you develop arguments based on evidence. There are three major types of reasoning: inductive, deductive, and cause-effect.

Inductive reasoning involves using specific pieces of information to make a general conclusion. It moves from specifics to a generalization. When using inductive reasoning, a speaker lists many pieces of evidence to help listeners draw a conclusion. The following is an example of inductive reasoning: "Last week, every fourth customer ordered a vegetarian meal in our restaurant. Meatless dishes are becoming a part of everyday eating around here."

It is important to test inductive reasoning by looking at the connection between the evidence and the conclusion. You need to consider these factors: (1) Are there enough examples? (2) Are they typical? (3) Are there important exceptions or special cases?

To test the vegetarian example, you need to ask, "Have enough orders been counted?" "Were there new or different customers at the restaurant because of a special event in town?" "Was last week a typical week?"

Deductive reasoning involves using a general idea to reach conclusions about a specific case. It moves from a generalization to a specific situation. When using deductive reasoning, a speaker states a generalization, which is then applied to an individual example. The following is an example of deductive reasoning: "Employees who work at the Harvest Store are paid very well. Rachel works at the Harvest Store. Rachel has lots of spending money."

This example represents three steps of reasoning. You may think through the three steps, but most people leave out the middle step when they use this type of reasoning: "Harvest Store employees are paid very well. So Rachel has lots of spending money."

When you use deductive reasoning, you need to test it by asking yourself the following questions: (1) Is the general statement true? (2) Is the specific example true? (3) Does the specific example apply to the general statement?

Look at the second example. To test the truth of the general statement, you need to check if the overall pay at Harvest Store is very good or if only certain

Dilbert reprinted by permission of United Feature Syndicate, Inc.

groups of employees are well paid. To check the truth of the specific example, you would first need to know if Rachel is well paid. If she is well paid, you would still need to know if she is free to spend her money any way she wants. Finally, to determine if the specific example applies to the general statement, you would have to find out if Rachel's spending money comes from her job or from another source (for example, an allowance from her parents).

Cause-effect reasoning suggests that one event produces a second. It suggests that an effect (what happens) can be tied to a specific cause—for example, "If you buy this sports car, your social life will improve in months."

To test cause-effect reasoning, you need to look carefully at the relationship between the first and second events. You should ask the following questions: (1) Is the cause connected to the effect? (2) Is the cause capable of producing the effect by itself? (3) Could some other cause produce the same effect?

Emotional Appeals

Emotional appeals use listeners' feelings to persuade them. Sometimes this is called an appeal to the heart. Listeners are moved by the emotional stories of victims of natural disasters and human tragedies. Seeing the face of a poor, innocent child left hungry by famine moves people to donate money. Many of these appeals are connected to situations involving the basic human needs that make up Maslow's hierarchy of needs.

Emotional appeals rely on evidence such as quotes, stories, personal examples, or images. Many persuasive speakers who deal with controversial subjects use emotional appeals thoughtfully to tap into their listeners' feelings. On the other hand, some persuaders use emotional appeals irresponsibly. They ignore reason or logic.

Here are some common emotions to which speakers often appeal:

Emotional appeals use people's feelings to persuade them. These appeals are sometimes called appeals of the heart. Emotional appeals are often connected to the basic human needs that make up Maslow's hierarchy of needs.

- **Guilt** "You attend a good high school, while just three miles away less fortunate kids are in an elementary school with overcrowded classes and few textbooks. Join the tutoring group that works every Wednesday night with fifth and sixth graders from that school."

- **Fear** "Do not walk through the parking lot after dark without a buddy or a security guard. Remember that Tamar was robbed last month by someone who was hiding behind a parked van."

- **Freedom** "No matter how hard it is to hear the words of racists marching through our streets, this is the price of freedom in our country. It is a symbol of our precious right to free speech, no matter how strongly we oppose the message."

- **Justice** "This is so unfair. Sandy had to miss soccer practice because of her sister's illness. Everyone was at the hospital. Sign this petition for the principal to override Coach Smith's decision to drop her from the team."

- **Greed** "If you work five minutes into a new hour, you can claim that hour and add $8.00 to your paycheck each day. The manager never looks carefully at those sheets."

- **Patriotism** "The Memorial Day ceremony is always underattended. We are taking our way of life for granted and forgetting the men and women who died to make it a reality. Join us for the 3 P.M. ceremony honoring our flag and our country."

- **Belonging** "Conway's is a great place to work because the staff is young. We hang out after hours, and it's like a family there. You really ought to consider applying."

- **Anger** "If you saw the small children brought into our hospital with broken bones and severe bruises, your blood would boil. It's time we stop this kind of brutality."

The Persuasive Process

- **Happiness** "A day at Six Flags theme park is just what you need. You will have a great time and forget about the problems at home. A little laughter will help your mood."

As you can tell, many of these appeals involve ethical issues. Appeals to greed are always a problem. You don't want to exaggerate fears or guilt, but you want to be honest. Appeals to justice, happiness, and fears of real danger can move your listeners to take important actions. You are very likely to encounter listeners who will be persuaded more easily by a mix of logical argument and emotion than just by reasoning alone. The key is to appeal to a listener's heart as well as to a listener's head.

Credibility Appeals

Why should anyone listen to you? On what national topics are you well informed—the civil rights movement? year-round school? global warming? What are some local controversial topics you can talk about with authority? The most effective persuaders know a great deal about their subject and appear to care about it. To be effective, persuaders must be credible, and they must demonstrate an understanding of and respect for ethical standards. **Credibility** is the quality or power of inspiring belief. **Credibility appeals** are qualities that make a speaker believable. Credible persuaders are both believable and trustworthy.

Believability You can become believable by demonstrating your knowledge of the topic and your interest in the topic. If you come across in your delivery as interested and involved in your topic, your listeners will take you seriously.

Knowledge You can become an expert on a topic through firsthand experience or through study. For example, suppose you choose to talk about providing relief to communities devastated by hurricane damage. If you have lived through a hurricane, you know about the devastation firsthand. In addition, you might interview a disaster relief expert. If you have never experienced a hurricane, you can still give a fine persuasive speech on the subject using current information researched from reliable sources.

Interest Persuasive speakers appear believable when they express an enthusiasm for the topic and when they convey a connection and a commitment to the topic. If you really care about animal rights, your nonverbal messages should convey this to your listeners. When speakers show little nonverbal energy for

Credible persuaders are believable. You will be believable to your listeners if you demonstrate that you know your topic and that you are interested and involved in it.

their topic, listeners tend to doubt their involvement. If you have a personal connection to the topic, this connection will reinforce and support the interest and commitment you convey.

Ethical Standards Sometimes you leave an argument thinking, "That was a very strong argument but there has to be another side." An ethical speaker is a person who conforms to accepted standards of conduct and is considered trustworthy. Ethical persuaders recognize competing or opposing points of view. They demonstrate that they have done careful research and have weighed pro and con evidence in reaching their position.

Think about various sales situations you have experienced. Did the salesperson try to put you at ease and assure you that he or she was sincere and honest? A good salesperson will show personal care and concern for your needs and advise you on the best choice to make. Ethical speakers do the same. However, remember the expression "buyer beware." Some speakers or salespeople may appear to be honest and ethical, but not all are.

Credibility is central to an effective persuader. Broadcasting pioneer Edward. R. Murrow eloquently expressed this point when he said, "To be persuasive, we must be believable; to be believable, we must be credible; to be credible, we must be truthful."

Eye-to-Eye

With a partner, choose one of the following situations and determine how you would develop your credibility: (1) You wish to convince your manager that you are underpaid. (2) You wish to convince an audience that the minimum wage level needs to be raised.

Identify False Persuasive Strategies

Sometimes speakers use incorrect or misleading strategies, called **faulty appeals,** to try to persuade their audience members. Faulty appeals are based on poor, inaccurate, inappropriate, or illogical evidence. Listeners must be prepared to recognize evidence that is based on faulty appeals so that they are not misled. Examples of faulty appeals include defective evidence, slippery-slope fallacies, red-herring claims, glittering generalities, card stacking, band-wagon appeals, unrelated testimonials, and name calling.

Defective Evidence Defective evidence is flawed information. It may be outdated, inappropriate, misleading, or simply incorrect. Quoting Dr. Smith (a Ph.D. scholar in history) as an expert on a medical topic is one example. Tampering with statistics to create data useful to your point is another example: "The average temperature in Barton City is 80 degrees—perfect for holding your outdoor events." (This average was calculated by combining night and day temperatures. The actual daytime average is over 90 degrees.)

Slippery Slope The slippery-slope fallacy suggests that once something happens it establishes a trend and other things, usually bad, will automatically follow: "If we let servers pierce their ears, by next month we'll have servers coming to work with pierced eyebrows and nose rings."

Red Herring A red herring is a claim that is not related to the topic. It ignores the issue under discussion. (It is named red herring after the fish that is dragged along a trail for the purpose of leaving a smell that confuses hunting dogs.) For example, in an argument over what effect requiring school uniforms would have on student self-expression, one student might contend that uniforms are desirable because "students would no longer need to shop for school clothes at that overpriced downtown department store."

Glittering Generalities Glittering generalities are vague, general statements. These generalities are not supported with specific information and are not linked to the main point. What are some questions you would ask after reading the following generalizations?

- Teenage employees are more irresponsible than older ones.
- TV shows aren't as good as they used to be.

Card Stacking Card stacking refers to piling up information in favor of one idea or one side of an issue, with very little backing. The speaker gives examples or reasons for one side of the issue without explaining them carefully— for example, "Abe Froman Productions creates commercials with a youthful, fresh perspective. The partners have won numerous awards at film festivals. It is the hottest production company in town." What questions would you ask after reading such claims?

Bandwagon Appeal A bandwagon appeal suggests that you should "jump on the bandwagon"—in other words, do something because everyone else is doing it. When you hear arguments that include statements such as "Everyone has one" or "We're all going," be aware that you are receiving a bandwagon appeal.

Unrelated Testimonials A testimonial is an opinion expressed by a well-known person on a particular subject. Testimonials try to persuade listeners by linking positive feelings for one person, thing, idea, or event to a related person, thing, idea, or event. Unrelated testimonials try to link things that are not related obviously or validly. If there is no direct, valid connection between the

person and the thing receiving the testimonial, you need to question the testimonial: for example, "Football great Barry Gardner shops at Tag's. You should too." or "Be like Andy. Sign up for Universal phone service."

Name-Calling Name-calling attacks a person rather than the person's ideas by using unpopular names or labels. This is also called an *ad hominum* argument, that is, attacking the person rather than the argument. Here are several examples: "Don't listen to him. He's a throwback—a real dinosaur." "Jana is an inefficient worker—just a dumb kid." "That double-crossing backstabber! He doesn't deserve your vote."

When you hear labels such as *liar, geek, bleeding-heart liberal, retro-conservative, hick,* and others, you need to pay careful attention. Is the label just an attempt to attack the person?

Although it is tempting to use some of these faulty appeals to convince your listeners, the ethical speaker uses evidence honestly. This means the speaker does not exaggerate, use misleading statistics, rely on unrelated testimonials, resort to name-calling, or use biased information. The speaker tries to present the best argument with accurate information, careful reasoning, and ethical strategies.

Organize and Deliver the Persuasive Message

Although you can use many different organizational forms in a persuasive speech, the most commonly used forms are (1) statement of reasons, (2) problem-solution, and (3) the motivated sequence, or "Hey-You-See-So" form. Your choice will depend partly on the listeners' position, that is, their attitude toward your topic.

Career Communication *College Recruiter*

At a time when many students are able to continue their education on the Internet or through distance-learning programs, many colleges are developing sophisticated persuasive approaches to fill their freshman classes with students who will fit well at their schools. In fact, many schools are actively recruiting high school juniors and seniors. College admissions recruiters need to develop many different persuasive strategies aimed at potential students and, in many cases, their parents.

Many college recruiters work out of their cars, traveling from high school to high school, giving presentations about their college. They arrive with visual aids that help them describe their schools, the academic programs, and housing facilities. Each student who attends a session leaves with glossy brochures on the college. During the next week, the recruiter may drop a note to specific students who seemed particularly interested, encouraging them to visit the campus.

A few times a year, college recruiters staff booths at college fairs, where they talk with scores of high school students and parents, hoping to convince them to send in applications or come for a campus visit. College recruiters work with campus media staff to develop videotapes and campus web sites designed to interest prospective students. As the competition for good students increases, successful college recruiters are becoming highly skilled as strategic persuaders.

Statement of Reasons

For supportive audiences, just listing three or four reasons may be enough to get across your message and inspire them to act on your proposal. For example, everyone may agree that recycling at the office is a good idea. When you make your presentation, you may list the benefits of recycling. First, precious trees and natural resources will be saved. Second, recycling requires little effort—a recycling bin can be placed at each workstation. Third, the money earned by selling the used paper and aluminum cans could go to the employees' activity fund. Your co-workers will be impressed by reasons that are clearly organized and that logically support your argument.

Problem-Solution

When using a problem-solution organization, the speaker describes a problem and then describes a way to solve the problem. He or she tries to convince the listeners that the problem is serious and that the proposed solution is the best way to solve the problem. The following rough outline shows how a problem-solution organization can be applied to a speech dealing with inequities among schools in providing advanced-placement (AP) courses.

Problem:

Our state has a two-tier educational system in which wealthy districts offer many advanced-placement courses, and poor districts, like ours, offer only two or three.

Consequences/Reasons to Be Concerned:

- Our students are less competitive when they apply to prestigious colleges.
- Our students can't reach 4.5 grade-point averages like students in other schools can.
- Our students must spend more time and money taking additional courses in college because they have fewer AP courses to use for college credit.
- Our top students are not challenged to their highest potential.

Solution:

- Increase funding from the state for AP courses.
- Increase the number of AP courses, so that each school in the state offers at least six.

Notice that the speaker included everything necessary for good problem-solution organization. The outline includes four points explaining why the problem is serious and presents solutions to solve the problem.

Hey-You-See-So

Although the title seems silly, the words *Hey, You, See,* and *So* create an easy and effective outline for persuasive speeches. This model is based on a more elaborate persuasion model called Monroe's Motivated Sequence. The steps in the formal motivated sequence include (1) getting the attention of your receivers, (2) explaining the need for your proposal, (3) suggesting what can be done to relieve the problem, (4) helping receivers picture the benefits of solving the problem, and (5) showing what actions your listeners can take to solve the problem. A simplified version can be remembered by memorizing the first word in each of the following statements:

1. "Hey, look or listen to me!"
2. "You need to hear what I'm saying."
3. "See what it can do for you!"
4. "So, what are you going to do about it?"

Hey Pay attention. We have problems due to our small number of AP classes. Our students are less competitive in terms of advanced placement classes and grade-point averages.

You You need to hear this, since it affects how colleges will look at your application and how much time and money college will cost you.

Evaluate the Message's Effectiveness

As you listen to persuasive messages, you need to ask

- How credible is this speaker?
- What logical appeals are being used by the speaker?
- What emotional appeals are being used? Are they appropriate?
- To what extent does the message reflect an understanding of both sides of the issue?
- What, if anything, is unsaid or overlooked?

As you listen to a persuasive speech, you will use the critiquing skills you learned in Chapter 13. When you provide a critique, you should not make up your mind on the topic before you hear the speech. Listen carefully for logical, emotional, and credibility appeals. Then you can decide how well the speech worked.

Feedback forms can help you to evaluate your own speeches and those of others. Forms A and B in this chapter are examples of forms that are useful for evaluating persuasive speeches. Form A allows you to rate parts of a speech. Comments can be written on the bottom of the sheet. Form B allows you to describe the parts of the speech that worked well, the parts that did not work well, and suggestions for improvement.

Evaluation Form A: Persuasive Speech Feedback

Speaker's Name_____

Speaker's Topic_____

Rate each item either *poor, fair, good, very good,* or *excellent.* Use the space at the bottom of this form to offer suggestions for improvement.

	Poor	Fair	Good	Very Good	Excellent
Clear audience goal	☐	☐	☐	☐	☐
Use of evidence to support points	☐	☐	☐	☐	☐
Topic appropriate to audience and occasion	☐	☐	☐	☐	☐
Organizational structure	☐	☐	☐	☐	☐
Language appropriate to audience and occasion	☐	☐	☐	☐	☐
Use of logical appeals	☐	☐	☐	☐	☐
Use of emotional appeals	☐	☐	☐	☐	☐
Demonstrate credibility	☐	☐	☐	☐	☐

Comments

_____

Evaluation Form B: Persuasive Speech Feedback

Speaker's Name_____

Speaker's Topic_____

The parts of your speech that were most persuasive were

(**Example:** Comparison of possible grade-point averages between our school and others due to AP courses. Examples of other AP classes we could offer.)

The parts of your speech that were least persuasive were

(**Example:** I wanted more-specific things I could do now. Suggestions were very long-term.)

To make the speech stronger, you could

(**Example:** Give names of people to contact. Give a sheet with main points to use when contacting the school board or state legislature.)

Chapter 14   *Summary*

In this chapter you learned about the persuasive process. Persuasion is a communication process with a goal of influencing other people. In developing persuasive competence you need to consider the ethics of persuasion and the impact of persuasion.

Effective persuaders use the following steps:

1. Decide on an audience goal. Determine what your listeners should believe or do when your message is completed.
2. Analyze the listeners. Pay attention to general listener needs, using Maslow's hierarchy of needs, and determine the position of your listeners. Are they supportive, uncommitted, indifferent, or opposed?
3. Create logical, emotional, and credibility appeals. Develop arguments based on evidence, using sound inductive, deductive, and cause-effect reasoning. Use appeals to feelings such as guilt, fear, patriotism, greed, happiness, and the like. Demonstrate qualities that make you believable and trustworthy. Recognize and reject faulty appeals.
4. Organize and deliver the message. Use a statement-of-reasons, problem-solution, or a Hey-You-See-So organization. Deliver the message with conviction, emphasizing delivery techniques that force your listeners to focus on your message.
5. Evaluate the message's effectiveness. Critique your own presentation and that of others.

Review Questions

1. What does *persuasion* mean? What is a persuasive message?
2. What are the five steps in the persuasive process?
3. What two factors must you know about your audience before you can select a persuasive strategy?
4. According to Abraham Maslow, what does every human need?
5. How does the persuasive speaker convince the uncommitted listener?
6. What is one strategy that speakers use with opposing listeners?
7. What types of supporting material would be considered logical arguments?
8. What types of supporting material would be considered emotional appeals?
9. Describe inductive reasoning, deductive reasoning, and cause-effect reasoning. Give one example of each.
10. How does a speaker demonstrate credibility?

Critical Thinking Activities

Speaking/Doing

1. Create a poster illustrating Maslow's hierarchy of needs, with visual examples illustrating each level. You can draw your own images to illustrate the poster or cut them out of old magazines. Present your poster to the class, explaining each level.
2. Listen to a persuasive speech on video or CSPAN-TV. Complete a persuasive-speech feedback form, evaluating the effectiveness of the speaker.
3. Select a commercial from television. Either record it on video or describe it in detail to the class. Analyze the persuasive strategy that the company is using to sell its product or service. Do the appeals in the commercial relate to Maslow's needs? Does the commercial use logical appeals, emotional appeals, or both? Who is the intended audience? Give an analysis of the commercial in a one- to two-minute presentation to the class.

Writing

1. Choose a controversial topic and write a brief essay, discussing the strategy for presenting that topic to each of the four types of listeners: supportive, uncommitted, indifferent, and opposed. First state your position on the topic. Then, explain how you would adjust your

message in order to convince each type of listener to adopt your position on the topic.

2. Collect examples of faulty appeals from old newspapers and magazines. The examples can be from news stories, feature articles, or advertisements. Number and label each example. Record your examples on paper. List them by number, identify the type of faulty appeal, and explain why the reasoning is faulty. Attach the examples to the back of your list.

Group Activities

1. Divide into small groups of three students. Select a persuasive speech or a persuasive essay from the newspaper, Internet, or library. Using colored highlighters, mark passages that use emotional appeals, logical arguments, inductive reasoning, deductive reasoning, and cause-effect reasoning. Determine what type of listener was the intended audience and write a brief paragraph supporting your choice. Make a color key for the highlighted passages.

2. Work in groups of six students. Select a controversial topic. Three people should take one side of the issue, and three should take the opposing viewpoint. Develop persuasive arguments to represent each side of the issue. Give a group presentation, arguing the pros and cons. One member of the pro side should present the first arguments in a two- to three-minute speech. A member of the con side should present that team's first arguments and attack the pro arguments in two to three minutes. Continue until each team member has spoken at least once; then open up the discussion for debate among the six team members for another three to five minutes. Allow the audience to ask questions at the end of the presentation and to participate in the discussion.

Practical Application: Case Challenge

Today even some Girl Scout troops are learning persuasive techniques in order to sell more Girl Scout cookies. As part of the training, a sales expert discussed a practice role-play sale, saying, "Notice, I didn't ask 'Would you like to buy?' but 'How many would you like to buy?'" He taught the girls to use a final close, such as "Do you have any friends who want cookies?" He created a cookie-wheel—a nine-step sales process that begins with "Smile" and ends with "Thank you very much."

If you were to develop a persuasion training wheel for a group that needed to raise money, what steps would you put in your wheel? List each step and provide a one-sentence explanation of each.

Celebrate! Celebrate!

Congratulations on successfully completing this course. You deserve a pat on the back. Why not organize an awards ceremony? You can do any or all of the following:

- Have your teacher assign you a classmate. Prepare a short speech honoring your classmate. Deliver your speech and present your classmate with a diploma at a class "graduation ceremony." Every student should present a diploma, and every student should receive a diploma.
- Students can prepare short acceptance speeches to deliver when they receive their diplomas.
- One or more students can prepare and deliver short welcoming remarks at the beginning of the ceremony.
- Students can prepare announcements to be delivered during the ceremony. The announcements can relate to the ceremony, or they can relate to real upcoming school events.
- Students can prepare introductions to the speakers delivering welcomes and announcements.
- Students can prepare toasts to your teacher and to the class.
- Students can tell stories illustrating amusing moments during the course.

Pull Out All the Stops!

If time and resources permit, turn this ceremony into a grand celebration. Reserve the cafeteria or a nearby banquet room. Hold the ceremony in the evening. Include a dinner. Dress up and invite a date or a good friend as a guest. Decorate the tables with candles and flowers. Hire a deejay and end the ceremony with an informal dance. Live it up. You deserve it!

Bibliography

The following books are useful sources of additional information on a variety of topics related to the workplace, including job interviews, business etiquette, workplace cultures, internships, workplace presentations, and career opportunities.

Bloch, D. P. *How to Have a Winning Job Interview*, 3rd ed. Lincolnwood, IL: VGM Career Books, 1999.

Bolles, R. N. *What Color Is Your Parachute?* Berkeley, CA: Ten Speed Press, 2000.

Borden, G. A., et al. *Kiss, Bow, or Shake Hands*. Holbrook, MA: Adams Media Corporation, 1994.

Connellan, T. *Inside the Magic Kingdom*. Austin, TX: Bard Press, 1996.

Green, M. E. *Internship Success: Real-World, Step-by-Step Advice on Getting the Most Out of Internships*. Lincolnwood, IL: VGM Career Horizons, 1997.

Hutton, D. B. *Guide to Military Careers*. Hauppauge, NY: Barrons, 1998.

Kelsey, J. *VGM's Career Portraits: Science*. Lincolnwood, IL: VGM Career Horizons, 1997.

Kenig, G. *Best Careers for Bilingual Latinos*. Lincolnwood, IL: VGM Career Books, 1999.

Love, J. *Behind the Arches*. New York: Bantam Books, 1995.

Marler, P., and J. B. Mattia. *Choosing a Career Made Easy*. Lincolnwood, IL: VGM Career Horizons, 1997.

McCormack, M. *What They Don't Teach You at Harvard Business School*. New York: Bantam Books, 1984.

Murray, A. *Teach Yourself Business Presentations*. Lincolnwood, IL: NTC Publishing Group, 2000.

O'Connor, J. R. *High-Impact Public Speaking for Business and the Professions*. Lincolnwood, IL: NTC Business Books, 1997.

Pitz, M. E. *Careers in Government*. Lincolnwood, IL: VGM Career Horizons, 1994.

Glossary

A

active listening: the ability to recognize another person's feelings and to reflect those feelings back to the speaker.

agenda: an outline of a meeting prepared by the leader, showing topics to be addressed so that members know what will be discussed and in what order.

alliteration: the repetition of initial sounds in closely connected words.

articulation: the clear expression of one's words and sounds.

audience analysis: part of the process a speaker uses to create a message appropriate for a specific audience.

audience goal: a description of what the listeners should be able to do after a speech is completed.

B

behavioral questions: questions asking for specific examples or descriptions of actions taken in the past.

brainstorming: the process of quickly generating as many ideas as possible without evaluating them.

buzz groups: small groups formed by audience members in which ideas presented by the speakers are discussed and evaluated.

C

cause-effect reasoning: type of reasoning that suggests one event produces a second event.

chronological order: the arrangement of points in a speech in the order in which they happen.

clarity: the clearness of a speaker's words.

cliques: subgroups whose members tend to associate with each other and avoid others.

collaborating: a conflict style that involves looking for a solution that will satisfy both or all individuals.

committee: a subgroup formed to study or manage a specific task within an organization.

communication: the process of sending and receiving messages in order to share meanings.

communication acts: specific communication behaviors that are the major reasons for communicating.

communication strategy: the use of a carefully selected message to reach a goal.

competence steps: steps that a communicator follows to select and act on a strategy for handling a particular communication situation.

competent communicators: people who are skilled at speaking and listening.

confirming message: an appropriate, relevant response indicating that one recognizes the other person's existence.

conflict: an occurrence involving two or more persons who believe that their beliefs or desires are incompatible.

connected information: new information that is related to information the audience already knows.

connotative meaning: a person's emotional or personal response to a word.

constructive criticism: stating what is not working or what is bothering someone and making thoughtful suggestions for change.

context: the setting or situation in which one is communicating.

credibility: quality or power of inspiring belief.

credibility appeals: qualities that make a speaker believable.

critique: the formal feedback given by a critic.

culture: values and beliefs of a group or organization.

cyberspace resources: a wide range of resources provided by the Internet.

D

deductive reasoning: reasoning that uses a general idea to reach conclusions about a specific case.

demonstration: a speech in which a speaker explains or physically demonstrates how something works.

denotative meaning: the definition of a word found in a dictionary.

discomfirming message: a message indicating that the other person is invisible or is ignoring the speaker.

downward communication: the sending of messages from superiors to subordinates.

E

effective listening: situation in which the message sent by the speaker is the same message decoded by the listener.

emotional appeals: appeals that use listeners' feelings to persuade them.

empathic listening: listening to another's feelings.

entrepreneurs: persons who start up and manage their own businesses.

ethics: principles that one believes in regarding right or wrong conduct.

eulogy: a speech honoring and remembering the life of a person who has died.

extemporaneous speech: a speech in which speakers use a prepared outline but do not write out each word or sentence.

external distractions: factors outside the listener that interfere with listening and distract his or her attention.

eye contact: the visual connection between people; the act of looking someone in the eye.

F

fabrication: the act of making up information as part of the research process.

facial expressions: movements of the eyes, eyebrows, and mouth that communicate one's attitudes and feelings to others.

faulty appeals: incorrect or misleading strategies.

feedback: the verbal and nonverbal messages, which can be positive or negative, that listeners send, telling speakers how they are doing.

formal feedback: planned written or oral comments, often referred to as critiques, that evaluate a speech.

formal language: the use of standard English with careful pronunciation and full sentences.

formal networks: the sending of messages throughout an organization using downward or upward message directions.

forum: the involvement of the audience in panel discussions or symposiums.

functional messages: the managing of day-to-day necessities and sharing of basic information.

G

gestures: movements of the hands and arms to help make a point.

group: people who communicate with each other over time and share an interest in the same things or share a common purpose.

group communication: interaction among a group of people who share an interest in the same thing or share a common purpose.

group consensus building: providing a framework for satisfying as many interests as possible.

group norms: standards for behavior within a group.

group role: a pattern of communication that characterizes one's place in a group.

gunnysacking: the storing up of one's anger at someone and dumping it all at once when the other person does one more annoying thing.

H

hearing: a biological process created when sound waves hit the eardrum.

hierarchy of human needs: Maslow's list of five basic human needs: physical, safety, belonging, self-esteem, and self-actualization.

horizontal communication: the sending of messages between peers.

hyperbole: an intentional exaggeration.

I

impromptu speech: a speech that is delivered with little or no preparation.

inductive reasoning: reasoning that uses specific pieces of information to draw a general conclusion.

informal feedback: verbal or nonverbal messages given spontaneously to the speaker during or after a speech.

informal language: a relaxed language style usually used among friends or in casual situations.

informal network: the sending of information throughout an organization based on relational connections between people rather than power in an organization.

informative speech: a speech that is intended to increase listeners' knowledge of a subject.

interference: something that blocks a listener's ability to receive a message.

internal distractions: factors inside the listener that interfere with listening.

interns: young people, often students, who are hired to gain workplace experience.

interpersonal communication: ongoing interaction between two people.

interview: a formal face-to-face meeting between two or more persons to share information for a specific purpose.

irony: the use of words to represent the opposite of the literal meaning.

J

job interview: a conversation between two or more persons that may determine if one of them should join the organization that the other represents.

L

labeling: giving a derogatory evaluation of another person.

listening: an active process including receiving, interpreting, evaluating, and responding to a message.

logical appeals: appeals that use solid evidence and sound reasoning to support ideas.

M

manuscript speech: a speech written out entirely and delivered word-for-word from a typed or handwritten paper.

mediation: the use of an objective or neutral third person to help others resolve their conflict.

memorized speech: a speech the speaker learns and delivers word-for-word without notes or a manuscript.

mentor: a person who serves as a role model or career counselor to a younger member of an organization.

metaphor: an implied comparison of two things that are not alike.

mixed message: a message in which the speaker's words imply one meaning but his or her nonverbal cues imply something entirely different.

N

negotiation: a formal problem-solving process in which persons voluntarily discuss their differences, work out a settlement, and come to an agreement.

nonverbal communication: messages sent or received without the use of words.

nurturing messages: messages that indicate supportiveness and a valued relationship.

P

panel discussion: a discussion in which a subject is explored by group members addressing an audience.

personal questions: questions asking for the background and personal qualities of the applicant.

personification: a figure of speech that gives human characteristics to nonhuman things.

persuasion: a communication process with a goal of influencing other people.

persuasive speech: a speech that is intended to change the beliefs or behaviors of listeners.

phone scripts: predictable lines or scenarios that callers use for business purposes.

pitch: the highness or lowness of a voice.

plagiarism: the act of representing words or ideas of others as one's own.

posture: the body's position as one sits or stands.

procedural statements: statements that give direction to a discussion and keep a discussion on the desired path.

pronunciation: the act of saying words correctly.

proxemics: the use of space and its influence on relationships and communication.

proximity: physical closeness or distance.

pseudolistening: the act of pretending to listen and conveying it nonverbally.

public speaking: communication involving one speaker or a group of presenters talking to an audience.

purpose statement: a summary of the main ideas and goal of the speech.

Q&A: a question-and-answer time following a presentation.

qualifier questions: questions asked by interviewers to determine if an interviewee meets certain qualifications for a position.

rate: how fast or slowly a person talks.

references: other persons who can speak about an individual's personal and workplace qualifications.

relational skills: interpersonal communication skills used to build or maintain a good relationship through the transmission of confirming messages.

résumé: a summary of one's academic and employment background as well as job qualifications.

sexual harassment: language or behavior that puts down a person because of his or her gender.

simile: a comparison of two things that are not alike that includes the word *like* or *as*.

slang: a particularly informal language style that is unique to a group and is subject to frequent changes.

social rituals: a culture's rules for everyday interaction, such as rituals for greetings, leavings, and small talk.

social-ritual speeches: short speeches that have a specific social function and follow a predictable pattern.

source credibility: the establishment of a source as trustworthy and believable.

spatial use: the manner in which space is used between persons and how the arrangement and design of space affects communication.

speech community: a community in which people share norms about how to talk.

stage fright: extreme nervousness when talking to an audience.

strategies: methods or plans to reach a goal.

subgroups: smaller units within a group.

supporting material: information that develops the main points of a speech.

symposium: a discussion in which members give short speeches to an audience.

synergy: the combination of individual ideas of two or more persons to create something new.

T

team: a group consisting of two or more people who coordinate their activities as they work in a task-oriented, interdependent manner toward a common goal.

technical language: specialized language used by people with expertise in a particular field.

tone: the style or manner of expression in speaking.

training speech: a speech that is intended to teach specific procedures or skills.

transitions: words, phrases, or sentences that form links between ideas.

U

upward communication: the sending of messages from subordinates to superiors.

V

verbal communication: the spoken or written words one sends or receives when communicating.

visualizing: seeing a picture in the mind.

vocal quality: the sound or tone of a voice.

voiced pauses: verbal hesitations or interruptions.

volume: the loudness or softness of a voice.

W

win/lose outcome: a situation in which a conflict is resolved with only one person satisfied.

win/win outcome: a situation in which a conflict is resolved to the satisfaction of all individuals.

workplace: any location where paid or unpaid work is accomplished.

workplace culture: the way in which things are done in a particular workplace.

Glosario

acoso sexual lenguaje o conducta peyorativos hacia una persona debido a su género

actos de comunicación comportamientos de comunicación que representan las principales razones para comunicarse

acumulación de enojo ir guardando el enojo hacia alguno y verterlo todo de una sola vez cuando esa persona hace una cosa más para molestarnos

aliteración repetición de sonidos en palabras cercanas y/o relacionadas

análisis de audiencia proceso de identificar información sobre una audiencia que ayuda a un hablante a crear un mensaje ajustado a esa audiencia

apelación a la credibilidad apelación que usa las cualidades que hacen creíble a un hablante

apelación a la lógica apelación que usa evidencia sólida y razonamiento válido en apoyo de una idea

apelación a las emociones apelación que usa los sentimientos del oyente para persuadirlo

apelación defectuosa apelación que se vale de una estrategia inválida o engañosa

articulación producción y pronunciación clara de las palabras y sonidos

audición proceso biológico que se produce cuando las ondas sonoras chocan con el tímpano del oído

brainstorming proceso que consiste en generar la mayor cantidad de ideas posible sin detenerse a evaluarlas

charla/discusión de panel charla/discusión en la que los miembros de un grupo exploran un tema dirigiéndose a una audiencia

claridad nitidez en las palabras del hablante

clique subgrupo cuyos miembros tienden a asociarse entre sí y a excluir a los demás

colaboración estilo de conflicto en el cual se busca una solución que satisfaga a ambos o a todos los participantes

comité subgrupo formado con el fin de estudiar o dirigir una tarea específica dentro de una organización

comunicación proceso de envío y recepción de mensajes con el propósito de compartir significados

comunicación grupal interacción que se da entre un grupo de personas que comparten un interés u objetivo común

comunicación hacia abajo envío de mensajes de superiores a subalternos

comunicación hacia arriba envío de mensajes de subalternos a superiores

comunicación horizontal envío de mensajes entre colegas del mismo rango

comunicación interpersonal interacción en desarrollo entre dos personas

comunicación no verbal mensajes enviados o recibidos sin que intervenga uso de palabras

comunicación verbal palabras dichas o escritas que se envían o reciben durante el proceso de comunicación

comunicadores competentes personas que poseen gran destreza para hablar y escuchar

comunidad de habla comunidad en la que sus miembros comparten normas referentes a cómo hablar

conflicto situación en la que intervienen dos o más personas que opinan que sus creencias o deseos son incompatibles

contacto ocular conexión visual entre las personas; acto de mirar a alguno a los ojos

contexto ambiente o situación en la que uno se está comunicando

credibilidad calidad o poder de ser creíble

credibilidad de la fuente determinación de la veracidad y confiabilidad de una fuente

crítica retroalimentación formal dada por un crítico

crítica constructiva manifestar algo que no marcha bien o que molesta a alguno y hacer sugerencias razonadas para lograr un cambio

cultura valores y creencias de un grupo o de una organización

cultura del lugar de trabajo modo en que se hacen las cosas en un determinado lugar de trabajo

currículum vitae resumen del historial académico, experiencia de trabajo y aptitudes de un individuo

D

declaración de propósito resumen de las ideas principales y el objetivo del discurso

declaración procedimental aseveración que direcciona una charla/discusión y la mantiene dentro de su objetivo establecido

demonstración discurso en el cual el hablante explica o muestra físicamente cómo funciona algo

destrezas relacionales destrezas de comunicación interpersonal empleadas para edificar y mantener una buena relación mediante la transmisión de mensajes de confirmación

discurso con manuscrito discurso escrito en su totalidad y pronunciado palabra por palabra leyendo de un papel

discurso de capacitación discurso cuyo fin es enseñar procedimientos o destrezas específicos

discurso de ritual social discurso que posee una función social y sigue un patrón predecible

discurso extemporáneo discurso en el cual el hablante utiliza un esquema escrito previamente preparado pero no escribe el discurso palabra por palabra

discurso improvisado discurso pronunciado con poca o ninguna preparación

discurso informativo discurso cuyo fin es ampliar el conocimiento de los oyentes acerca de un tópico

discurso memorizado discurso aprendido y pronunciado palabra por palabra sin leer

discurso persuasivo discurso cuyo fin es modificar las creencias y conductas de los oyentes

distracciones externas factores que están fuera del oyente que interfieren con el proceso de escucha y distraen su atención

distracciones internas factores que están dentro del oyente que interfieren con el proceso de escucha

E

edificación de consenso de grupo suministrar un marco de acción para satisfacer la mayor cantidad de intereses posibles

elogio funeral discurso en honor y recordación de un difunto

entrepreneur persona que monta y administra un negocio propio

entrevista reunión formal cara a cara entre dos o más personas a fin de compartir información con un propósito determinado

entrevista de trabajo conversación entre dos o más personas para determinar si la persona entrevistada es apta para incorporarse a la organización que la otra persona representa

equipo grupo formado por dos o más personas que coordinan sus actividades mientras trabajan en pro de un objetivo determinado de manera independiente y organizadas por tareas específicas

escucha proceso activo de recepción, interpretación, evaluación y respuesta a un mensaje

escucha activa capacidad de reconocer los sentimientos del hablante y de reflejar esos sentimientos hacia el mismo

escucha efectiva situación que se da cuando el mensaje enviado por el hablante es el mismo que el mensaje descodificado por el oyente

escucha empática acto de escuchar los sentimientos de otro

estrategia método o plan para lograr un objetivo

estrategia de comunicación uso de un mensaje cuidadosamente seleccionado con el propósito de lograr un objetivo determinado

ética principios que rigen lo que respecta a la buena o mala conducta

etiquetado hacer una evaluación despectiva de otra persona

expresiones faciales movimiento de los ojos, cejas y boca que comunica nuestras actitudes y sentimientos a los demás

F

fabricación inventar información como parte del proceso de investigación

foro participación de la audiencia en charlas/discusiones de panel o simposios

G

gestos movimiento de las manos y brazos para enfatizar una idea

grupo personas que se comunican entre sí en el curso del tiempo que comparten un interés en las mismas cosas y tienen un objetivo común

grupo "buzz" pequeño grupo formado por miembros de la audiencia en el que se comentan y evalúan las ideas presentadas por los ponentes

H

hipérbole exageración intencional

I

información conexa información nueva relacionada con información que la audiencia ya posee

interferencia algo que obstaculiza la capacidad del oyente de recibir un mensaje

ironía empleo de palabras para expresar lo contrario del significado literal de las mismas

J

jerarquía de necesidades humanas las cinco necesidades humanas básicas: física, de seguridad, de ser parte de algo, de autoestima y de autosuperación

jerga estilo informal de lenguaje que caracteriza a un grupo y está supeditado a frecuentes cambios

L

lenguaje formal español normativo con pronunciación cuidada y oraciones completas

lenguaje informal estilo coloquial de lenguaje que se suele emplear entre amigos o en situaciones informales

lenguaje técnico lenguaje especializado empleado por personas expertas en un campo determinado

libretos telefónicos textos o situaciones predecibles que utilizan los que llaman por teléfono con fines de negocio

lugar de trabajo toda situación en la que se realiza trabajo remunerado o no remunerado

M

material de apoyo información que desarrolla los puntos principales del discurso

mediación uso de una tercera persona objetiva y neutral para ayudar a otros a resolver su conflicto

mensaje de confirmación respuesta apropiada y relevante que indica que uno reconoce la existencia de la otra persona

mensaje de desconfirmación mensaje que indica que la otra persona es invisible o que ignora al hablante

mensaje mixto mensaje en el cual las palabras del hablante implican un cierto significado pero sus señales indicadoras no verbales implican algo totalmente distinto

mensajes funcionales el lidiar con las necesidades del día a día y el compartir información básica

mensajes nutricios mensajes que indican apoyo y valoración de la relación

mentor persona que sirve de ejemplo o guía a un nuevo o joven miembro de una organización

metáfora comparación tácita de dos cosas que no son semejantes

miedo escénico sentimiento de nerviosismo extremo al hablar ante una audiencia

N

negociación proceso formal de resolución de problemas en el cual las personas hablan voluntariamente de sus diferencias, negocian una transacción y llegan a un acuerdo

normas de grupo directrices que reglamentan la conducta interna de un grupo

O

objetivo para la audiencia lo que los oyentes deberán ser capaces de hacer después de terminado el discurso

oratoria comunicación en la que interviene un hablante o un grupo de hablantes que se dirige a una audiencia

orden cronológico organización de los puntos del discurso según el orden en que suceden

orden del día esquema de una reunión preparado por el líder que contiene los tópicos a ser abordados, de manera que los miembros sepan lo que se va a tratar y en qué orden

P

P&R sesión de preguntas y respuestas que sigue a una presentación

pasante persona, por lo general estudiante, contratada para trabajar en una empresa con el fin de que adquiera experiencia laboral

pasos de competencia pasos que sigue el comunicador para seleccionar y ejecutar una estrategia destinada a manejar una situación de comunicación

pausas abruptas vacilaciones o interrupciones verbales

personificación figura del habla que otorga características humanas a seres no humanos

persuasión proceso de comunicación cuya meta es influenciar a otros

plagio utilizar palabras o ideas de otros como si fueran de uno

postura posición del cuerpo al estar la persona sentada o de pie

preguntas calificadoras preguntas que hace el entrevistador para determinar si el entrevistado reúne ciertas aptitudes para ocupar un puesto determinado

preguntas conductuales preguntas que piden ejemplos o descripciones concretas de acciones tomadas en el pasado

preguntas personales preguntas que indagan sobre el pasado y aptitudes personales del solicitante

pronunciación acto de emitir o decir las palabras correctamente

proxémica uso del espacio y su influencia en las relaciones y la comunicación

proximidad cercanía o distancia física

R

razonamiento causa-efecto tipo de razonamiento que sugiere que un suceso produce un segundo suceso

razonamiento deductivo razonamiento que parte de una idea general y llega a conclusiones acerca de un caso particular

razonamiento inductivo razonamiento que parte de datos particulares y llega a una conclusión general

recursos de ciberespacio la amplia gama de recursos que provee el Internet

redes formales envío de mensajes dentro de una organización que se desplazan en dirección vertical hacia arriba y hacia abajo

redes informales envío de mensajes dentro de una organización que se basa en las conexiones relacionales entre las personas antes que en el poder

referencias personas que pueden dar informes acerca de las aptitudes personales y laborales de un individuo

resultado gane o gane situación en la cual se resuelve un conflicto dejando a todos los individuos intervinientes mutuamente satisfechos

resultado gane o pierda situación en la cual se resuelve un conflicto dejando a una sola persona satisfecha

retroalimentación formal comentarios planificados, escritos u orales, comúnmente conocidos como reseñas o críticas, que evalúan un discurso

retroalimentación informal mensajes verbales o no verbales comunicados espontáneamente al hablante durante o después de un discurso

retroalimentación mensajes verbales y no verbales, tanto positivos como negativos, que envía el oyente comunicando al hablante qué tal éste está realizando su discurso

ritmo rapidez o lentitud con que habla una persona

rituales sociales normas de una cultura determinada que rigen la interacción diaria, como son los rituales de saludo, de despedida, y de conversación de relleno

rol de grupo patrón de comunicación que caracteriza el sitio que ocupa un miembro dentro del grupo

S

seudoescucha acto de fingir estar escuchando y comunicarlo de forma no verbal

significado connotativo respuesta emocional/personal de una persona a una palabra

significado denotativo definición de la palabra que encontramos en los diccionarios

símil comparación de dos cosas que no son semejantes en la que se utilizan las expresiones: *como, así, igual que,* etc.

simposio charla/discusión en la que los miembros hacen discursos cortos dirigiéndose a una audiencia

sinergia combinación de las ideas individuales de dos o más personas con el fin de crear algo nuevo

subgrupo subunidad de un grupo

T

timbre cualidad del sonido que caracteriza a una voz

tono estilo o manera de expresarse al hablar

tono lo aguda o grave que es una voz

transiciones palabras, frases u oraciones que forman enlaces entre las ideas

U

uso espacial modo en que se usa el espacio entre las personas y modo en que la distribución y diseño del espacio afectan la comunicación

V

visualizar proceso de formarse una imagen en la mente

volumen lo fuerte o débil que es una voz

Index

persuasive, 33–34
of public speaker, 250
of words, 60
worker handling of, 9
Message direction, 152–154
downward communication, 153
horizontal communication, 153–154
upward communication, 153
Metaphors, 288–289
Microphone, 312–313
Mindfulness, listening and, 126
Mixed message, 102
Models, as media aids, 322, 323
Moderate-control leaders, 207
Moderators, 195, 208
Monroe's Motivated Sequence model, 373
Morrison, Terri, 100
Movement, 309
Multimedia training program developer, 22

Name calling, 228, 371
as destructive conflict strategy, 228, 232
Navy officer, 174
Needs
hierarchy of, 360–361, 367
of listeners, 360–361
Negotiation, conflict resolution through, 233–234
Networks, formal and informal, 205
Newspapers, for research, 263
Nominations, 334
Nonverbal communication, 82–105
analyzing corporate patterns of, 48
attending to cues, 125
body language and, 86–92
definition of, 86
elements of, 86–101

eye contact and facial expressions, 93–94
joint functions of, with verbal messages, 102–103
messages of, 14, 16
by navy officer, 174
spatial use and time as, 98–101
vocal cues and, 94–96
Norms, of groups, 191
Note taking
listening and, 115
research and, 267–268
Numbers, as presentation support, 283
Nursing, 77
Nurturing messages, 138

OAR process (Observe, Ask, Reveal), 140
Objects
as media aids, 322, 323
in physical environment, 100
Office clerk, 121
Opinion questions, 77
Oral communication
importance of, 7–9
problems with skills, 6
Ordering, of ideas in speeches, 314
Organization
analyzing goals of, 48
of informative speech, 340
Organizational messages, 152–154
Organizational patterns
cause-effect order, 278–279
chronological (time) order, 277
problem-solution order, 279
process order, 278
spatial order, 278
topical order, 278
Organizational stories, 79
Originality, of language, 287
Outlining, 279–281
guidelines for, 281
key-word outline, 279, 280

sentence outline, 279–280
web-style outline, 281
Out-of-the-box thinking, 223
Overhead transparencies, 321, 323

Panel discussions, 210, 211
Paramedic, 231
Paraphrase response, listening and, 125–126
Parentheses searches, 266
Part-time jobs, of teens, 10–12
Pathos, 363
Patterns of organization. *See* Organizational patterns.
Pauses, voiced, 311–312
Peer mediator, 236
Periodicals, for research, 263
Personal biases, as barrier to listening, 124
Personal experience
as information source, 260
in presentation, 283, 292
sharing, 148–149
Personal introductions, verbal skills for, 69–70
Personal questions, in job interview, 171
Personal delivery style, 308–313
Personification, 289
Persuasion
appeals to credibility and, 368–369
audience goal and, 359
definition of, 356–357
emotional appeals and, 366–368
ethics of, 358
evaluating message effectiveness, 376–377
false persuasive strategies and, 369–371
Hey-You-See-So organization for, 373–374

R

Q

Y

Z

Photo Acknowledgments

Table of Contents